Jim Coleman's
flavors

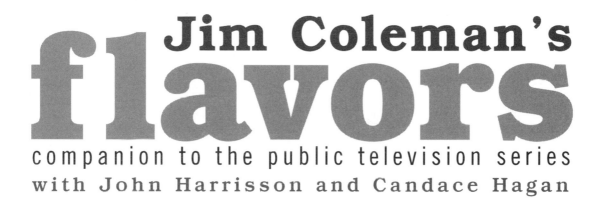

Jim Coleman's flavors

companion to the public television series

with John Harrisson and Candace Hagan

Clarkson Potter/Publishers
New York

Published by Clarkson Potter/Publishers, New York, New York.
Member of the Crown Publishing Group.

Random House, Inc. New York, Toronto, London, Sydney, Auckland
www.randomhouse.com

Clarkson N. Potter is a trademark and Potter and colophon are registered
trademarks of Random House, Inc.

Printed in the United States of America

Design by Jan Derevjanik

Library of Congress Cataloging-in-Publication Data
Coleman, Jim.
    Flavors / Jim Coleman, with John Harrisson and Candace Hagan.
    1. Cookery, American. 2. Cookery, International. I. Title: Jim Coleman's
flavors. II. Harrisson, John. III. Hagan, Candace. IV. Flavors of America
(Television program) V. Title.
TX715.C692 2001
641.5973—dc21   2001032895

ISBN 0-609-60972-6

10 9 8 7 6 5 4 3 2 1

First Edition

I could not have accomplished the television series without the support of the Rittenhouse Hotel in Philadelphia, where I am executive chef. It is one thing to research interesting food stories, capture them on film, and create relevant and exciting recipes. It is another to meet the expectations and incredibly high standards of the guests at an independent Five-Diamond hotel. Specifically, I am indebted to general manager and vice president David Benton for his patience and foresight in allowing me to participate in the series so that I could bring back with me a greater understanding and appreciation for both the ingredients I work with and my craft. Also, I extend heartfelt thanks to David's executive assistant, Lori Simon, for her help in turning my recipes into print and for successfully coordinating so much that went on behind the scenes relating to the TV show. I have to thank my talented kitchen staff for their considerable support and help, and especially Jeff McKay, my executive sous-chef, a star in his own right.

I am grateful also to Stanley Keenan, our pastry chef, for suffering through the recipe perfection process. Louis Miraglia, our intrepid purchasing director, makes sure all the food gets where it's supposed to go . . . and never gets thanked for anything. My thanks also to the Restaurant School at Walnut Hill College, and especially to Collin Clifford and Kimberly Cambra, for being our home away from home for five weeks.

I also thank Jim Davey, executive producer, the Spielberg of food television, for his fearless dedication to "getting the shot." At least now he knows what mussels are! And big thanks to Maiken Scott, producer of *A Chef's Table*, for her endless grace under pressure, and to Melissa Jacobs, a true princess.

Finally, to my family, Candy, Katie, and Jimmy, thanks for putting up with the biggest kid of all.

acknowledgments

contents

This book is, in part, the companion volume to my second series of food shows on public television, *Flavors of America.* The series, consisting of fifty-two programs, is the sequel to my first series of twenty-eight shows, broadcast with the same title. I have also included in this book a number of representative recipes from my weekly public radio show, *A Chef's Table,* broadcast nationally from WHYY in Philadelphia. This one-hour radio show has been running for more than four years, and each week I feature a simple recipe related to one of the topics discussed on the air.

Each show in the new television series of *Flavors of America* follows a particular food theme, be it a particular ingredient, a city or region, a special holiday or occasion, or a sampling of a guest chef's recipes. With my TV crew, I have traveled the length and breadth of the United States to showcase the way this country cooks, shooting on location. We even filmed one memorable show in France to bring a glimpse of the unique food culture and traditions to our American audience. The show also proved that French food can be just as user-friendly as American regional food and can be prepared easily at home. Whatever our theme, we inevitably ended up focusing on the men and women working behind the scenes to bring the food to our tables—the fishermen, farmers, growers, suppliers, and chefs. These individuals invariably possessed a passion for what they did, and their personal histories and anecdotes made the series a labor of love for me. I could spend all day talking with them and learning, and in many cases, I did!

For each show, on average, I created three recipes, typically an appetizer, soup, or salad; a main course; and a dessert. A handful of shows presented more recipes, and some, fewer. The overriding philosophy behind the recipes was that they should be simple, relevant, and easy to re-create in the home kitchen. I want as many of them as possible to become your favorites and to be *used.* Just about anybody can make at least some of these recipes, and if you possess a few basic kitchen skills and experience as a home cook, you should have no problem preparing all of them. The most advanced recipes in this book are probably some of those contributed by guest chefs, but they are still straightforward and easy to follow, and well worth the effort.

notes on ingredients

In the recipes that follow, a number of assumptions are understood.

Onions, garlic, shallots, and carrots are peeled.

Potatoes are scrubbed clean.

Salt refers to kosher or sea salt.

Pepper refers to freshly ground black pepper (unless *white pepper* is specified).

Flour is all-purpose and unbleached.

Eggs are large.

Butter is unsalted.

Sugar is white and granulated, unless otherwise specified.

Heavy cream is pasteurized, but not ultrapasteurized.

All ingredients and cooking pans are medium, unless otherwise specified.

Grated means freshly grated.

Chicken stock may be homemade or a good-quality, low-sodium canned brand.

soups

Hearty Spinach Soup with Beets and Potatoes

Spinach

Artichoke Soup with Pine Nuts

Acorn Squash Soup with Honey and Cinnamon

Spinach, Shiitake, and Tofu Soup

Chicken Tortilla Soup with Avocado and Grated Cheese

Broccoli

Broccoli-Chardonnay Soup with Apple and Tarragon

Polish Sauerkraut Soup

Greek Egg and Lemon Chicken Soup

Oyster and Swiss Chard Bisque

Irish Sorrel Soup

Salmon Bisque

Korean Cucumber Soup

New Jersey Clam Chowder

Peanut Butter Soup

Peanuts

Charleston Shrimp Bisque

Celeriac and Pear Soup

Crab Soup with Green Onion–Rice Fritters

Chilled Tomato and Avocado Soup

Tomatoes

Summer Gazpacho with Texas Blue Crab and Cilantro

Indian Dhal Soup

I am a card-carrying soup lover. Virtually every region in every country of the world claims a soup as its own, and America is no different. Soups are easy to prepare and they are an underrated way to begin a meal, in my opinion. They are the natural prelude to a three-course meal, and I appreciate their versatility. There's nothing like a hot, hearty, nourishing soup in the middle of winter, yet chilled soups can lend an air of sophistication as well as welcome refreshment on the hottest summer day.

One of the many good things about soups is that there is an acceptable amount of trial and error involved, especially compared to the more precise techniques required in baking, for example. You can use leftovers, stretch ingredients, and include favorite foods—or leave out those you don't like—and the results can still be magnificent. Although best results can be gained from making soup bases from homemade stocks, it's by no means necessary. Some excellent premium low-sodium, additive-free stocks and broths are available on the market (especially chicken stock), and canned vegetable juice or bottled clam juice also make a fine, simple soup base.

Soup can also be a wonderful medium for flavors, textures, and even colors. I generally prefer smooth soups to chunky ones, perhaps because when I think of chunky, I think more of stews and main courses or lunch dishes, but this is only a matter of personal taste. I created most of the soups in this chapter along themes for the TV show, so they feature—or at least include—a certain ingredient or local cooking style. When people ask me how I come up with ideas for soups, I tell them that my first rule of thumb is to make the most of fresh, seasonal produce. Then if you use a good-quality stock or broth, you can't go far wrong. Don't be afraid to adapt to your taste the recipes that follow, or to include what's in your refrigerator.

hearty spinach soup with beets and potatoes

serves 4

When I lived in San Diego years ago, the Chino Farms produce stand in Del Mar was just a few minutes' drive away, and was it ever worth it! The fruits and vegetables on offer were incredible. Chino Farms is an institution in southern California, and their remarkable organic produce helped Alice Waters and her peers revolutionize American cooking thirty years ago. The company is still going strong today. I was fortunate enough to be able to interview Tom Chino, one of the second-generation family owners, for the TV show, and the information he shared with me about the cross-breeding programs, growing techniques, and handling procedures helped explain the remarkable quality of the farm's product. I created this soup using some of the vegetables they had available in April.

3 tablespoons butter

1 large onion, chopped

3 cloves garlic, minced

3 cups fresh spinach, cleaned and chopped

1 teaspoon paprika

4 cups Chicken Stock (page 266)

2 russet potatoes (about 1 pound), peeled and roughly chopped

4 beets (about 1 pound), peeled and chopped

1 large tomato, chopped

Salt and pepper, to taste

4 tablespoons low-fat sour cream

4 sprigs of fresh flat-leaf parsley

Place the butter in a large stockpot and melt over medium-high heat. Add the onion and garlic and sauté for 1 minute. Add the spinach and paprika and sauté for about 1 minute, until the spinach is wilted. Add the stock, potatoes, beets, and tomato and bring to a boil. Reduce the heat to a light simmer and cook for about 30 minutes, or until the potatoes and beets are tender.

Transfer the soup to a food processor in batches and purée until smooth. Season with salt and pepper. Ladle the soup into serving bowls and garnish with the sour cream and a parsley sprig.

Spinach was first found growing wild near ancient deserts in Persia and was initially picked to satisfy the appetites of Persian cats. People soon caught on and by the sixth century A.D. the "Persian herb" made its way through trade to China. The Chinese refined its usage and it was exported to India and Nepal as the "China flower." Six hundred years later the Moors took it to Spain and the taste for spinach spread throughout Europe. French dishes made with spinach were called Florentine in honor of Catherine de Médicis, the sixteenth-century French queen imported from Florence, who insisted that spinach be served at every meal.

Spinach can be prepared in numerous ways, but it is easy to overcook. As one food writer observed, "For years spinach was not cooked in American kitchens, it was punished." Modern chefs have learned from classic French preparations to cook spinach briefly in order to bring out its best flavor and color and its ability to merge with other flavors. It beautifully enhances recipes by receiving the effects of other ingredients rather than imposing its own taste.

As children, many of us learned that Popeye got his muscles from all the iron packed in his canned spinach. Spinach is also a wonderful source of beta-carotene and is rich in other anticancer compounds such as folic acid. Its health benefits and a renewed respect for the vegetable in the kitchen have tremendously boosted consumption. By the end of the twentieth century, more than 170 million pounds of fresh spinach a year were eaten in America alone.

artichoke soup with pine nuts

serves 4

The inspiration for this artichoke recipe comes from a Jerusalem artichoke soup I tasted once in Los Angeles. Although listed on the menu as artichoke soup, the dish that arrived at my table was in fact made with Jerusalem artichokes (also called sunchokes). These are not true artichokes at all, but a tuber belonging to the sunflower family. It was a good soup, though, and I have adapted the flavors to create this real artichoke soup! For a simpler recipe, use a half cup of frozen artichoke halves instead of fresh artichokes. Don't be tempted to use bottled artichokes, which come in a flavored brine that would not work well here.

4 fresh artichokes

3 tablespoons olive oil

½ onion, diced

2 stalks celery, diced

3 tablespoons brandy

4 cups Chicken Stock (page 266)

1 russet potato (about 8 ounces), peeled and coarsely chopped

2 teaspoons dried tarragon

½ cup heavy cream

Salt and white pepper, to taste

¼ cup toasted pine nuts (see page 269)

Cut off the top of each artichoke about one quarter of the way down and discard. Trim off the tougher outer leaves, leaving the tender pale inside leaves exposed. Open up the center of the artichoke and remove the prickly core. Cut each artichoke into sixths.

In a large saucepan, heat the oil and sauté the artichokes, onion, and celery over medium-high heat for 4 or 5 minutes, or until golden. Add the brandy and deglaze the pan. Add the stock, potato, tarragon, and cream. Continue cooking until the potatoes and artichokes are tender and the soup has thickened, 30 to 40 minutes.

Transfer the soup to a food processor or blender in batches and purée until smooth. Using a medium mesh sieve, strain the soup into a clean saucepan. Season with salt and white pepper and reheat the soup. Ladle into soup bowls and sprinkle the pine nuts over the top.

acorn squash soup with honey and cinnamon

serves 4

Whenever I make this soup in fall or winter, I think of my children, Katie and Jimmy, who love baked acorn squash. At home, I'll cut one in half, brush it with butter and honey, season it with salt and pepper, and bake it at 375°F. for 30 to 40 minutes, or until fork tender. This rich and creamy dish is a good example of creating soups using favorite flavors. The tarragon cuts the richness just enough. If you prefer, you can use a hand blender to purée the soup, rather than a food processor.

1 tablespoon butter

1 large carrot, roughly chopped

1 stalk celery, roughly chopped

½ large onion, roughly chopped

1 large acorn squash, peeled, seeded, and chopped (about 3 cups)

2½ cups Chicken Stock (page 266)

½ teaspoon ground cinnamon

1 tablespoon chopped fresh tarragon

2 teaspoons salt

1 teaspoon pepper

¼ cup heavy cream

1½ tablespoons honey

Place the butter in a large stockpot and melt over medium-high heat. Add the carrot, celery, and onion and sauté for 4 or 5 minutes; do not burn the butter. Add the squash, stock, and cinnamon, cover the stockpot, and lower the heat to a simmer. Cook for 20 to 30 minutes, or until the squash is soft.

Transfer the soup to a food processor in batches and purée until smooth. Return the soup to a clean saucepan and reheat. Stir in the tarragon, salt, and pepper. In a mixing bowl, whisk the cream until lightly whipped and add the honey. Ladle the soup into serving bowls and swirl in the honey-cream mixture.

tip Everyone wants to get rid of unwanted fat! An easy way to remove fat from soups and stews is to drop ice cubes into the pot after it has cooled slightly. The fat will cling to the cubes as you stir. Remove the cubes before they melt. You can also wrap the cubes in cheesecloth and skim them over the top of the pot.

spinach, shiitake, and tofu soup

I featured this soup on our show about the Chinese New Year, an event that is traditionally celebrated by preparing lots of different courses. Typically, the first course is vegetarian, like this one, symbolizing regeneration and a fresh beginning. Chinese New Year usually falls at the end of January, and in Philadelphia, as in many large cities in the United States with a sizable Chinese community, there is a big parade with firecrackers, dancing paper dragons, and colorful costumes.

5 cups Chicken Stock (page 266)

8 ounces spinach, cleaned and roughly chopped

8 ounces firm tofu, drained and cut into ½-inch dice

4 ounces shiitake mushrooms, thinly sliced

1 teaspoon ground ginger

1 teaspoon toasted (dark) sesame oil

Salt and pepper, to taste

Pour the stock into a large saucepan and bring to a boil. Add the spinach, tofu, mushrooms, and ginger, return to a boil, and cook for 2 to 3 minutes. Remove the pan from the heat and stir in the sesame oil. Season with salt and pepper and serve hot.

chicken tortilla soup with avocado and grated cheese

serves 4 to 6

The subtitle for this recipe could be "Mexican Chicken Noodle Soup," with tortilla strips playing the role of the noodles. This is a heart-healthy soup, especially if you choose a low-fat cheese. Kids love it, and although it isn't spicy, you can always add a little hot sauce. For the TV show, which we filmed in San Antonio, I made the soup with both corn and flour tortillas.

2 tablespoons olive oil

1 small red onion, chopped

3 cloves garlic, minced

2 boneless, skinless chicken breasts (4 to 6 ounces each), cut into bite-size pieces

4½ cups Chicken Stock (page 266)

½ green bell pepper, seeded and chopped

1 teaspoon red pepper flakes, or to taste

2 tablespoons chopped fresh basil leaves, or 1½ tablespoons dried

1½ cups tomato sauce

½ cup corn oil

12 corn tortillas (6 inches across), sliced into strips

1 cup grated Monterey Jack cheese

1 avocado, peeled, pitted, and thinly sliced

Heat the oil in a large saucepan or soup pot, add the onion and garlic and sauté over medium-high heat for 2 or 3 minutes. Add the chicken, chicken stock, bell pepper, red pepper flakes, basil, and tomato sauce. Bring to a boil, reduce the heat, and simmer for 30 minutes.

In a skillet, heat the corn oil, and when hot, add the tortilla strips. Fry for 30 seconds to 1 minute, or until light golden brown. Divide the tortilla strips among serving bowls (save a few for garnish) and ladle in the soup. Garnish with the grated cheese, avocado, and reserved tortilla strips.

broccoli

In the first century A.D., Roman patricians were noted for the prodigious amounts of food they consumed at every meal. Yet the emperor Tiberius's young son stepped over the line when he gorged himself on broccoli at an important banquet. His father felt compelled to publicly reprimand him, and the scolding went into the history books as the first written mention of broccoli. Modern parents who have a difficult time coaxing their children to eat vegetables may have a hard time swallowing this anecdote, but it attests that broccoli was popular for as long as we have a record of eating it.

Broccoli is thought to have originated in Asia Minor, where it was grown for its floral shoots. Navigators took it to Italy, where it is believed that the expert gardening techniques of the Etruscans honed it into the vegetable so enjoyed later in Rome. The English word for the vegetable is derived directly from the Italian term that means "little arms" or "little shoots." The Italians are credited with devising numerous delicious broccoli preparations, which were later introduced to France by Catherine de Médicis.

Broccoli did not make much of an impression in the United States until after World War Two, when Italian immigrants began to plant the vegetable so prized in their homeland. Most of the modern crop comes from California, and today it is one of America's most familiar produce items. Broccoli's popularity soared after a 1992 article in the *New York Times* quoted research citing the vegetable as containing "the most powerful anticancer compound ever discovered." Subsequent studies allow that besides fighting carcinogens, broccoli has the highest concentration of calcium found in any vegetable and is rich in a variety of other minerals and vitamins.

broccoli-chardonnay soup with apple and tarragon

serves 4

In this wine-inspired recipe, it is the apple that makes all the difference. It gives the soup a wonderful flavor and texture, but it's subtle enough that you may not realize it's there. Broccoli might not normally be the perfect marriage with white wine, but they work really well together here. Avoid using an assertive, oaky Chardonnay for this recipe. Garnish the soup with a blanched broccoli floret, if you like.

2 tablespoons olive oil

2 tablespoons chopped white onion

1 tablespoon minced garlic

1 pound broccoli, roughly cut into chunks

2 scallions, green and white parts, roughly chopped

1 large apple (such as Granny Smith), peeled, cored, and roughly chopped

¼ cup diced small carrots

4 cups Chicken Stock (page 266)

¾ cup Chardonnay wine

¼ teaspoon cayenne

Salt and white pepper, to taste

½ cup heavy cream

2 tablespoons chopped fresh tarragon leaves

Heat the oil in a sauté pan, add the onion and garlic, and sweat the vegetables over medium heat for 1 minute. Add the broccoli, scallions, apple, and carrots and sauté for 2 minutes longer, stirring often. Add the stock and wine and bring to a boil. Reduce the heat to a simmer and cook for 10 minutes.

Transfer the soup to a food processor or blender in batches and purée until smooth. Return to a clean saucepan and season with the cayenne, salt, and pepper. Stir in the cream and bring to a simmer. Reduce the heat and simmer for 5 minutes. Ladle the soup into serving bowls and garnish with the tarragon.

polish sauerkraut soup

serves 4

One old turn-of-the-twentieth-century volume in my collection of several thousand cookbooks is a fascinating collection of recipes for Polish-Americans. I adapted this comfort-food recipe from that source for the show about Polish food that we filmed in Chicago. It's a mild soup, and not at all overpowering as the title might suggest. I love sauerkraut, which can be purchased in refrigerated bags or cans. A little-known fact about sauerkraut is that due to the high vitamin C content of cabbage, it was commonly used by seafarers in the nineteenth century to prevent scurvy.

4 or 5 slices of bacon, diced

3 tablespoons flour

¼ cup chopped smoked ham

4½ cups Beef Stock (page 267)

2 russet potatoes (about 1 pound), peeled and finely diced (about 2½ cups)

2 cups sauerkraut, drained and rinsed

¾ teaspoon caraway seeds, ground

1 teaspoon sugar

Pepper, to taste

Place the bacon in a saucepan and cook over medium-high heat for 3 or 4 minutes, until crispy and all the fat is rendered. Remove the bacon, drain on paper towels, and set aside. Add the flour to the pan and stir, while cooking, for 2 minutes to make a roux. Add the ham, stirring constantly, and add the beef stock cup by cup until the ingredients are well blended. Add the potatoes and reduce the heat to a light simmer. Cook for 10 to 15 minutes, or until the potatoes are soft. Add the sauerkraut, caraway, sugar, pepper, and cooked bacon and cook for 5 minutes, or until heated through. Ladle into serving bowls.

tip Use a colander for rinsing sauerkraut under cold running water; a spray nozzle attachment is perfect for a thorough wash.

greek egg and lemon chicken soup

serves 4

Think of this dish as the Greek version of Chinese egg-drop soup! In Greek cuisine, this hearty, tangy rice soup is called avgolemono, *a name also given to a thick sauce made from similar ingredients but without the rice. One of my favorite places to eat out with my family is a Greek restaurant in southern New Jersey, and I think that Greek food and wine is seriously underrated in the United States. I predict that the cuisine, and especially Greece's better wines, will become very fashionable in the near future.*

for the chicken and soup

¼ cup rice

Salt, to taste

5 cups Chicken Stock (page 266)

2 chicken breasts (6 to 8 ounces each), diced

1 carrot, diced

½ onion, diced

1 stalk celery, diced

1 teaspoon dried thyme

1 teaspoon dried oregano

Pepper, to taste

for the lemon sauce

2 eggs, separated

Juice of 2 lemons

To prepare the soup, place the rice, ½ cup water, and salt in a small saucepan and bring to a boil. Reduce the heat to low, cover the pan, and simmer for about 15 minutes, or until the water is evaporated. Fluff with a fork and set aside.

Pour the stock into a saucepan set over medium-high heat. Bring to a simmer and add the chicken, carrot, onion, celery, thyme, oregano, salt, and pepper. Cook for about 30 minutes, or until the vegetables and chicken are tender. Stir in the cooked rice and remove from the heat.

Meanwhile, to prepare the sauce, whisk the egg whites in a bowl until soft peaks form. Add the egg yolks and whisk for 2 minutes, until well blended. Slowly add the lemon juice while gently whisking. Add 1 ladle of the hot soup to the egg mixture while whisking and then add the warmed lemon–egg yolk mixture back into the soup. Stir well; do not reheat the soup. Ladle into serving bowls.

oyster and swiss chard bisque

serves 4

When the City of Philadelphia recently embarked on a major road-repair program for the Old City section of downtown, mechanical diggers uncovered several feet of crushed oyster shells in layers below the paved roadway. Oysters were so abundant in the eighteenth and nineteenth centuries that they were given away in bars and saloons, and the shells were simply discarded in the streets. Crushed and broken up by carts and wagons, the shells made a natural road surface that was a big improvement on the mud that had prevailed before. This recipe is a variation of a Chinese-American stir-fry recipe that I have transformed into a soup. Shucked oysters can be purchased in plastic containers in the chilled seafood section of most good supermarkets.

2 cups freshly shucked oysters (including the liquid)

3 tablespoons butter

1 onion, diced

3 cloves garlic, finely minced

3 tablespoons flour

2½ cups Chicken Stock (page 266)

1 pound Swiss chard (or spinach), washed, stemmed, and chopped

½ teaspoon dried thyme

½ teaspoon dried dill

1 cup heavy cream

½ teaspoon minced lemon zest

¼ teaspoon sugar

Pinch of nutmeg

Salt and pepper, to taste

Using a colander, drain the oysters over a bowl, reserving the liquid. Roughly chop or quarter the oysters and set aside. Melt the butter in a saucepan over medium-high heat. Add the onion and garlic and sauté for 2 minutes. Add the flour and cook while stirring for 1 or 2 minutes to make a roux. Whisk in the stock and reserved oyster liquid and bring to a boil. Cook while whisking for 4 or 5 minutes, or until thick.

Add the chard, thyme, and dill and simmer for 5 or 6 minutes. Transfer the soup to a blender or food processor in batches and purée until smooth. Return the soup to a clean saucepan and set the heat to medium. Add the cream and the reserved oysters and heat through but do not bring to a boil. Stir in the lemon zest, sugar, and nutmeg and season with salt and pepper. Ladle into warm serving bowls.

irish sorrel soup

Sorrel is an herb related to rhubarb and buckwheat that finds itself in many traditional Irish dishes. It has a tart flavor—the name is based on an archaic form of the word sour—*and sorrel has been used as a green vegetable since ancient times. This dish adapts a classic spinach soup recipe, and you can vary the texture and flavors by using milk rather than cream and compensating by adding a little more flour; or by omitting the bread crumbs, which are used as a thickening agent.*

for the bouquet garni

- 1 leek, green part only, about 6 inches long
- 1 sprig of fresh flat-leaf parsley
- 1 sprig of fresh thyme
- 2 peppercorns
- 1 whole clove

for the soup

- 6 tablespoons butter
- 8 ounces sorrel, stemmed, washed, and chopped
- 1/2 yellow onion, diced
- 2 1/2 tablespoons flour
- 5 cups Chicken Stock (page 266)
- 2 tablespoons plain dried bread crumbs
- 2 tablespoons chopped fresh tarragon leaves, or 1 1/2 tablespoons dried
- Salt and pepper, to taste
- 3/4 cup heavy cream

To prepare the bouquet garni, place the leek, parsley, thyme, peppercorns, and clove in a piece of cheesecloth and tie with twine. Set aside.

To prepare the soup, melt the butter in a large saucepan over medium-high heat. Add the sorrel and onion and cook for 1 or 2 minutes, stirring constantly. Shake the flour over the sorrel mixture and cook for 2 minutes longer, stirring occasionally. In a separate saucepan, bring the stock to a boil, then add it to the sorrel mixture. Return to a boil and reduce the heat to a simmer. Add the bouquet garni, bread crumbs, tarragon, salt, and pepper and simmer the soup for 30 minutes to 1 hour, or until the liquid is reduced and the sorrel is cooked through.

Remove the bouquet garni. Transfer the soup to a food processor or blender and purée until smooth. Return to a clean saucepan, stir in the cream, and bring just to a simmer; do not boil. Ladle the soup into warm serving plates.

soups

salmon bisque

serves 4

One thing that amazes me about France is the high standard of food offered at the roadside and motorway truck stops. Show me a little restaurant in the middle of nowhere with a LES ROUTIERS sign outside, denoting an officially sanctioned level of food and service, and I'll show you at least one big-rig parked outside. In honor of a delicious salmon bisque I enjoyed recently at a French autoroute service station, I created this recipe for our show on French food, filmed on location in Burgundy. This is a terrific bread-dunking soup, if that's your thing.

2 tablespoons butter

½ yellow onion, chopped

½ leek, white part only, cleaned and chopped

2 small carrots, chopped

2 stalks celery, chopped

1 teaspoon tomato purée, tomato paste, or ketchup

1 tomato, cored and chopped

3½ cups fish stock or bottled clam juice

1 cup dry white wine

2 teaspoons chopped fresh dill leaves

2 teaspoons chopped fresh oregano leaves

10 ounces boneless, skinless salmon, cut into large chunks

¾ cup heavy cream

Salt and pepper to taste

Melt the butter in a saucepan or soup pot, add the onion, leek, carrots, and celery and sauté for 3 to 5 minutes, or until soft. Add the tomato purée, tomato, fish stock, wine, dill, and oregano and simmer for 15 to 20 minutes. Add the salmon and cook for 15 minutes longer. Transfer the soup in batches to a food processor or blender, and purée until smooth. Return to a clean saucepan, add the cream, and simmer gently for 15 minutes. Season with salt and pepper and ladle into warm serving bowls.

tip

If using bottled clam juice, omit or carefully limit the amount of salt used, because clam juice is notoriously salty. In addition, you can thin the juice with water to dilute its intensity.

korean
cucumber soup

serves 4

For the program on Korean cuisine, we took the show to Koreatown in Los Angeles. Daniel Oh, the president of the Korean Restaurant Coalition there, took me on a guided tour of the local Korean food market. It was a unique experience: I saw ingredients I'd never seen elsewhere, from vegetables and fruits to pickles, salads, dried seafood, and prepared foods of all kinds. For the show, I made kimchi, the spicy condiment (see page 154), as well as this simple soup that amounts to much more than the sum of its parts.

3 cucumbers, peeled, seeded, and diced

1½ cups Chicken Stock (page 266)

½ cup rice wine vinegar

¼ cup soy sauce

1 tablespoon toasted (dark) sesame oil

1½ teaspoons sugar

1½ teaspoons white pepper

4 scallions, sliced (green parts only)

1 tablespoon toasted white sesame seeds

1 tablespoon toasted black sesame seeds

Place 2 of the cucumbers in a food processor or blender and add the stock, 1½ cups water, the vinegar, soy sauce, sesame oil, sugar, and white pepper. Purée until smooth and transfer to a mixing bowl. Stir in the remaining cucumber and the scallions. If the consistency of the soup is too thick, add more water. Ladle the soup into serving bowls and garnish with the sesame seeds.

new jersey
clam chowder

serves 4

As much as 70 percent of all the clams enjoyed in soups and sauces worldwide are harvested off the New Jersey coastline. Most of them are Quahog clams, and while filming the show about the state's important seafood industry, I came to appreciate that clamming can be a precarious and sometimes dangerous activity. I serve a variation of this soup at the Rittenhouse Hotel in Philadelphia, where I use pancetta bacon; you might consider making this substitution, too.

2 russet potatoes (about 1 pound), peeled and diced (about 2½ cups)

Salt

6 slices bacon, cut into ¼-inch strips

2 cloves garlic, minced

1 small onion, chopped

2 tablespoons flour

2 cups bottled clam juice

2 cups milk

½ cup heavy cream

Pepper, to taste

1 teaspoon chopped fresh dill

1 tablespoon chopped fresh flat-leaf parsley

1½ cups chopped fresh or bottled clams

Place the potatoes in a large saucepan and add enough salted water to cover by 1 inch. Bring to a boil, reduce the heat to a simmer, and cook for 10 to 15 minutes, or until almost done. Drain and set aside.

Meanwhile, in a separate dry sauté pan, sauté the bacon until almost crisp. Leave the rendered bacon fat and the bacon in the pan, add the garlic and onion, and sauté over medium heat for 2 minutes. Add the flour and cook for 3 to 4 minutes, being careful not to burn the flour. Add the clam juice, milk, cream, pepper, dill, and parsley and bring to a boil, stirring well. Add the potatoes and chopped clams and return to a boil for 1 minute. Ladle into warm serving bowls.

peanut butter soup

serves 4

For our television show on Savannah, Georgia, I felt duty bound to include a peanut recipe. Jimmy Carter, for one, wouldn't want it any other way! Peanut butter soup may sound unusual, but it's a Southern tradition, and Savannah is very much the old South. I grew up in Texas, and although my parents are originally from Atlanta, I had never tasted a peanut butter soup until a few years ago, at Marcel Desaulniers's restaurant, The Trellis, in Williamsburg, Virginia. It may have been my first, but it remains the best I have ever tried.

1 tablespoon butter

½ onion, finely diced

2 tablespoons flour

2 cups milk

2 cups Chicken Stock (page 266)

1 cup smooth peanut butter

¼ cup finely diced celery

2 tablespoons chopped fresh flat-leaf parsley leaves

Salt and pepper, to taste

¼ cup toasted peanuts (see page 269), roughly chopped

Melt the butter in the top of a double boiler set directly on the stovetop over medium heat. Add the onion and sauté for 2 to 3 minutes. Stir in the flour and cook for 2 minutes. Separately, in the bottom part of the double boiler, heat the milk and stock and bring to a simmer. Stir the milk mixture into the flour mixture and whisk over the heat until thick. Clean the bottom half of the double boiler, add water, and bring to a boil. Cover with the top half of the double boiler and whisk in the peanut butter, celery, parsley, salt, and pepper. Heat through for 2 or 3 minutes. Ladle the soup into serving bowls and garnish with the toasted peanuts.

peanuts

Hot roasted peanuts may today be associated with ball games, but the snack is nothing new. As early as 800 B.C., the Incas in Peru were the first to cultivate peanuts, which they used liberally in their largely vegetarian meals. They would also seal them in decorated jars placed inside tombs, making these gourmet gifts for the afterlife the very first packaged peanuts.

Spanish explorers who visited Peru returned home with peanuts in their cargo and began to trade them in other parts of the world, including India and China. In Africa, peanuts found perfect growing conditions and became a vigorous crop across that continent. They were a critical food source for victims of slave trading, who in turn became the first to grow peanuts in North America. The term *goober* is an Americanization of an African word for peanut.

The peanut is actually a member of the legume family and is not a nut at all. The flowers of the peanut bush droop after blooming, and the stalks then grow into the ground, where the peanuts form. Thomas Jefferson experimented with peanut propagation in the 1790s, prompting southern farmers to grow the crop for personal use and livestock feed. During the Civil War, protein-rich peanuts provided sustenance to soldiers on both sides. When Union veterans returned home, they introduced the food to the northern states. After the boll weevil destroyed American cotton crops in the 1890s, botanist George Washington Carver promoted the peanut as a replacement in the fields. From that point it became a viable commodity in the United States.

charleston shrimp bisque

serves 4

After the success of the movie Forrest Gump, *most people recognize Charleston, South Carolina, as the shrimp capital of the East Coast. The restaurants, the local seafood, and the style of Lowcountry cuisine (see page 196) make Charleston one of my favorite cities, and this soup is typical of what you might find served there.*

¼ cup (½ stick) butter

2 cloves garlic, minced

1½ teaspoons chopped fresh rosemary leaves, or ¾ teaspoon dried

1 tablespoon chopped fresh thyme leaves, or 1½ teaspoons dried

½ onion, diced

2 stalks celery, diced

1 pound fresh small shrimp, peeled and deveined

¼ cup flour

3 tablespoons tomato paste

4 cups Chicken Stock (page 266)

1 cup milk

½ cup dry sherry

Salt, to taste

3 tablespoons brandy

½ cup heavy cream

Pepper, to taste

Pinch of ground nutmeg

Melt the butter in a large saucepan over medium-high heat and add the garlic, rosemary, thyme, onion, and celery. Stir well. Coarsely chop half of the shrimp in a food processor and add to the pan. Cook for 4 to 5 minutes, stirring often. Add the flour and tomato paste and continue cooking for 3 or 4 minutes. Add the stock, milk, and sherry, bring to a simmer, and turn down the heat to low. Cook for 15 to 20 minutes, stirring occasionally, or until thickened.

Meanwhile, cook the remaining shrimp. Bring a saucepan of salted water to a boil. Add the shrimp, reduce the heat, and simmer for 3 minutes. Drain and rinse under cold running water to stop the cooking. Drain completely and set aside.

Transfer the soup in batches to a blender or food processor and purée until smooth. Strain through a fine strainer into a clean saucepan and add the reserved cooked shrimp. Stir in the brandy and cream, season with salt and pepper, and add the nutmeg. Heat through for 2 minutes; do not boil. Ladle the soup into serving bowls.

soups

celeriac and pear soup

serves 6 to 8 *On the show's travels to San Francisco, we invited chef Laurent Man-rique, the executive chef of Campton Place restaurant in the Campton Place Hotel, to prepare a menu in the Gascony-based style of cooking that he has taken to the next level. This soup, with its duck garnish and cele-riac, is very much in the style of southwestern France. For a simpler presentation, use just one type of duck breast, although the three styles Laurent uses gives an appealing complexity of flavor. Celeriac, also called celery root, is an underrated vegetable with great flavor, and as this recipe proves, it combines well with the flavor of fruit.*

for the soup

3 tablespoons duck fat, chicken fat, or vegetable oil

5 cups diced peeled celeriac (about 2 celery roots)

1 onion, diced

4 cloves garlic, chopped

7 ripe pears (such as Anjou or Bartlett), unpeeled, cored, and diced

2 tablespoons chopped fresh thyme leaves, or more to taste

8 cups Chicken Stock (page 266)

Salt and pepper, to taste

To prepare the soup, heat the duck fat in a sauté pan. Add the celeriac, onion, and garlic and sauté over medium-high heat for 3 to 4 minutes, or until the onion turns translucent. Add the unpeeled pears and cook until they begin to soften, about 5 minutes longer. Add the thyme.

Meanwhile, in a saucepan, bring the chicken stock to a boil and turn off the heat. Add half of the boiling stock to the sauté pan, return to a boil, turn down the heat, and simmer for 15 to 20 minutes. Remove from the heat and transfer in batches to a food processor or blender. Purée until smooth and strain into a clean saucepan. Add the remaining chicken stock in small increments until the soup reaches the desired consistency (it is not necessary to add all of the stock). Season the soup with salt and pepper and more chopped thyme if desired.

for the garnish

Salt

¼ cup finely diced peeled celeriac

¼ cup finely diced peeled pear, such as Anjou

1 tablespoon olive oil

¼ cup finely diced skinless duck breast

¼ cup finely diced skinless smoked duck breast

¼ cup finely diced duck-breast prosciutto

To prepare the garnish, bring a small saucepan of salted water to a boil. Add the diced celeriac and blanch for 2 to 3 minutes. Add the diced pear and blanch for 2 minutes longer. Remove and drain. Heat the olive oil in a sauté pan set over medium-high heat. Add the skinless (unsmoked) duck breast and sauté for 2 to 3 minutes, tossing occasionally. Remove and drain on paper towels. Place equal amounts of smoked duck breast, prosciutto, sautéed duck breast, blanched celeriac, and blanched pear in the center of each serving bowl. Ladle the soup over.

crab soup with green onion–rice fritters

serves 4

South Carolina is famous for its she-crab soup, made with the meat and roe of blue crabs, but this soup—made without roe—is also typical of Carolina cooking. By all means add ¼ cup of crab roe when it's in season during the spring and early summer. Many cooks in the region hold strong opinions about whether male or female crabs have tastier, sweeter meat, but scientists have concluded that there is precious little difference. The fritters that accompany the soup are also a Southern tradition, and they make this dish almost a meal in itself.

for the soup

¼ cup (½ stick) butter

2 tablespoons chopped onion

2 tablespoons chopped carrot

¼ cup chopped celery

¼ cup flour

2 cups crab stock, fish stock, or bottled clam juice

2 cups milk

½ cup heavy cream

2 teaspoons Tabasco sauce

2 teaspoons Worcestershire sauce

2 tablespoons dry sherry

8 ounces lump crabmeat

Salt and pepper, to taste

To prepare the soup, melt the butter in a large saucepan or soup pot and sauté the onion, carrot, and celery over medium heat for 4 or 5 minutes, or until soft. Stir in the flour to make a roux and continue to cook for 2 or 3 minutes, or until light golden in color. Add the stock, milk, and cream and bring to a low boil. Add the Tabasco sauce, Worcestershire sauce, and sherry, reduce the heat, and simmer for 20 minutes. Add half of the crabmeat and season with salt and pepper (reserve the remaining crab to garnish the fritters).

for the fritters

¼ cup flour

¼ teaspoon ground cumin

¼ teaspoon crab-boil seasoning, such as Old Bay

    Pinch of baking powder

    Salt and pepper, to taste

1   egg, beaten

3   scallions (white and green parts), finely sliced

⅓ cup cooked Carolina or other long-grain rice

2   tablespoons vegetable oil

Prepare the fritters while the soup is cooking. Sift the flour, cumin, crab-boil seasoning, baking powder, salt, and pepper into a mixing bowl. Fold in the beaten egg, scallions, and rice, taking care not to overwork the batter or it will toughen. Pour the vegetable oil into a nonstick sauté pan set over medium-high heat. Spoon the batter into the pan in 1-tablespoon dollops (the fritters should be the same size as silver-dollar pancakes). Turn the fritters once when the batter begins to bubble and the underside is golden brown. When golden brown on both sides, remove the fritters from the pan and pat dry on paper towels.

Ladle the soup into 4 serving bowls and float 2 fritters on the soup in each bowl. Top the fritters with the remaining crabmeat.

tip Crab stock is a welcome by-product of boiling your own crabs to derive the crabmeat. Simply add some sliced onion, celery, and carrot to the water and sprinkle in some crab-boil seasoning.

chilled tomato and avocado soup

I learned many new things when we traveled to Florida and California to produce our show about avocados. Two main types are sold commercially: the darker, bumpy skinned Hass (which is properly pronounced to rhyme with pass*); and the larger, rounder, green Fuerte avocado. Hass avocados are grown almost exclusively in California. I prefer their softer, more buttery texture for most uses, and especially for this soup. (For more on avocados, see page 202.) Add a few drops of hot sauce to the finished product, if you like.*

2 cups tomato juice or vegetable juice

2 cloves garlic, minced

⅓ cup freshly squeezed lime juice

2 ripe avocados, peeled, pitted, and diced

Salt and white pepper, to taste

¾ cup cold water

1 tomato, diced

1 tablespoon chopped fresh basil leaves

1 tablespoon chopped fresh cilantro leaves

¼ cup finely sliced fresh chives

½ cup plain yogurt, optional

In a food processor or blender, purée the tomato juice, garlic, lime juice, and one of the avocados. Season with salt and white pepper and thin with up to ¾ cup of cold water (depending on the ripeness of the avocados) to achieve the desired texture and consistency. Transfer the mixture to a mixing bowl and add the diced tomato. Fold the remaining avocado into the soup together with the basil, cilantro, and chives. Ladle the soup into serving bowls and serve with a dollop of yogurt, if desired.

tip

Avocado oil can be found in specialty or gourmet food stores. Keep a small bottle of oil on hand just in case you can find only the drier variety of avocado for recipes that call for them to be mashed. Adding a little oil will make them smoother, richer, and less mealy.

The plant that modern gardeners spend hours nurturing in their gardens first took root as a weed in South America and was ignored by the agriculturally adept Incas. It spread northward to Mexico, whose natives were the first to try it as a food, probably because it resembled the tomatillo already in their diet. Called *tomatl* after their green cousins, they were ground with chiles to make sauces that have remained popular in Central America to this day.

Spanish explorers returned home with seeds they called *tomate* and the plant got its Old World start, as peasant fare. The nobility was slow to warm to the new food, and botanists warily noted that the tomato belonged to the same family as deadly nightshade. Despite its questionable culinary value, the tomato made its way to Italy via the Spanish-held port of Naples. It was there in the sun-baked soil that the tomato found its European home. Italians began to incorporate the tomato in simple sauces, founding a cooking tradition that came to rival the use of tomatoes in Central American cuisine.

Back in North America, the tomato was once again the object of suspicion. Few Colonial gardeners had the desire to grow them, and many held on to the European notion that they might be poisonous. Even though the gardening visionary Thomas Jefferson championed the tomato, early American cookbooks suggested cooking them for at least three hours to ensure that they could be safely eaten. For years people argued about whether the tomato was a fruit or vegetable. Botanically, the tomato is indeed a fruit, but legally the debate was settled in 1893 when the U.S. Supreme Court ruled that the tomato was a vegetable due to its culinary uses. By World War One, tomatoes were accepted across the country, and improved transportation made the summertime delicacy available year-round. Today they are second only to potatoes in U.S. vegetable production, and the misunderstood tomato is the reigning star of produce counters from coast to coast.

summer gazpacho
with texas blue crab and cilantro

serves 8

This refreshing soup was created by Scott Cohen, the executive chef at the historic La Mansión del Rio Hotel in San Antonio. The Gulf Coast of Texas supplies more blue crab than anywhere else in the country, so Scott is well placed to take advantage. This soup contains the perfect combination of summer flavors and crab, and bear in mind that even if you don't consider yourself a cook, you can still make gazpacho: You have to mix, but there's no cooking involved! Note that you will need to start the recipe a day in advance.

3 English (seedless) cucumbers, peeled and roughly chopped

1 red bell pepper, seeded and chopped

1 yellow bell pepper, seeded and chopped

1 red onion, roughly chopped

4 cloves garlic, minced

7 or 8 beefsteak tomatoes, roughly chopped

1 bunch of cilantro, leaves roughly chopped (about ½ packed cup), 8 whole leaves saved for garnish

1 bunch of basil, leaves roughly chopped (about ½ packed cup)

½ cup olive oil

½ cup sherry vinegar

3 tablespoons premium tequila

Juice of 1 lime

Salt and pepper, to taste

Tomato juice, if necessary

4 ounces lump crabmeat (preferably Texas blue crab)

Place the cucumbers, bell peppers, onion, garlic, tomatoes, chopped cilantro and basil, oil, vinegar, tequila, and lime juice in a large mixing bowl and marinate in the refrigerator for 24 hours, tossing occasionally if possible.

Transfer in batches to a food processor and pulse until smooth but still a little chunky. Season with salt and pepper. If necessary, thin the consistency with a little tomato juice. Transfer to blue-rimmed Mexican martini or margarita glasses, or serving bowls. Add the crabmeat and garnish with the reserved cilantro leaves.

tip

If you wish, also garnish the gazpacho with finely diced endive and mixed red, yellow, and green bell peppers.

indian dhal soup

serves 4

Dhal is an Indian lentil side dish that often accompanies curry, and its naturally moist texture makes it easy to adapt as a soup. Use vegetable stock for a vegetarian version, and yellow lentils if you'd like to give the soup a different color. I was surprised that during my first PBS television series, the most feedback I received followed a segment on Indian food. It seems that there are as many opinions on the subject as there are devotees of the cuisine, which is perhaps less surprising when you consider the diverse regional cooking styles and recipes to be found across such a large country.

2 cups Chicken Stock (page 266)

1 cup red lentils, washed and picked through

1 small onion, diced

1½ cups cold water

2 tablespoons vegetable oil

2 teaspoons ground cumin

3 cloves garlic, finely minced

Salt and pepper, to taste

4 teaspoons plain yogurt

tip

Once I gave a plastic container of carrot soup to a neighbor. She loved the recipe but was embarrassed to give back the container because the soup had stained it. Now I always coat my plastic containers with vegetable-oil spray before I fill them. The only thing the food leaves behind is a smile.

Pour the stock into a saucepan and bring to a boil. Add the lentils and onion, stir, and reduce the heat to a simmer. Cook for about 15 minutes, or until the lentils have become soft, and the liquid is almost absorbed. Remove the pan from the heat and stir in the cold water, a little at a time, until the consistency is smooth. Return the pan to the heat and continue to simmer for 20 minutes.

Meanwhile, in a small sauté pan, heat the oil over medium-high heat and add the cumin, garlic, salt, and pepper. Cook for about 3 minutes, or until the oil begins to smoke. Remove from the heat and slowly stir the mixture into the lentils, being careful not to burn yourself with the hot oil. Thin with a little more water if the consistency is too thick. Ladle the soup into serving bowls and garnish each serving with 1 teaspoon of the yogurt, using a toothpick or the tip of a sharp knife to swirl it into the soup, if desired.

soups

salads

Stuffed Avocado Salad with Avocado Vinaigrette

Artichokes

Jamaican Jerk Asparagus and Artichoke-Heart Salad

West Texas Cole-Slaw Salad

Fresh Tomato Salad with Basil, Tarragon, and Sweet Onion

Warm German Potato-Herb Salad

Roasted Beet, Spinach, and Walnut Salad

Jícama-Citrus Salad

Pear and Mint Chicken Salad

Lobster and Mixed-Herb Salad with Watercress Dressing

Lettuce

Strawberry and Goat Cheese Salad with Poppy-Seed Dressing

Spinach Salad with Smoked Portobellos and Balsamic Vinaigrette

Cantaloupe and Shrimp Salad with Tarragon-Dijon Vinaigrette

Chamomile-Marinated Vegetable Salad

Tomato and Red-Onion Salad with Bruschetta

Coffee-Barbecued Shrimp Salad

Coffee

July Fourth Artichoke Salad

Salmon and Asparagus Salad with Dijon, Lime, and Caper Dressing

Boston Bean and Shrimp Salad with a Molasses Dressing

Butterhead and Mesclun Salad with Grilled Star Fruit and Edible Flowers

Apricot, Arugula, Sweet Onion, and Blueberry Salad

Blueberries

Asparagus and Beet Salad with Watercress and Frisée

Sorrel Salad with Herbs

Tossed Hearts of Romaine with Roasted Peppers and Honey-Lemon Dressing

New Potato, Corn, and Cherry Tomato Salad with Basil-Balsamic Dressing

Corn

Grilled Southern Smoked Chicken Salad with Endive, Carolina Shrimp,
   and Yogurt-Walnut Dressing

It was during Roman times that salads became an intrinsic part of every meal. Initially, they were served at the end of the meal, but they soon were served as a first course when it was observed that raw greens boosted the appetite. To this day, when a salad is presented at the beginning of a meal, it is called Roman style. The English word *salad* comes from the Latin word for salt, because Romans were fond of eating this course simply dressed with the seasoning and a splash of oil and vinegar.

Still today, when most people think of salads, they imagine a pile of dressed lettuce, perhaps with some tomatoes and onion tossed in. As this chapter demonstrates, the ingredients that can be used in salads and the combinations of flavors, colors, and textures are endless. Among the unexpected but pleasingly tasty salad flavorings here are coffee, chamomile, molasses, and mint jelly. The main ingredients featured in the salads in this chapter range from beef to chicken, shellfish, fish, and fruit, as well as herbs and different kinds of greens. The dressings I have created draw from diverse culinary styles, bringing further variety to the plate. And just to dispel the salad stereotype further, a number of these recipes don't involve any lettuce greens at all.

I have placed emphasis here on creating salads that are simple to prepare, composed of ingredients that most people really enjoy and that are readily available. I admit that I particularly enjoy shrimp, asparagus, and onions, for example, which explains their presence in more than one recipe. In most cases, as I note where appropriate, you can make all kinds of adjustments and substitutions according to personal taste, so don't be afraid to experiment and use your favorite ingredients.

stuffed avocado salad with avocado vinaigrette

Growing up in Dallas, my idea of a fancy lunch dish was avocados stuffed with shrimp salad. This summery dish is an updated version, with a light, herbed ricotta replacing the shrimp. This first-course salad can also be served with grilled chicken or fish as an entrée. It's important to use ripe, firm avocados. If they are a little overripe and mushy, use them instead for guacamole or Chilled Tomato and Avocado Soup (page 26).

serves 4

for the avocado vinaigrette

1½ tablespoons rice wine vinegar

1 teaspoon Dijon mustard

¼ teaspoon sugar

Salt and pepper, to taste

1 tablespoon white wine (or water)

3 tablespoons olive oil

2 tablespoons finely diced avocado

for the stuffed avocados

½ cup fresh corn kernels (from 1 ear of corn)

½ cup ricotta cheese

2 tablespoons finely chopped fresh chives, plus 8 long chives, for garnish

Salt and pepper, to taste

2 avocados, cut in half and pitted (skin left on)

Juice of 1 lemon

2 cups mesclun salad mix or other mixed greens, washed

To prepare the vinaigrette, place the vinegar, mustard, sugar, salt, and pepper in a mixing bowl and mix together. Stir in the wine until well blended. Slowly whisk in the olive oil until well incorporated and then fold in the diced avocados. Set aside.

To prepare the avocados, place the corn kernels, ricotta, chives, salt, and pepper in another mixing bowl and mix together. Brush the avocado halves with lemon juice. In a mixing bowl, toss the mixed greens with the vinaigrette and arrange on serving plates. Spoon the ricotta mixture on top of the avocado halves and garnish the ricotta with 2 chives, leaning across each other. Place the avocados on the greens.

jim coleman's flavors

32

The globe artichoke is the culinary crown of the thistle family and the world's largest edible flower. The choke, which we remove before eating the delectable bottom, is actually a mass of florets that turn a beautiful violet blue if left to develop.

Artichokes are thought to have originated in Africa, though some historians believe they are native to Sicily. It was in Italy that they evolved into a culinary art form, and Italians are credited with teaching the world to eat the dangerous-looking vegetable. In 1533, Catherine de Médicis introduced the artichoke to France when she traveled from Florence to marry the future King Henri II. There it was prized not only for its culinary attributes, but also because it was considered an aphrodisiac. Perhaps it was no coincidence that in 1947 Marilyn Monroe was crowned California's first Queen of Artichokes.

Artichokes made their way to America via a Philadelphia seed catalog in 1806, but it was not until 1922, when Italian immigrant Angelo Del Chiaro began to cultivate them near San Francisco, that they gained popularity in the United States. Most of the artichokes served in America are still harvested in Castroville, California, where the cool nightly fog offers perfect growing conditions. The perennial plants are relatives of the sunflower family and can grow to be three to five feet tall. The most productive growing seasons are in the spring and fall, but the huge, tasty flower buds of the artichoke plant can be harvested year-round.

jamaican jerk asparagus and artichoke-heart salad

serves 4

Spicy Jamaican jerk seasoning has been such a popular food trend during the 1990s that by now, it has entered the American mainstream. Jerk seasonings can range from relatively mild (like this one) to incendiary; the heat of the chiles used is what makes all the difference. If you like it hot, substitute one or two habanero chiles for the jalapeño. Although this dish calls for only two teaspoons of the jerk rub, make the entire recipe so you can use it for the grilled chicken recipe on page 150. The rub will keep in a jar in the refrigerator for at least a week. This is a dish that is best accompanied by beer, as asparagus and artichokes are notoriously incompatible with wine.

for the jerk marinade rub

- 1 jalapeño or 2 serrano chiles, seeded and minced

  Juice of 1 lime

- 2 teaspoons soy sauce

- ½ cup sliced scallions (green and white parts)

- 1 teaspoon ground allspice

- 1 teaspoon dried mustard

- 2 cloves garlic, roughly chopped

- 2 teaspoons (packed) light brown sugar

- 1 teaspoon dried thyme

- ½ teaspoon ground cinnamon

  Salt and pepper, to taste

To prepare the jerk marinade rub, combine the chile, lime juice, soy sauce, scallions, allspice, mustard, garlic, sugar, thyme, cinnamon, 1 tablespoon water, and the salt and pepper in a blender and purée until smooth.

To prepare the salad, fill a bowl with water and ice and bring a saucepan of salted water to a boil. Add the asparagus and artichoke hearts to the boiling water. Blanch for 1 or 2 minutes, depending on the thickness of the asparagus and size of the hearts, and transfer to the ice bath to stop the cooking process. Drain and set aside. In a bowl, blend the olive oil, vinegar, and 2 teaspoons of the jerk rub.

for the salad

Salt

20 asparagus spears, stems trimmed

8 ounces frozen artichoke hearts

½ cup olive oil

¼ cup balsamic vinegar

1 large butterhead lettuce, such as Bibb or Boston, washed, leaves separated

2 plum tomatoes, diced

Arrange 5 asparagus spears in the top center of each serving plate. Arrange the artichoke hearts on either side of the asparagus. Place the lettuce below the asparagus spears in the center of each plate. Drizzle the jerk dressing over the whole salad and garnish with the diced tomatoes.

west texas
cole-slaw salad

serves 4

This dish is more salad than slaw, and it's best eaten the same day, because the romaine is prone to wilt after a while. For the TV show, I paired the salad with the traditional San Antonio Easter dish of cabrito: grilled kid goat or lamb. The goat cheese in the dressing gives the slaw element a different spin, and it's appropriate here because plenty of goats are raised on the sparse terrain of West Texas and the Hill Country. As a result, plenty of local goat milk and goat cheese are available in the region.

for the dressing

3 tablespoons balsamic vinegar

¼ cup olive oil

¼ cup crumbled goat cheese

for the slaw

2 cups very finely sliced green cabbage

2 cups sliced romaine leaves

1½ cups fresh corn kernels (from 3 ears of corn)

1 small red onion, finely sliced

1 green bell pepper, roasted, peeled, seeded, and diced (see page 268)

1 red bell pepper, roasted, peeled, seeded, and diced

Salt and pepper, to taste

To prepare the dressing, place the balsamic vinegar, olive oil, and goat cheese in a blender or food processor and blend well.

To prepare the slaw, place the cabbage and romaine in a mixing bowl and add the corn, onion, and bell peppers. Mix well and season with salt and pepper. Drizzle the goat cheese dressing over, toss well, and divide onto serving plates.

fresh tomato salad with basil, tarragon, and sweet onion

serves 4

While we were on location with the TV show in Texas, we took the opportunity to devote a program to culinary herbs. The star of the show was the extensive Fredericksburg Herb Farm, owned by Bill and Sylvia Varney. Located in the Hill Country about one and a half hours (by car) west of San Antonio, it's well worth a visit, not only for the vast array of herbs, but also for the incredible tomatoes and sweet onions they grow. While visiting, I was inspired to create this summer salad.

for the dressing

- 1 teaspoon Dijon mustard
- 1 tablespoon balsamic vinegar
- Juice of 1 lime
- 2 cloves garlic, finely minced
- 1/4 cup olive oil
- 3 tablespoons julienned fresh basil leaves
- 3 tablespoons julienned fresh tarragon leaves

for the salad

- 4 tomatoes, cored and cut into 1/2-inch-thick slices
- Salt and pepper, to taste
- 1 large sweet onion, cut into 1/4-inch-thick slices and separated into rings
- 4 fresh basil leaves, for garnish

To prepare the dressing, place the mustard, vinegar, lime juice, and garlic in a mixing bowl and whisk together. Slowly add the olive oil in a steady stream and whisk until well blended. Stir in the julienned basil and tarragon.

Fan the tomato slices around the edges of each serving plate and sprinkle with salt and pepper. Toss the onion rings in the dressing and arrange over the tomatoes. Drizzle some of the remaining dressing over the salads and garnish with the basil leaves.

warm german
potato-herb salad

serves 4

The herbs at the Fredericksburg Herb Farm (see page 37) also inspired me to prepare this salad for my show. One of the largest immigrant groups that first settled in Texas Hill Country were Germans, as many of the town names (such as Fredericksburg and New Braunfels) suggest. They brought potatoes and other crops, such as kohlrabi, which prospered in their new surroundings. Traditionally, German potato salad contains bacon, vinegar, and sugar, rather than the mayonnaise and bell peppers that characterize the typical American potato salad. This salad, which makes a fine accompaniment for grilled foods, especially pork, can be served warm or at room temperature.

2 pounds small new or red potatoes, washed well and cut into eighths

Salt

7 slices bacon, cut into ¼-inch strips

1 small red onion, finely chopped

2½ tablespoons cider vinegar

½ teaspoon sugar

¼ cup Chicken Stock (page 266)

Pepper, to taste

1 tablespoon fresh flat-leaf parsley leaves, chopped

1 tablespoon fresh rosemary, chopped

1 tablespoon fresh thyme, chopped

Place the potatoes in a large saucepan and add enough salted water to cover by 1 inch. Bring to a simmer and cook for 6 to 8 minutes, or until soft. While the potatoes are cooking, heat a large nonstick sauté pan over medium-high heat and cook the bacon until crispy and golden brown. Remove the bacon and drain on paper towels; leave 3 tablespoons of the fat in the pan. Add the onion to the pan and sauté over medium-high heat for 2 or 3 minutes, or until soft. Add 1½ tablespoons of the vinegar, the sugar, and stock, reduce the heat to medium-low, and simmer for 3 minutes.

Drain the potatoes and place in a mixing bowl. While still warm, add the onion mixture and season with salt and pepper. Add the remaining 1 tablespoon of vinegar and the parsley, rosemary, and thyme. Crumble the reserved bacon and sprinkle over the salad.

roasted beet, spinach, and walnut salad

serves 4

I created this recipe to showcase the perfect beets and spinach grown by Chino Farms (see page 4). Since this recipe contains few ingredients, it's important that they be of high quality. For this reason, it makes the most sense to prepare this salad in peak season—late spring through fall. Roasting beets has become popular over the past few years. This cooking technique eliminates any slight bitterness the beets may have, while bringing out their nutty quality. Serve the salad at room temperature.

5 tablespoons olive oil

4 beets (about 1 pound)

1 large onion, cut in half

1/2 cup walnut pieces

2 tablespoons balsamic vinegar

2 cloves garlic, minced

Salt and pepper, to taste

2 cups baby spinach, washed

1/2 cup crumbled blue cheese, such as Stilton or Gorgonzola

Preheat the oven to 400° F. Lightly brush a roasting pan or cookie sheet with 1/2 tablespoon of the olive oil. Place the beets and onion in the pan and roast in the oven for about 30 minutes, or until the beets are tender. Add the walnuts to the roasting pan for the last 5 minutes.

In a mixing bowl, whisk the remaining 4 1/2 tablespoons of olive oil with the balsamic vinegar, garlic, salt, and pepper until well blended. Peel the beets and onion, slice, and add to the bowl with the toasted walnuts. Add the spinach and toss together. Transfer the salad to serving plates and sprinkle with the blue cheese.

tip

If you want to use up some unshelled walnuts or hazelnuts in a recipe, but dread the chore of cracking them, make it easy on yourself. Cover them with water in a saucepan and bring to a boil. Remove the pan from the heat, cover, and let the nuts cool for at least 15 minutes. After you wipe them dry, you will find them much easier to crack.

jícama-citrus salad

serves 4

Herbie Yamamura owns one of the largest lime groves in Florida as well as the only commercial kumquat orchard. His Homestead-based company, LimeCo Inc., is also the largest packer and shipper of limes in the country, and he deserves his nickname, the Lime King. Most of his orchards have had to be replanted over the past few years following the devastation of Hurricane Andrew in 1992, and, more recently, of a citrus canker that has crippled the state's lime industry. Jícama is a crisp root vegetable that's also known as "the Mexican potato," and citrus juice highlights its marvelously refreshing quality.

for the dressing

- 2 tablespoons rice wine vinegar
- 1 tablespoon honey

  Salt and pepper, to taste
- 2 tablespoons chopped fresh cilantro leaves
- 5 tablespoons olive oil

for the salad

- 2 oranges, peeled and sectioned
- 2 limes, peeled and sectioned
- 1 jícama (about 14 ounces), peeled and julienned (about 2¾ cups)
- 1 red onion, finely sliced
- 1 head of Boston lettuce (or other butterhead lettuce), washed and leaves separated
- 6 kumquats, cut lengthwise into 4 quarters, or 1 additional small orange, sectioned

To prepare the dressing, place the vinegar, honey, salt, pepper, and cilantro in a mixing bowl and slowly whisk in the olive oil in a steady stream.

To prepare the salad, add the orange and lime segments, jícama, and red onion to the bowl containing the dressing and toss until completely coated. Evenly arrange the lettuce leaves on four serving plates and mound the dressed ingredients over the lettuce. Spoon an additional 1 teaspoon of the dressing over the lettuce leaves and garnish the plate with the kumquats.

tip

If your local supermarket or specialty produce store does not carry kumquats, look for them in Asian markets. Kumquats have a sweet-tart flavor, and they are eaten whole, skin and all.

pear and mint
chicken salad

serves 4

This light, flavorful salad is a good choice if you need a do-ahead first course. The marriage of pears and walnuts is traditional, but pears with mustard and horseradish is unusual. The sweet-and-hot combination works well, though, and the cooling mint rounds out the flavors nicely. This salad, from my weekly radio show, A Chef's Table, *also features contrasting but complementary textures. I really enjoy cooking with mustard at home. I experiment by flavoring prepared mustard to complement whatever I'm cooking on the grill or on the stove, and the results are real taste treats.*

⅓ cup mint jelly

3 tablespoons Dijon mustard

1 tablespoon horseradish

4 skinless, boneless chicken breast halves, about 6 ounces each

4 cups mesclun salad mix or other mixed greens, washed

2 pears, cored and sliced

⅓ cup coarsely chopped walnuts

1 tablespoon cider vinegar

1 tablespoon olive oil

Prepare the grill.

In a small saucepan, cook the mint jelly over low heat until melted. Remove the pan from the heat and stir in the mustard and horseradish. Set aside, reserving 2 tablespoons of the jelly-mustard mixture separately.

Grill the chicken breasts over medium heat on the uncovered grill for 12 to 15 minutes, or until no longer pink. Turn the breasts once during cooking, brushing with the reserved 2 tablespoons of jelly-mustard glaze. Transfer the cooked chicken to a cutting board, let cool slightly, and then cut the breasts into diagonal slices.

While the chicken is grilling, toss the greens with the pears and walnuts in a salad bowl. To prepare the dressing, stir together the remaining jelly-mustard glaze, the vinegar, and the oil. Arrange the greens on serving plates and place the sliced chicken on top. Drizzle the dressing over each salad.

lobster and mixed-herb salad with watercress dressing

serves 4

This elegant salad is refreshing and energizing. I really enjoy the palate-cleansing qualities of herb salads, and if you do too, you might want to double the herbs in this recipe and reduce the amount of greens—or omit them entirely. The puréed watercress dressing is versatile and can be used for most other salads, especially those with grilled chicken.

for the dressing

- 1 bunch of watercress, stems trimmed
- ½ small onion, chopped
- ¼ cup rice wine vinegar
- 1 sprig of fresh chervil
- ¼ cup olive oil
- Salt and white pepper, to taste

To prepare the dressing, place the watercress, onion, vinegar, and chervil in a food processor and purée. With the machine running, pour in the oil in a steady stream until emulsified. Season with salt and pepper and set aside.

To prepare the salad, bring a large saucepan of water to a boil and add the lemon, peppercorns, and salt. Skewer each lobster tail lengthwise with a bamboo skewer and add to the pan. Poach for 3 or 4 minutes, or until the lobster is cooked through. Using tongs, remove the lobster tails and hold under cold running water to stop the cooking process. Pull out the skewers. Remove the meat from the shells by cutting the underneath membrane with scissors and cut the lobster meat into ¼-inch slices.

for the salad

- 1 lemon, quartered
- 1 tablespoon black peppercorns
- 1 tablespoon kosher salt
- 4 frozen lobster tails (6 to 8 ounces each), thawed
- ½ cup coarsely chopped fresh chervil leaves
- ½ cup coarsely chopped fresh basil leaves
- ½ cup coarsely chopped fresh flat-leaf parsley leaves
- ½ cup coarsely chopped fresh tarragon leaves
- 2 cups mesclun salad mix or other mixed greens, washed
- 1 tomato, cut in half, seeds and pulp removed, and julienned
- ½ red bell pepper, seeded and julienned
- ½ yellow bell pepper, seeded and julienned

Place the chervil, basil, parsley, tarragon, and greens in a mixing bowl. Pour in the watercress dressing and toss to coat completely. Mound the dressed greens in the center of serving plates and fan the lobster slices around the greens. Garnish the salad with the slices of tomato and red and yellow bell peppers.

tip When chopping herbs, use a very sharp knife and chop gently to avoid bruising them.

lettuce

Before airfreight became standard in the 1970s, iceberg lettuce was the only salad material hearty enough to withstand cross-country shipping. Back then, the crispy, green globes were trucked in cases of ice, which is how they got their nickname. These days even the produce sections of good small-town markets are well stocked with all kinds of greens, and upscale salads are routinely served on ordinary kitchen tables. Americans have come a long way from the days of iceberg wedges drizzled with bottled dressing, but salads were tossed centuries before that first container of Thousand Island hit the shelves.

Salad greens were cultivated in the gardens of Babylon, and lettuces were a constant menu item in the courts of Persian kings. In Egypt, lettuces were carefully grown in checkerboard patterns divided by irrigation canals, and four varieties were served up on ancient Greek tables. It was the Romans (see also page 31) who developed some of the types of head lettuce we enjoy today. Columbus is credited with introducing lettuce to the New World, but it was largely ignored for generations. After the Revolutionary War, many European traditions, including that of a daily salad, were abandoned in the Western Hemisphere. Green salads were only consumed on a small scale out of home gardens. Between the Civil War and World War One, salads in our country tended to consist of mostly meat and cooked vegetables with a few lettuce leaves used as garnish. It was not until European trends were repopularized in the middle of the twentieth century that green salads got regular billing on menus in the United States.

Americans now graze on more salads per capita than do diners anywhere else in the world. The two main types of lettuce we enjoy are the crisp-leafed varieties such as iceberg and romaine, and the softer-textured butterhead lettuces, like Bibb or Boston. Dozens of lettuce varieties are raised commercially in twenty of the states; California tops the list with 70 percent of the production. The combination of American creativity and exotic international ingredients has created almost as many kinds of salads as there are salad eaters. Perhaps as far as salads are concerned, we have only seen the tip of the iceberg.

strawberry and goat cheese salad with poppy-seed dressing

serves 4

While preparing to film a show about strawberries at a family farm in northern California, I learned that the fruit has been cultivated in Europe since the fourteenth century. The popularity of the fruit really took off when the larger and more flavorful New World strawberry was taken to Europe and hybridized. In developing the idea for this unusual salad, I embellished the successful flavor combination for an hors d'oeuvre I sometimes serve at the Rittenhouse Hotel: a crouton topped with goat cheese and a strawberry.

for the dressing

2 tablespoons rice wine vinegar

1 tablespoon Dijon mustard

1 tablespoon sugar

2 tablespoons poppy seeds

Salt and pepper, to taste

¼ cup olive oil

for the salad

1 head of red leaf lettuce, washed, 4 large leaves removed and the rest roughly chopped

1 pint strawberries, hulled and sliced

4 ounces goat cheese, preferably Montrachet, crumbled (about ⅔ cup)

¼ cup pine nuts, toasted (see page 269)

1 red onion, thinly sliced

To prepare the dressing, place the vinegar, mustard, sugar, poppy seeds, salt, and pepper in a mixing bowl and combine. Pour in the olive oil in a steady stream while whisking and continue to whisk until emulsified.

To prepare the salad, in a separate mixing bowl, toss together the chopped lettuce, strawberries, goat cheese, pine nuts, and onion. Add the dressing and toss the salad until well coated. Place the reserved large lettuce leaves on each serving plate and top with the tossed salad.

spinach salad with smoked portobellos
and balsamic vinaigrette

serves 4

One of my guests on Flavors of America *was Dr. Deborah Chud from The Children's Hospital in Boston, author of the successful* Gourmet Prescription *cookbook. Suffering from chronic pain and high blood sugar levels, Dr. Chud tried various diets without success. She developed her own regimen, reducing her carbohydrate and fat intake and using common sense. She replaces the taste of added fat with flavor-enhancing techniques such as stovetop smoking. Available at kitchen stores, smokers are an inexpensive means of giving everyday ingredients a deliciously different spin.*

2 portobello mushrooms (about 5 ounces each), stemmed

Salt and pepper, to taste

for the vinaigrette

1 clove garlic, chopped

1 tablespoon chopped shallot

¼ cup balsamic vinegar

¼ cup olive oil

Salt and pepper, to taste

2 pounds fresh spinach, stemmed and washed

½ red onion, sliced into rings

2 cups cherry tomatoes, halved

Prepare a stovetop smoker with 1 tablespoon of hickory chips sprinkled with 1 tablespoon of water. Place the mushrooms on the smoker rack and half-close the lid. Set the smoker on medium-high heat and when smoke first appears, close the lid. Smoke the mushrooms for 8 minutes. Turn off the heat and keep the smoker closed for 10 minutes. Remove the mushrooms and let cool. Cut on the bias into ½-inch-thick slices and season with salt and pepper.

To prepare the vinaigrette, place the garlic, shallot, and vinegar in a food processor and purée. With the machine running, slowly add the olive oil in a steady stream until emulsified. Season with salt and pepper. Place the spinach in a large mixing bowl and toss with the vinaigrette. Arrange the spinach on serving plates and top with the mushrooms and red onion. Arrange the cherry tomatoes around the salad.

cantaloupe and shrimp salad with tarragon-dijon vinaigrette

serves 4

Combine a shrimping center such as Charleston, South Carolina, with a hot and humid climate for much of the salad season, and it's no wonder that pairing fruit and shrimp is popular in the region. Melon and shrimp make a particularly refreshing combination. Cantaloupe is one of my favorite fruits, and this seemed like the perfect opportunity to use it in a salad. I use the mild rice wine vinegar in this dressing to keep acidity low; the lemon juice and the vinegar in prepared mustard already provide some sharpness.

for the vinaigrette

- 1 tablespoon Dijon mustard
- 1 tablespoon rice wine vinegar
- 1 tablespoon freshly squeezed lemon juice
- 1 clove garlic, finely minced
- 1 tablespoon chopped fresh tarragon leaves

  Pinch of cayenne pepper
- ¼ cup olive oil

for the salad

- 12 extra-large shrimp (10 to 12 ounces total)
- 1 tomato, cored and chopped
- 2 cups mesclun salad mix or other mixed greens, washed
- 1 large cantaloupe melon, cut in half, seeded, peeled, and thinly sliced into half-moons

To prepare the vinaigrette, combine the mustard, vinegar, lemon juice, garlic, tarragon, and cayenne in a small mixing bowl until well blended. Slowly add the olive oil in a steady stream and whisk until emulsified.

To prepare the salad, fill a bowl with water and ice. Bring a saucepan of water to a boil, add the shrimp, and cook for 3 to 4 minutes, or until cooked. Transfer the shrimp to the ice bath to stop the cooking process. Peel, devein, and chill the shrimp. Place the tomato and lettuce greens in a large mixing bowl and toss together. Add the vinaigrette and toss until well coated. Arrange the cantaloupe around the perimeter of each serving plate and mound the tossed greens in the center. Place three large shrimp on top of the greens at the 2 o'clock position, 6 o'clock, and 10 o'clock. Drizzle with any remaining vinaigrette left in the bowl.

chamomile-marinated vegetable salad

The first tea estates in the New World were planted in the Charleston area of South Carolina. The only remaining commercial tea farm in the United States, Charleston Tea Plantation, owned by American Classic Tea, is located twenty-five miles south of Charleston. That was good enough reason for me to dedicate a show to cooking with tea. Chamomile is a popular herbal tea made with a type of dried daisy, and its floral, grassy tones certainly give this salad a summery feel. You can substitute mint or jasmine tea for this recipe, which also works well without the tea infusion.

for the dressing

2 tablespoons balsamic vinegar

2½ tablespoons brewed chamomile tea, at room temperature

1½ tablespoons julienned fresh basil leaves

2 cloves garlic, minced

2 tablespoons olive oil

for the salad

2 plum tomatoes, cut into wedges

½ large green bell pepper, thinly sliced

1 yellow squash, cut into ½-inch slices

½ red onion, thinly sliced

2 tablespoons chopped fresh tarragon leaves

1 tablespoon chopped walnuts

1 head of red leaf lettuce, washed and separated into leaves

To prepare the dressing, combine the vinegar, tea, basil, and garlic in a small mixing bowl and whisk in the olive oil until emulsified.

To prepare the salad, place the tomatoes, bell pepper, squash, onion, and tarragon in a large mixing bowl and combine. Add the dressing and toss to combine. Let the salad marinate at room temperature for about 1 hour. Stir in the walnuts. Arrange 3 or 4 lettuce leaves on each plate and top with the vegetable mixture.

tip To brew chamomile tea, add ¼ cup of boiling water to a cup containing 2 teabags and let the tea infuse until cool. Strain off the amount needed for this recipe and save the rest to drink (you will need to dilute it). Chamomile makes a relaxing, caffeine-free tea that soothes the digestive system.

tomato and red-onion salad with bruschetta

serves 4

Bruschetta—bread toasted with olive oil in the Italian tradition—is another welcome food trend that has entered the American culinary mainstream, and it makes an interestingly different way to present a tomato and onion salad. In summertime, I serve a version of this salad at the Rittenhouse Hotel, and I always include a tomato and red-onion salad for my family's July Fourth celebration, not least to celebrate the onset of peak tomato season. So it is no surprise that I included this recipe on our Independence Day TV show.

for the salad

3 tablespoons balsamic vinegar

2 tablespoons extra-virgin olive oil

1 teaspoon minced garlic

1 red onion, sliced lengthwise and julienned

4 plum tomatoes, roughly chopped in ½-inch pieces

1 teaspoon chopped fresh flat-leaf parsley leaves

1 teaspoon chopped fresh basil leaves

Salt and pepper, to taste

2 tablespoons sugar (optional)

for the bruschetta

8 slices French baguette, cut on the bias about ¾ inch thick

3 tablespoons olive oil

Salt and pepper, to taste

4 cups mesclun salad mix or other mixed greens, washed

To prepare the salad, place the vinegar, oil, and garlic in a mixing bowl and whisk together. Add the onion, tomatoes, parsley, basil, salt, and pepper and thoroughly combine. Add the sugar if you wish, or if the tomatoes are acidic. Cover the bowl and refrigerate for at least 1 hour before serving to allow the flavors to marry.

Preheat the broiler.

To prepare the bruschetta, brush both sides of the bread with the oil and season with salt and pepper. Toast the bread under the broiler until crisp and golden brown.

Arrange the salad greens on serving plates. Spread the salad on top of the bruschetta and gently lean 2 bruschetta against the greens on each plate, crossing each other.

salads

49

coffee-barbecued shrimp salad

Coffee is often the surprising secret ingredient in prize-winning barbecue sauces; another is chocolate. Using coffee in barbecue sauce as well as in "redeye" gravy is an authentic Texan tradition, dating back to the days of the open range and cowboy cooking. I'm sure that originally, it was added for economy rather than flavor—the camp cook preferred not to throw out leftover coffee. It's not as strange as it may seem and you'll enjoy the results. This sauce can be used with chicken or ribs, and it can be stored in the refrigerator in an airtight container for at least three months.

for the coffee barbecue sauce

- 3 tablespoons butter
- 5 cloves garlic, minced
- 1 jalapeño chile, seeded and minced
- ½ onion, chopped
- 1 teaspoon pure red chili powder
- 2 tablespoons tomato paste
- Zest and juice of 1 lime
- ¾ cup fresh brewed strong coffee
- ½ cup rice wine vinegar
- 1 cup tomato ketchup
- ¼ cup chopped fresh cilantro leaves
- ¼ cup (packed) dark brown sugar
- 1 teaspoon ground cumin
- 2 tablespoons Worcestershire sauce
- Salt and pepper, to taste

Soak 4 bamboo skewers in water for at least 30 minutes (this will prevent them from burning up while cooking).

To prepare the barbecue sauce, melt the butter in a nonstick sauté pan over medium heat. Add the garlic, jalapeño, onion, and chili powder and sauté for 2 to 3 minutes, stirring often. Add the tomato paste and lime zest and cook for 2 to 3 minutes longer. Add the coffee, vinegar, ketchup, lime juice, cilantro, brown sugar, cumin, Worcestershire sauce, salt, and pepper and turn down the heat to low. Simmer for 20 to 30 minutes, or until thickened, stirring constantly.

Preheat the broiler.

for the salad

16 jumbo shrimp (about 1¼ pounds), peeled and deveined

1 tablespoon rice wine vinegar

3 tablespoons olive oil

2 cups mesclun salad mix or other mixed greens, washed

To prepare the salad, place 4 shrimp on each bamboo skewer and place on a baking dish under the broiler (alternatively, grill the shrimp). Broil or grill the shrimp for about 2 minutes on each side or until cooked through. Brush both sides of the shrimp with the barbecue sauce during the last minute of cooking.

Place 1 tablespoon of the barbecue sauce and the vinegar in a large mixing bowl, add the oil, and whisk together. Add the greens and toss well to coat. Arrange the greens in a mound in the center of each serving plate and arrange the shrimp on top of the greens. Drizzle with some of the remaining barbecue sauce.

coffee

From cities to the suburbs, coffeehouses are the new hot spots. People who used to ask for nothing more than a "cup of joe" are now connoisseurs who know their espressos from their mochaccinos. Coffee may be hip, but it is not new; this beverage has livened up cultures around the world for centuries.

Legend has it that coffee was discovered around A.D. 850 when Ethiopian goatherds noticed that their flocks had an extra spring in their step after eating coffee plants. Looking for an explanation, they took one of the plants to a local holy man, who was the first to brew a drink from the beans. He found it was just the thing to keep him awake during lengthy prayer sessions. People knew a good thing when they saw it, and after Arab growers began cultivating the plant around 1575, coffee was soon in demand across the Middle East and Europe.

In the 1700s coffee was introduced in South America and Central America, where it flourished in ideal growing conditions. The establishment of the large coffee plantations in this region marked the beginning of the highly competitive coffee trade around the world. Second only to oil as an item of world trade, coffee's price is listed in commodity and stock exchanges. The World Bank has even used coffee instead of currency on occasion, and some countries that produce the crop have exchanged it for foreign aid from wealthier nations.

Americans first turned to coffee as a means to protest the high English tax levied on tea, and it has warmed our hearts ever since. In 1878, James Sanborn and Caleb Chase were the first to market ground coffee sealed in cans, and in 1907 President Theodore Roosevelt coined the first coffee slogan when he proclaimed the coffee at Nashville's Maxwell House Hotel "good to the last drop." Americans made a patriotic sacrifice in 1942 when coffee was rationed. But in postwar years, the thirst for coffee was stronger than ever, and amid the booming job market the great American coffee break was born.

july fourth
artichoke salad

serves 4

If it's July Fourth, the chances are that you'll be grilling, and you'll need a salad that stands up well to smoky, robust flavors. This one certainly fits the bill, as it has plenty of body and flavor of its own. My family enjoys artichokes and fennel, so we often celebrate July Fourth at home with barbecued burgers, ribs, and this salad. You can serve this salad as a starter, with or without lettuce greens. Note that for best results, this salad should marinate for at least three hours ahead of time.

¼ cup white vinegar

2 tablespoons freshly squeezed lemon juice

¼ cup virgin olive oil

2 tablespoons chopped fresh flat-leaf parsley leaves

1 fennel bulb (about 12 ounces), cored and finely sliced

1 red onion, finely sliced

6 artichokes, cooked, cleaned, and quartered (see page 6)

2 tablespoons chopped fresh dill leaves

Salt and pepper, to taste

4 cups mesclun salad mix or other mixed greens, washed

1 tomato, cut in half, seeds and pulp removed, chopped

4 sprigs of fresh dill

In a mixing bowl, whisk together the vinegar, lemon juice, oil, and parsley. Add the fennel, onion, artichokes, and dill; combine thoroughly; and season with salt and pepper. Cover the bowl with plastic wrap and transfer to the refrigerator. Let it sit for at least 3 hours for the flavors to marry.

Arrange the salad greens on serving plates and top with the artichoke salad. Garnish with the tomato and dill and drizzle the salads with any vinaigrette remaining in the mixing bowl, if desired.

tip

If you only need a little bit of lemon juice in a recipe, try this. Break the skin of the lemon with a toothpick and squeeze out the amount of juice you need. Reinsert the toothpick and place the lemon in a plastic bag to store in the refrigerator. It will keep in this manner for a long time and can be used repeatedly.

salmon and asparagus salad with dijon, lime, and caper dressing

serves 4

I chose this combination of ingredients for a show about Mother's Day brunch simply because my wife loves salmon and asparagus! The month of May is also a perfect time of year for both ingredients. The idea behind this recipe is that the loving husband puts the salad together while the helpful kids wash the dishes and set the table. If they are old enough, get them to help with the dressing. The deserving mother will certainly be impressed!

for the dressing

Zest of 2 large limes

Juice of 1 lime

1/2 tablespoon capers, drained

2 1/2 tablespoons Dijon mustard

2 tablespoons chopped fresh tarragon leaves

1 teaspoon sugar

Salt and pepper, to taste

1/3 cup olive oil

To prepare the dressing, place the lime zest, lime juice, capers, mustard, tarragon, sugar, salt, and pepper in a mixing bowl. Add the oil in a steady stream and whisk until emulsified.

To prepare the salad, pour the wine into a nonstick skillet and bring to a boil. Add the salmon, reduce the heat to a simmer, and cover the pan. Poach for about 8 minutes, or until the salmon is cooked through. Remove the lid and let cool. Meanwhile, place the potatoes in a saucepan and add enough water to cover. Lightly salt the water. Bring to a boil and cook for 10 to 15 minutes, or until the potatoes are tender. Strain and place in a covered dish to keep warm. Add some water to the same pan and using a steamer basket, steam the asparagus for 3 or 4 minutes, or until tender. Remove the asparagus and cool under cold running water to stop the cooking process. Transfer to a mixing bowl and set aside.

for the salad

½ cup white wine

1 pound salmon fillet

1 pound small new potatoes, quartered

Salt

1 pound asparagus, trimmed and cut into 2-inch pieces

1 head of green leaf lettuce, leaves separated and washed

2 hard-boiled eggs, shelled and cut into quarters

Arrange the lettuce leaves on serving plates. Add the eggs decoratively around the lettuce leaves. Add ⅓ cup of the dressing to the bowl containing the asparagus and toss together. Flake the salmon into large chunks, add to the bowl, and gently toss again. Place the salmon mixture on top of the lettuce and drizzle the salad with the remaining dressing (or to taste).

tip My mother always taught me that throwing ice cubes in the garbage disposal would sharpen its blades, but my plumber informed me that is an old wives' tale. He may be right, but it still makes me feel better. I do know that tossing in excess citrus rinds will deodorize your appliance, especially after disposing of anything with a strong smell.

boston bean and shrimp salad with a molasses dressing

serves 4

I have always wondered why Boston is known as Beantown. While filming our show on historic Boston, I learned that baking beans with molasses was a Saturday tradition in the Puritan-influenced city, as cooking on Sunday was frowned upon. In honor of that, I have added authentic baked-bean flavorings to this dressing, and I paired navy beans (favored for Boston baked beans) with the same type of shrimp that we filmed being landed at the commercial fish auction in Gloucester, Massachusetts.

for the dressing

¼ cup olive oil

1½ teaspoons red wine vinegar

1 tablespoon dark molasses

1 teaspoon ground cumin

1 teaspoon garlic powder

1 teaspoon onion powder

Salt and pepper, to taste

for the salad

1 can (15 ounces) navy beans, rinsed and drained

1 red bell pepper, seeded and cut into very thin strips

8 ounces precooked small shrimp

2 scallions, green part only, chopped

1 butterhead lettuce, such as Boston or Bibb, washed, 4 large leaves reserved and the rest finely chopped

To prepare the dressing, place the oil, vinegar, molasses, cumin, garlic powder, onion powder, salt, and pepper in a mixing bowl. Whisk together until well blended.

To prepare the salad, add the beans, bell pepper, shrimp, and scallions to the dressing and combine to coat well. Place a lettuce leaf on each of 4 serving plates and top with the chopped lettuce. Spoon the bean and shrimp mixture over the lettuce and drizzle with any remaining dressing left in the bowl.

**roasted beet,
spinach, and
walnut salad**
(page 39)

**jícama-citrus
salad**
(page 40)

maine rock crab cakes with tartar sauce
(page 101)

coffee-barbecued shrimp salad
(page 50)

roasted pork loin with honey-orange glaze
(page 130)

grilled pepper pork chops with mango-corn salsa
(page 133)

butterhead and mesclun salad with grilled star fruit and edible flowers

serves 4

This is a delicate, colorful, and pretty salad that sets the mood for a Valentine's Day dinner and goes perfectly with a glass of champagne. These days, edible flowers such as nasturtiums, chive blossoms, pansies, and mint flowers are available at upscale grocery stores, even in February, when they are sure to be hothouse-grown. They are not only a romantic touch that looks good on the plate; the flowers also contribute peppery or herbal flavor tones to the salad.

for the dressing

3 tablespoons champagne vinegar

1 teaspoon minced garlic

¼ cup finely chopped mixed fresh herbs, such as chives, tarragon, parsley, and thyme

Salt and pepper, to taste

⅓ cup olive oil

for the salad

1 star fruit, cut crosswise into ¼-inch slices

1 butterhead lettuce, such as Boston or Bibb, washed and leaves separated

2 cups mesclun salad mix or other mixed greens, washed

½ head radicchio, finely sliced

16 edible flowers

To prepare the dressing, combine the vinegar, garlic, herbs, salt, and pepper in a mixing bowl and allow to steep for 15 minutes. Slowly whisk in the oil until completely emulsified.

Prepare the grill (or alternatively, use a grill pan or broiler). Lightly grill or broil the star fruit for about 3 minutes on each side. Place the lettuce leaves on 4 serving plates and mound the mesclun greens on top. Garnish with the radicchio and arrange the edible flowers and star fruit on the lettuce leaves around the edge of the salad. Drizzle the dressing over the salad.

apricot, arugula, sweet onion, and blueberry salad

serves 4

Carole Peck, chef-owner of the Good News Cafe in Woodbury, Connecticut, created this salad recipe. I enjoyed filming our show from New England with Carole, whose trademark is cooking with garden-fresh local ingredients, many of which are supplied by small organic family farms located near her restaurant. Blueberries thrive in New England, where they are frequently used in salads as well as in desserts. The intense flavors of the grilled apricots, the peppery arugula, and the sweet onion make a deliciously unique combination of flavors. You will not need all of the vinegar, but it keeps for at least one month, refrigerated, and is useful for other vinaigrettes and marinades. If you are using frozen blueberries in the salad, eat it up the same day, as they will lose their texture and become too mushy otherwise.

for the blueberry vinegar

1 cup fresh or frozen blueberries

½ cup sugar

2 cups white wine vinegar, warmed

To prepare the blueberry vinegar, place the blueberries, sugar, and vinegar in a food processor or blender and purée. Strain through a fine-mesh strainer into a large glass bottle or jar and store in the refrigerator until ready to use.

To prepare the salad, place the onion in a shallow dish and sprinkle with the salt, followed by the basil, lemon juice, and oil. Cover the dish with plastic wrap and marinate in the refrigerator for at least 2 hours and up to 3 days.

for the salad

1 Vidalia onion (or other sweet onion), very finely sliced

1 tablespoon kosher or sea salt

¼ cup chopped fresh basil leaves

Juice of 1 lemon

2 tablespoons extra-virgin olive oil

4 fresh apricots, cut in half and pitted

1¼ cups fresh or frozen blueberries

2 cups packed arugula, washed

⅓ cup vegetable oil

Prepare the grill (alternatively, use a grill pan or broiler). Grill or broil the apricots for 30 seconds to 1 minute on each side. Remove and cut into ¼-inch slices. Remove the onion mixture from the refrigerator, transfer to a serving bowl, and add the blueberries. Toss together and add the arugula. In a bowl, whisk together ¼ cup of the blueberry vinegar with the vegetable oil and pour the vinaigrette over the salad. Toss again to combine thoroughly. Transfer to serving plates and garnish with the apricots.

blueberries

Blueberries were a treat just waiting to be discovered when humans first arrived in North America. When nomads began to cross the Bering Strait, they became big fans of this indigenous fruit. These first Americans enjoyed the berries in season and learned to dry them for the lean times in winter. In the late eighteenth century Captain James Cook made note of blueberry preparations of the Indians of the Pacific Northwest, who by then had developed a variety of recipes.

Taking a cue from their predecessors, Europeans who settled in America began to tuck blueberries into their favorite Old World recipes. Calling them hurtleberries, and then huckleberries, the Colonial cooks created American standards like the cobblers, buckles, and crisps that we still enjoy today.

The Indians and Colonists picked their berries from the plentiful supply of wild bushes. Commercial cultivation did not begin until 1920 in New Jersey, where acres of acid, marshy soil that were unfit for other crops were transformed into productive blueberry farms. Much of the modern blueberry crop is still grown in New Jersey, which, along with a handful of other states, annually produces more than 200 million pounds of the fruit. The berry is now being farmed in parts of Europe, and the summer crops in New Zealand warm American hearts during the coldest months of the year here.

asparagus and beet salad with watercress and frisée

serves 4

Brian Scheehser, the executive chef at The Sorrento Hotel in Seattle and its award-winning restaurant, Hunt Club, is known for pairing Pacific Northwest–style cuisine with Mediterranean influences. His dishes emphasize seasonal regional ingredients, and in addition to local suppliers, artisans, and farmers, Brian is lucky to have Pike's Market close by; he shops there at least twice a week for his hotel kitchen ingredients. This lively, flavorful salad, with its peppery crispness, is a great example of Brian's creativity.

for the dressing

- ½ cup freshly squeezed orange juice
- ¼ cup sherry vinegar
- 2 shallots, minced
- 1 cup extra-virgin olive oil
- Salt and pepper, to taste

for the salad

- 10 beets (about 2½ pounds), unpeeled
- 24 asparagus spears, trimmed to 4 or 5 inches
- 2 cups loosely packed frisée lettuce, washed and trimmed
- 2 cups loosely packed watercress, washed and trimmed

To prepare the dressing, place the orange juice, vinegar, and shallots in a blender and purée. Add the oil in a steady stream, until combined thoroughly, and season with salt and pepper. Set aside.

To prepare the salad, place the beets in a saucepan of boiling water and cook for 20 to 25 minutes, until fork-tender. Drain, and when cool enough, peel and dice the beets. Meanwhile, fill a bowl with water and ice. Steam the asparagus in a vegetable basket set over a saucepan of boiling water for 2 to 3 minutes, until al dente. Transfer the asparagus to the ice bath to stop the cooking process, and drain.

Transfer half of the dressing to a bowl and add the beets. Place the frisée, watercress, and asparagus in a mixing bowl and toss with the remaining dressing. Fan out the asparagus on serving plates and cover the stems with the greens. Garnish with the beets.

salads

61

sorrel salad with herbs

serves 4

Sorrel, like lemon verbena, has become a fashionable herb over the past few years (for more on sorrel, see page 15). This salad recipe is taken from my radio show on growing and using culinary herbs—a popular subject. I encourage everyone to grow herbs. You only need a window box, and if you have a backyard, you can grow a lot of flavoring and seasoning in a small space. You'll also save a lot of money by growing your own herbs. I don't have a green thumb, but even I have luck raising them.

for the salad

    4 ounces sorrel, washed

    1 small head of red leaf lettuce, washed

    ⅓ cup fresh basil leaves, minced

    4 fresh tarragon leaves, minced

    2 sprigs of fresh chervil, minced

    1 teaspoon sliced fresh chives

for the dressing

    ¼ cup olive oil

    2 tablespoons tarragon vinegar

       Salt and pepper, to taste

Tear the sorrel and lettuce into bite-size pieces and place in a mixing bowl. Add the basil, tarragon, chervil, and chives and toss together. Place the bowl in the refrigerator to chill for 10 minutes. Meanwhile, to prepare the dressing, whisk together the oil and vinegar in a bowl and season with salt and pepper. Pour the dressing over the salad, toss to coat thoroughly, and arrange on serving plates.

tossed hearts of romaine with roasted peppers and honey-lemon dressing

serves 4

I created this simple recipe for my weekly radio show. Listeners appreci-ate short and snappy recipes, and a salad with just seven ingredients certainly meets those criteria! Although you can make this salad with other types of lettuce if you prefer, the sturdy, crisp romaine holds the peppers well and gives the whole dish some substance. It also lends itself well to the kind of unusual presentation called for in this recipe.

for the dressing

Juice of 2 lemons

2 tablespoons honey

½ tablespoon chopped fresh rosemary leaves

for the salad

2 hearts of romaine lettuce, trimmed, leaves separated and washed

½ small red bell pepper, roasted (see page 268), peeled, seeded, and finely sliced

½ small yellow bell pepper, roasted, peeled, seeded, and thinly sliced

½ small green bell pepper, roasted, peeled, seeded, and thinly sliced

To prepare the dressing, thoroughly whisk together the lemon juice, honey, and rosemary in a mixing bowl.

To prepare the salad, thoroughly dry the romaine leaves and place in a large mixing bowl with the bell peppers. Add the dressing and toss to coat completely. To serve, stack the romaine leaves on serving plates in crosswise layers (each leaf should be at a 90-degree angle to the leaves above and below it). Top each serving with any bell peppers that do not cling to the leaves.

new potato, corn, and cherry tomato salad
with basil-balsamic dressing

serves 8

One of my weekly public radio shows, A Chef's Table, *was devoted to the subject of organic produce and the desirability of government guidelines to set recognized standards. It's a subject that interests a great many listeners, especially as there is a lot of confusion over what the term* organic *means. I created this recipe for that show, but of course, you can use produce grown conventionally just as well. This salad is wonderful as a starter on its own, or paired with grilled meat for a summer weekend cookout.*

for the dressing

2 tablespoons balsamic vinegar

½ cup olive oil

1 cup packed fresh basil leaves

¼ cup packed fresh flat-leaf parsley leaves

Salt and pepper, to taste

for the salad

2½ pounds small new potatoes, about 2 ounces each

Salt, to taste

6 ears fresh sweet corn (preferably white corn)

8 ounces cherry tomatoes, cut in half

Pepper, to taste

To prepare the dressing, pour the vinegar and oil into a blender and add the basil, parsley, salt, and pepper. Purée until the dressing is completely emulsified.

To prepare the salad, place the potatoes in a large saucepan and add enough water to cover. Bring to a boil, season with salt, and reduce the heat to a simmer. Cook the potatoes for about 15 minutes, until tender. Drain the potatoes in a colander, let cool, and transfer to a large mixing bowl.

Meanwhile, bring a large saucepan of water to a boil and add the corn. Return to a boil and cook for 2 or 3 minutes, or until just tender. When the corn is cool enough to handle, remove the kernels with a sharp knife (there should be about 3 cups). Add the corn, tomatoes, and dressing to the potatoes, and toss to coat evenly. Season with salt and pepper and arrange on serving plates.

The first fresh corn of the summer is always an eagerly awaited treat. If today's harvest makes our mouths water, imagine how European settlers felt about the crop when they first reached this land. Back then, only Native Americans had any knowledge of corn. They taught the Colonists that corn grew faster and provided more food than wheat. When the hungry newcomers planted their first cornfields, they were already on their way to becoming Americans.

Corn has been nourishing civilizations in this hemisphere for more than 7,000 years. Research shows that it originated in the Mexican highlands as a wild grain. It was so important to the Mayans and Aztecs that the grain was incorporated into their religions, and the Incas based their calendar on the corn crop cycle. As of 3,000 years ago, corn had been sown from South America all the way to southern Canada. Beyond food, Native Americans used it for medicines, jewelry, and currency.

Today, the many uses of corn have made it a $20 billion commodity in the United States, where cornfields blanket the Midwest and Great Plains states. A surprising 85 percent of the crop is used mainly as animal feed, which in turn benefits the meat and poultry industries. A large portion of the harvest is thought of as "hidden corn," utilized in a variety of products like corn syrup, corn oil, and corn dogs. Yet the small amount of corn that we eat fresh off the cob is the image Americans treasure most. Just like our forefathers, Americans today continue to savor the flavor that leaves us smiling from ear to ear.

tip

The addition of salt to the water before boiling most vegetables helps to retain color, but it doesn't work for fresh corn. Freshly shucked corn is prized for its tenderness, and salt in the cooking water will only make it tough.

grilled southern smoked
chicken salad with endive, carolina shrimp, and yogurt-walnut dressing

serves 4

Bob Waggoner, executive chef at Charleston Grill at the Charleston Place Hotel, successfully fuses South Carolina Lowcountry cooking (see page 196) with classical French technique, which he acquired through working for several years in the kitchens of a constellation of Michelin-rated restaurants. He is still the only American to have received a Michelin star at his own restaurant in France. This salad is served family-style on a platter, and it has more dressing than most. I like the endive in the salad because its firmness holds up well to the weight of the chicken. Cooking the shrimp until just medium-rare gives the best tenderness and flavor. This makes an excellent lunch dish.

for the dressing

1 cup plain yogurt

Juice of ½ lemon

½ teaspoon salt

½ teaspoon white pepper

¼ cup walnut oil

To prepare the dressing, place the yogurt in a mixing bowl and whisk in the lemon juice. Add the salt and pepper and slowly add the walnut oil in a steady stream, while whisking. Set aside.

To prepare the salad, heat the olive oil in a large skillet and sauté the shrimp over high heat, while stirring often, for 2 or 3 minutes, or until lightly browned and medium-rare. Transfer the shrimp to a bowl and let them chill in the refrigerator. Cut the chicken into long strips and keep refrigerated.

for the salad

3 tablespoons olive oil

16 extra-large fresh shrimp (about 1 pound), peeled and deveined

1 pound cooked, smoked chicken breast meat

6 heads Belgian endive, washed

24 walnut halves

1 bunch of fresh chives, finely chopped (about ¼ cup)

Reserve 1 head of endive. Cut ¼ inch off the bottom of the remaining heads and then cut in half lengthwise. Cut each half head of endive into long julienne strips and transfer to a mixing bowl. Add the walnuts, shrimp, and chicken. Add the dressing and toss well to combine. Arrange 3 or 4 endive leaves from the reserved head on a platter, place the shrimp and chicken mixture on top, and garnish with the chives.

tip Smoked chicken is available at most high-end grocery stores. It's fine to substitute roast chicken, although the flavor will be different and not as intense.

appetizers

Asparagus, Portobello, and Goat Cheese Brie Strudel

Cheese

Family-Style Stir-Fry Eggplant

Gravlax of Striped Bass with a Mixed Greens Salad

Seafood Dumplings with Dipping Sauce

San Francisco Lo Mein

Cuban Marinated Sautéed Shrimp with Mangos and Avocados

Mangos

Escargot-Stuffed Mushrooms

Traditional New Hampshire Oyster and Spinach Pie

Davey's Chardonnay Mussels with Lemongrass, Ginger, and Herbs

Three-Cheese Soufflé with Mustard and Herbs

Mustard

Smoked Ham and Swiss Pitas

Pan-Fried Halibut Cakes

Grilled Turkey Sausage with Spiced Cranberry Relish and Watercress Salad

Little Havana Plantain-Pork Piononos

Papaya and Brie Quesadillas with a Crabmeat and Avocado Salad

Homemade Corn Dogs

Hot Dogs

Baked Artichoke Frittata with Two Cheeses

Creamed Chipped Beef with Buttermilk Biscuits

Marinated Salmon Skewers and Caesar Salad with Soy Dressing

New England Red Flannel Hash

Maine Rock Crab Cakes with Tartar Sauce

Caramelized Onion and Mushroom Tart on Mixed Greens with Balsamic Vinaigrette

Florida Lobster and Key West Shrimp Ceviche with Cayenne-Spiced Yuca Chips

Maryland-Style Striped Bass Cakes with Spinach Salad

Penn Cove Mussels with Curry Cream

Mussles

Foie Gras, Spinach, and Portobello Mushroom Purses

Fried Plantain Chips with Shrimp and Mango Salsa

Tortilla Chips with Hot Smoked Honey-Glazed Salmon

Fingerling Potatoes Stuffed with Curried Coconut Crab

Potato Latkes with Apple Compote

If there is one thing that home cooks can do to increase enjoyment of the dining experience, it's to serve an appetizer. It forces you to slow down and eat a little more deliberately. I find that when I'm at a dinner party or at a restaurant with my family, I eat more quickly if a salad and main course are served together than if there is an appetizer to begin with. This same principle is behind the "slow food" movement that began as a European response to the growing influence of American-style fast food. The movement has now turned into an organization with American chapters, with the objective of encouraging individuals to pace their meals, contemplate and appreciate the food they are eating, and put the enjoyment back into dining. I know from personal experience that there is more opportunity to talk about food and savor it over a leisurely meal. Of course, in this busy day and age, it's not always possible to take a relaxed, traditional approach, but if you are planning a special dinner, or if you know you have the time, I encourage you to think in terms of appetizers.

At the Rittenhouse Hotel, we usually have eight to ten appetizers on the menu at any one time—a sign that we take appetizers seriously! I know of several colleagues and friends who would gladly eat nothing but appetizers when eating out, and I feel that way too, on occasion. This relatively recent dining trend, also called grazing, remains a popular way of tasting lots of different dishes, rather like the tradition of Chinese dim sum. At home too, serving an appetizer is an obvious way to incorporate more flavors, textures, and ingredients into a single meal.

Most of the shows in my PBS television series, *Flavors of America,* feature appetizers, more so in fact than any other course. This chapter contains first-course appetizers as well as some hors d'oeuvres—finger foods to whet the appetite. Of course, you can always scale up hors d'oeuvre recipes and turn them into appetizers, and vice versa. In addition, a few of the appetizers here may look like salads and can be presented as such. However, the salad element of the dish is not the primary component—I just happen to enjoy appetizers that include some type of greens.

asparagus, portobello, and goat cheese brie strudel

serves 4

While filming in Boston, I visited Ihsan Gurdal to learn about cheese. Ihsan owns Formaggio Kitchen, a huge and impressive gourmet food store specializing in cheese, across the Charles River in Cambridge, Massachusetts. The store—a must for any connoisseur—features a unique natural cellar in which Ihsan ages an inventory of hundreds of imported cheeses until they are quite ripe and ready for sale. Temperature, humidity, and air flow are all carefully controlled, and the results are remarkable. I used goat cheese Brie for this recipe just because I was so impressed with it when I tasted it at Formaggio Kitchen, but any good melting cheese will work well.

Salt, to taste

8 ounces asparagus, trimmed and cut into 2- to 3-inch slices

5 tablespoons butter

12 ounces portobello mushrooms, thinly sliced

1 teaspoon freshly squeezed lemon juice

¾ cup diced goat cheese Brie, or Brie or goat cheese (crumbled)

Pepper, to taste

2 tablespoons fresh bread crumbs

¼ cup finely chopped walnuts

4 sheets of phyllo dough, thawed

Pour ½ inch of lightly salted water into a nonstick skillet and bring to a boil. Add the asparagus and blanch for 3 to 4 minutes, or until tender. Drain the asparagus, transfer to a mixing bowl, and let cool. Melt 1 tablespoon of the butter in the same skillet and add the mushrooms. Sauté the mushrooms over medium-high heat for about 5 minutes, or until the liquid is mostly evaporated. Remove the mushrooms from the heat and add the lemon juice. Let cool, add to the asparagus, sprinkle in the cheese, and combine. Season with salt and pepper.

Preheat the oven to 400°F. In a small saucepan, melt the remaining 4 tablespoons of butter. In a small bowl, combine the bread crumbs with the walnuts. On a flat work surface, place a phyllo sheet with the shorter side facing you. Using a pastry brush, brush the lower half of the sheet with a coating of the melted butter, sprinkle with about 1 tablespoon of the bread-crumb mixture, and fold the top half of the sheet over. Brush the lower half of the folded phyllo with a coating of the butter, sprinkle with about ½ tablespoon of the bread-crumb mixture, and fold over one more time. On the lower quarter of the dough, place one fourth of the asparagus mushroom mixture. Roll up the phyllo into a long, thin cannelloni shape. Repeat for the remaining ingredients, making 4 individual strudels. Place the strudels on a cookie sheet and bake in the oven for 15 to 20 minutes, or until golden brown.

cheese

Like many great culinary discoveries, the creation of cheese was most likely accidental. After cattle and goats were first domesticated in prehistoric times, liquids were customarily stored in bags made from their stomachs. When kept in these bags long enough, milk was converted to curds and whey through the enzyme called rennin found in the stomach's lining. Once they realized the product was palatable, people around the world refined the process and began their cheese making in earnest.

The desire for the finest product inspired wealthy Romans to build special kitchens for making cheese, while the common people brought their homemade renditions to public smokehouses for curing. The food was so appreciated that a special term of endearment in Rome and Greece was "little cheese," and Greek children were rewarded with bites of cheese much as candy is handed out today. The original Olympic athletes trained on a diet consisting primarily of cheese.

Although all cheese is produced from a basic recipe, its countless variations are due to the endless variety of conditions under which it is made. Flavor and texture are altered by temperature, the type of milk used, how the curds are cut, the draining process, the length of time it ripens, how often it is turned, and atmospheric conditions. Changing a single step can alter the taste of a cheese-maker's product, and the formulas for all varieties are carefully retained and often bound in secrecy.

family-style
stir-fry eggplant

serves 4

During our walking tour of San Francisco's Chinatown, our film crew and I enjoyed a wonderful, spicy, stir-fried eggplant dish that inspired this recipe. I have toned down the heat, but by all means add more chile paste or red pepper flakes. The long Asian eggplant works best here because it is much less bitter and more tender than its purple cousin, although baby purple or white eggplant would make good alternatives.

2 tablespoons Asian-style chile paste, or chile paste with garlic

1 tablespoon soy sauce

1 tablespoon rice wine vinegar

2 teaspoons sugar

½ cup canola oil or peanut oil

1 pound eggplant, preferably Japanese or Asian, cut into 1-inch cubes

1 tablespoon dry sherry

1½ tablespoons dried red pepper flakes

¼ cup Chicken Stock (page 266)

In a mixing bowl, combine the chile paste, soy sauce, vinegar, and sugar. Set aside. Heat the oil in a wok or large sauté pan set over high heat. When hot and almost smoking, add the eggplant and stir-fry for 1 minute. Add the sherry and pepper flakes and stir-fry for 3 minutes. Add the stock and cook for 2 minutes longer. Add the reserved chile paste mixture and cook for 2 to 3 minutes, or until the eggplant is tender and well coated.

tip As with most other Chinese dishes, I prefer serving beer rather than wine. In this case, the ingredients would make just about any wine unpalatable.

gravlax of striped bass with a mixed greens salad

serves 4

Traditional gravlax is raw salmon cured with a mixture of salt (to draw out moisture), sugar (to absorb it), and dill (for flavor), and then very finely sliced. The word gravlax *means "buried salmon" in Swedish, referring to the original technique of curing fish caught in summer before burying it for winter use. I enjoy making gravlax with other kinds of finfish such as freshwater bass, rockfish, and sea bass, so it seemed a natural choice when we visited High Rock Seafood in Ocean City, Maryland. This is the only fish farm in the country raising striped bass in saltwater, giving it a more realistic flavor than typical farm bass raised in freshwater (for more on High Rock, see page 205).*

for the gravlax

2 cups kosher salt

2 cups sugar

¼ cup peeled and minced fresh ginger

¼ cup pepper

¼ cup toasted and ground fennel seed (page 269)

2 tablespoons ground cumin

2 striped bass fillets, skin on (about 8 ounces each)

Vinegar (any kind) for wiping the cured fish

To prepare the gravlax, combine the salt, sugar, ginger, pepper, and fennel seed in a bowl until well blended. Place the striped bass on a rack set over a cookie sheet or in a roasting pan and pour the spice mixture over the bass meat. Rub it in to make sure the bass is very well coated. Wrap the bass in plastic wrap, transfer it to the refrigerator, and let it sit overnight, for at least 12 hours, and up to 24 hours.

Unwrap the bass and brush off the spice mixture by hand. Using a paper towel dampened with vinegar, wipe off the remaining mixture. Finely slice the bass crosswise at a very fine angle to give very thin slices, like smoked salmon. Cut through to the skin, but leave the skin off.

for the dressing and salad

1/3 cup olive oil

3 tablespoons balsamic vinegar

1 tablespoon minced garlic

Salt and pepper, to taste

2 cups mesclun salad mix or other mixed greens, washed

To prepare the dressing, whisk together the oil, vinegar, garlic, salt, and pepper in a bowl. Place the greens in a separate mixing bowl and toss with the dressing. Mound the greens in the center of 4 serving plates. Fold the sea bass slices into a tube shape and lean 3 or 4 slices against the greens. (Alternatively, lay the gravlax flat on the serving plates and mound the dressed greens on top.)

tip Ideally, let the fish marinate in the refrigerator for up to 24 hours, but no longer, otherwise too much moisture will be extracted during the curing process and the fish will become too tough. Note that the fresher the fish, the quicker it will cure.

seafood dumplings
with dipping sauce

serves 4

I was inspired to create this recipe after touring some dim sum restaurants in San Francisco's Chinatown with Shirley Fong-Torres. Shirley is a local food expert, chef, and author who conducts walking tours of the neighborhood, and she took us to some out-of-the-way places that non-Chinese people don't often get to. San Francisco is home to 100,000 Asians, making the city the largest Chinese community on the West Coast and second only to New York City nationally. I always have fun making dumplings, and they are easy to make. They are a popular party food, especially when you vary the fillings.

for the dumplings

- 4 ounces fresh sea scallops (or shrimp, or a firm white fish such as sea bass)
- 1 tablespoon peeled and minced fresh ginger
- 2 cloves garlic, minced
- 2 teaspoons rice wine vinegar
- 2 teaspoons soy sauce
- 2 scallions, finely sliced (green part only)
- 12 to 16 round wonton wrappers (Chinese dumpling skins)

for the dipping sauce

- ½ cup soy sauce
- 3 cloves garlic, minced
- 2 teaspoons rice wine vinegar
- 1 teaspoon hot chile oil

To prepare the dumplings, place the scallops, ginger, garlic, vinegar, soy sauce, and scallions in a food processor and purée until smooth. Fill each wonton wrapper with 1 teaspoon of the mixture and close tightly to form a half-moon shape, sealing the edges with water. Line a bamboo steamer or vegetable basket with cabbage leaves and steam the dumplings over a pan of boiling water for 4 or 5 minutes, or until done.

For the dipping sauce, place the soy sauce, garlic, vinegar, and chile oil in a blender and purée. Serve the sauce in individual ramekins or small dipping bowls alongside the dumplings.

tip

When using a bamboo steamer to cook dumplings and other Chinese foods, rub it with oil first. This prevents the steamer from warping with repetitive use. Also, lining the steamer with cabbage leaves stops foods such as dumplings from sticking to the steamer basket.

san francisco lo mein

serves 4

When San Franciscans claim that their Chinatown is the most vibrant, traditional, and culinarily diverse of any in the country, I have to agree. It also reminds me the most of China, where I worked for a year. For Flavors of America, *we filmed noodles being made from rice "milk" in a machine that resembled a shirt press—a fascinating experience.*

for the noodles and beef

- 8 ounces dried egg noodles
- 1 teaspoon cornstarch
- 1 tablespoon soy sauce
- 1 tablespoon dry sherry
- 8 ounces flank steak or skirt steak, cut into ⅛-inch strips

for the sauce mixture

- 1 tablespoon cornstarch
- 1 cup Chicken Stock (page 266)
- 1 tablespoon soy sauce
- 2 tablespoons oyster sauce

- 3 tablespoons toasted (dark) sesame oil
- 3 cloves garlic, minced
- 2 scallions, finely sliced (green part only)

Cook the egg noodles in rapidly boiling water according to the directions on the package. Drain in a colander and cool under cold running water. Set aside. Blend the cornstarch, soy sauce, and sherry in a mixing bowl, add the beef, and let marinate for 15 to 20 minutes.

To prepare the sauce mixture, place the cornstarch, stock, soy sauce, and oyster sauce in a mixing bowl and whisk together. Set aside. Keep a saucepan of water at a simmer to reheat the noodles at the last minute.

Heat 2 tablespoons of the sesame oil in a wok or large sauté pan set over high heat. When hot and almost smoking, add the marinated beef and the garlic and stir-fry for about 5 minutes. Add the sauce mixture and sauté for 3 or 4 minutes longer, or until the mixture thickens. Add the scallions and stir well.

Drop the cooked noodles into the pan of simmering water and heat through. Drain and stir into the beef mixture. Transfer to warm serving plates and drizzle the remaining 1 tablespoon of sesame oil over the top.

cuban marinated sautéed shrimp with mangos and avocados

serves 4

For the TV show about mangos, we made the pilgrimage to the Fairchild Tropical Garden in Coral Gables, Florida. The garden not only holds a seed bank of every type of mango in the world, but it also hosts an annual mango festival in the summer to celebrate harvest time. For the program we interviewed Dr. Richard Campbell, the curator of tropical fruit at the garden. Dr. Campbell is a globe-trotting horticulturist who probably knows as much about mangos as anyone in the world and who has an Indiana Jones–like instinct for tracking down rare varieties. This recipe demonstrates that mangos have a natural affinity for the flavors of both avocado and shrimp.

for the shrimp

¾ cup olive oil

3 tablespoons freshly squeezed orange juice

Juice of 1 lime

1 teaspoon ground cumin

2 cloves garlic, minced

1 jalapeño or serrano chile, minced, with seeds

Salt and pepper, to taste

12 jumbo shrimp (about 1 pound), peeled and deveined

To prepare the shrimp, place the oil, orange juice, lime juice, cumin, garlic, chile, salt, and pepper in a mixing bowl and whisk to combine. Add the shrimp and marinate in the refrigerator for 1 to 2 hours.

To prepare the dressing, whisk together the oil with the orange juice, garlic, honey, and soy sauce until well blended. Season with salt and pepper. Set aside.

To prepare the salad, heat the 3 tablespoons of olive oil in a sauté pan. Remove the shrimp from the marinade, drain, and add to the pan.

for the dressing

½ cup olive oil

⅓ cup freshly squeezed orange juice

½ tablespoon minced garlic

½ tablespoon honey

½ tablespoon soy sauce

Salt and pepper, to taste

for the salad

3 tablespoons olive oil

1 large head (or 2 small heads) red leaf or red oak lettuce, thinly sliced

2 large ripe mangos, peeled, pitted, and diced

2 large avocados, peeled, pitted, and diced

Sauté over medium-high heat for about 2 minutes per side, or until medium-rare. Place the lettuce in a mixing bowl. Add half of the dressing and toss to coat well. Mound the dressed lettuce on 4 serving plates and arrange 3 shrimp around each plate. Gently mix together the diced mangos and avocados in a mixing bowl and arrange in small mounds between the shrimp. Drizzle with a little of the remaining dressing.

tip

Chopping or mincing garlic can be a messy job. Try adding a little salt as you are chopping and the garlic won't stick to the knife as easily. Remember to adjust the amount of salt you are using in your recipe.

In some cultures it is believed that mango trees can grant wishes. Anyone who has savored a juicy, ripe mango will have at least one wish come true. The mango's sweet-tart, exotic flavor satisfies something in every fruit-lover's soul. Though their popularity is just beginning to rise in this country, it is no wonder that mangos are the most widely eaten fresh fruit in the world.

The evergreen mango tree originated in Southeast Asia, where it has flourished for more than 4,000 years. The fruit did not make its debut in the Western Hemisphere until Portuguese traders took seeds to Brazil in 1700. In this country they took root in Florida in the 1800s, and in 1888 David Fairchild of the United States Department of Agriculture introduced an improved grafted variety that kicked off that state's mango industry.

India is the world's leading mango producer, growing more than seven million tons of the juicy fruit annually, which accounts for almost a third of the global output. Mangos are so popular there that most of the massive Indian crop is consumed in that country. Mexico leads the list of mango exporters, with competition from countries in Central and South America, the Bahamas, and South Africa.

Many consumers are not sure how to handle the exotic fruit, but the mango is as simple to deal with as a tomato and should be handled the same way. Mangos are ready to eat when they give to the pressure of a thumb, and for superior flavor they should not be enjoyed until they are completely ripe. Like tomatoes, they should be stored at room temperature and only refrigerated when they cannot be eaten at their peak. Mangos are wonderful for making sauces, chutneys, and relishes, complementing everything from appetizers to desserts. Yet experts contend that the mystique of the mango is best experienced fresh and right out of the hand.

To peel and dice a mango, stand the fruit upright on a work surface and, with a sharp knife, cut down as close to the pit as possible on each side. Place the cut sections skin-side down and score the flesh in a crosshatch pattern, without cutting through the skin. Then cut horizontally beneath the fruit, as close to the skin as possible, to release the mango in diced form. Cut the remaining flesh around the sides of the mango pit, slice away the skin, and again dice the flesh.

escargot-stuffed mushrooms

serves 4

We filmed one of the segments of our show about France on an escargot farm in Burgundy. This was fitting because snails were popularized as a culinary delicacy by Antoine Carême, the early-nineteenth-century gourmet, and his classic dish, Escargots à la Bourguignonne (Escargots Burgundy-Style). Edible snails were prized long ago by the Greeks and Romans, who doubtless introduced them to the ancient Gauls, but until the time of Carême, snails were considered common food in France. Many people are wary of eating snails, which is understandable, but they are carefully washed several times and cooked twice before they are canned with a buttery sauce. Canned escargot are available at gourmet and specialty food stores.

8 tablespoons (1 stick) butter at room temperature, divided

½ shallot, minced

1 clove garlic, minced

2 teaspoons minced fresh thyme leaves

1 tablespoon minced fresh flat-leaf parsley leaves

1 tablespoon minced celery

½ teaspoon salt

¼ teaspoon pepper

12 large white mushrooms (about 10 ounces), stems removed

1 can (7 ounces) escargots or *petits gris* snails, drained

Preheat the oven to 400°F. In a mixing bowl, cream together 6 tablespoons of the butter, the shallot, garlic, thyme, parsley, celery, salt, and pepper to make an herb butter.

Heat the remaining 2 tablespoons of butter in a sauté pan and add the mushrooms. Sauté over medium heat for 3 or 4 minutes, turning to cook on all sides. Transfer the mushrooms to a baking dish, cap-side down. Place the escargots on the mushroom caps and top with a bit of the herb butter. Bake the stuffed mushrooms in the oven for 10 minutes. Remove and arrange 3 mushrooms on each serving plate.

appetizers

traditional new hampshire oyster and spinach pie

serves 4

This recipe is adapted from an old book of New England recipes that dates back to a time when oysters were plentiful and an everyday food. In the earliest Colonial days, oysters helped save the European settlers from starvation. This recipe calls for a puff-pastry crust, as a shortcut, and I have added bell peppers, garlic, and fresh herbs. Shucked oysters are available in the chilled seafood section of most supermarkets.

2 cups freshly shucked oysters (including the liquid)

¼ cup (½ stick) butter

1 red bell pepper, seeded and diced

1 clove garlic, minced

2 stalks celery, diced

1 cup roughly chopped spinach, washed

5 tablespoons flour

2 cups milk

1 tablespoon chopped fresh tarragon leaves

1 tablespoon chopped fresh flat-leaf parsley leaves

1 plum tomato, chopped

Salt and pepper, to taste

1 sheet puff pastry dough

Preheat the oven to 400° F. Place the oysters and their liquid in a warm sauté pan and cook over medium-high heat for about 2 minutes, or until the edges just begin to curl. Drain the oysters and set aside. Add the butter to the sauté pan and melt over medium heat. Add the bell pepper, garlic, celery, and spinach and sauté for about 2 minutes, or until soft. Sprinkle in the flour and stir for 2 to 3 minutes to form a roux. Add the milk and cook for 5 minutes, or until the mixture is thickened. Add the tarragon, parsley, and tomato and season with salt and pepper. Let the mixture cool and add the oysters. Pour the oyster and vegetable mixture into an oval ovenproof baking dish or casserole about 9 inches long and 2 inches deep.

On a flat work surface, roll out the puff pastry to make it large enough to cover the baking dish, with a little overhanging. Trim the pastry with a knife and pinch with a fork around the edges to seal. Make slits in the center of the pastry to allow the steam to escape. Bake for 20 to 25 minutes, or until the pastry is golden brown.

davey's chardonnay mussels with lemongrass, ginger, and herbs

serves 4

This dish is named after Jim Davey, the producer of our TV series. Jim is always lurking behind the scenes, working hard, even when the rest of the crew gets to taste the dishes I've cooked for the show. The exception to this rule is whenever I cook mussels. Then it's every crew member for himself or herself as Jim bears down on the plate of mollusks. I used a Washington State Chardonnay for this recipe as we were filming in Seattle, but whatever the source, choose a good-quality wine that is not too oaky or buttery; otherwise, it will prove too assertive for the other flavors. Scrub and debeard mussels just before you cook them to prevent spoiling.

2 tablespoons olive oil

1 stalk fresh lemongrass, minced

1 tablespoon peeled and minced fresh ginger

6 cloves garlic, minced

1 jalapeño or serrano chile, minced (with seeds)

Zest of 2 limes, minced

Juice of 3 limes

4 pounds mussels, debearded and scrubbed

1½ cups Chardonnay wine

3 tablespoons chopped fresh basil leaves

3 tablespoons chopped fresh mint

3 tablespoons chopped fresh cilantro

2 tablespoons butter

Heat the oil in a stockpot and add the lemongrass, ginger, garlic, chile, and lime zest. Sauté over medium-high heat for 2 to 3 minutes. Add the lime juice, mussels, wine, basil, mint, and cilantro and cover the pot. Cook for about 8 minutes, or until all the mussels have opened; throw away any mussels that do not open. Remove the mussels with a slotted spoon and transfer to 4 serving bowls. Add the butter to the stockpot and stir to incorporate. Spoon the mixture over the mussels in the bowls.

three-cheese soufflé with mustard and herbs

serves 4

"Only peril can bring the French together. One cannot impose unity out of the blue on a country that has 265 different kinds of cheese." Charles de Gaulle, the former president of France, might be even more concerned these days with the proliferation of cheeses, but the rest of us have cause to celebrate. As I discovered on our trip to France for the TV show, every small region in the country has its own official cheese. While filming, I met some young entrepreneurs who were reviving their local unpasteurized ash-covered cow cheese that had not been made for decades. This dish is my tip of the cap to them. This soufflé is easier to make than the traditional egg-white soufflé, so do not be put off. If the slightly tangy farmer's cheese is not marketed in your area, use any local fresh hard cow cheese.

6 eggs

½ cup heavy cream

⅓ cup grated Parmesan cheese

1 teaspoon dried mustard powder

2 tablespoons chopped fresh tarragon leaves

2 tablespoons chopped fresh flat-leaf parsley leaves

Salt and pepper, to taste

Pinch of cayenne pepper

8 ounces farmer's cheese (or Cheddar), diced

11 ounces cream cheese, diced

Preheat the oven to 375°F. Generously butter an ovenproof soufflé dish or baking dish about 9 inches long and 2 or 3 inches deep. Place the eggs, cream, Parmesan cheese, mustard, tarragon, parsley, salt, pepper, and cayenne in a food processor and blend. With the machine running, add the farmer's cheese, piece by piece, and then add the cream cheese, piece by piece. Process for another 30 seconds until well blended and thick. Using a spatula, scrape the mixture into the buttered baking dish.

Bake for 50 minutes to 1 hour, until golden brown and puffy; do not open the oven door for the first 50 minutes. Remove the soufflé, spoon onto warm serving plates, and serve immediately.

After black pepper, mustard is the most commonly consumed spice in America. Sports fans in stadiums around the country can attest to that. The fact that George J. French first sold his famous product in 1904, the same year that hot dogs were introduced, might suggest that mustard was first appreciated with ballpark food. Actually the condiment has been around so long that there is evidence that pre-historic people chewed mustard seeds with their meat. This universal spice has come a long way since then.

For centuries mustard has been cultivated all over the globe, and every culture's use of the spice is ideally suited to its own regional cuisine. In India the seeds are used to flavor cooking oil. The bold German mustards are natural partners for that country's hearty sausages, and fiery Chinese mustards add the perfect touch to intricate Asian dishes.

Two gentlemen by the name of Grey and Poupon put the city of Dijon, France, on the culinary map with their sophisticated blend. And when a fellow named Jeremiah Colman got interested in making mustard in the English city of Norwich in 1804, he virtually cornered the market in that country. Today a wide range of flavored mustards are available, or home cooks can "cut the mustard" themselves, creating their own family favorites by stirring a little imagination into a simple basic recipe.

smoked ham and swiss pitas

We had a lot of fun filming the show about food for children's parties. The best part was the performing magician, Brian Rykaczewski, who made food disappear (and not by eating it)! I think I enjoyed the whole thing even more than the kids did. From personal experience, I think some of the best children's parties involve cooking, and it's a great way to get the little ones interested in food. They just love to help make pizza, roll out cookie dough, and make their own sandwich fillings. Adult supervision is always important, and although this particular recipe isn't one suited for kids' participation, you'll appreciate them eating a wholesome ham and cheese melt rather than the usual party junk food.

1	pound smoked ham, chopped
12	ounces Swiss cheese, grated
1	tablespoon pickle relish
¼	cup diced onion
¼	cup yellow mustard
¾	cup low-fat mayonnaise
4	whole-wheat pitas, split

Place the ham and cheese in a food processor and grind together. Add the relish, onion, mustard, and mayonnaise and process briefly to blend. Stuff the mixture evenly into the pitas and wrap individually in foil. Refrigerate for 1 hour.

Preheat the oven to 325°F. Place the wrapped pitas on a cookie sheet and bake for about 25 minutes, or until the filling is melted. Unwrap the pitas and serve whole or sliced into quarters.

pan-fried halibut cakes

Crab cakes are ever popular, but I enjoy well-made fish cakes just as much. This is the perfect recipe for using up any leftover halibut or other firm, white-fleshed fish (such as sea bass or grouper), and if you buy a little extra for the recipes on pages 212 or 214, consider making this appetizer. Halibut caught in Alaska and on the West Coast is surprisingly different in quality from that landed on the East Coast. The former is bigger with a moister, flakier texture that takes particularly well to grilling. Either variety works fine here.

1 pound boneless, skinless halibut fillet

5 tablespoons butter

½ onion, minced

2 cloves garlic, minced

½ cup plain dried bread crumbs

3 eggs, beaten

½ teaspoon minced lemon zest

1 tablespoon freshly squeezed lemon juice

¼ teaspoon ground ginger

Salt and pepper, to taste

¼ cup flour

⅛ teaspoon cayenne pepper

Tartar Sauce (page 101; optional)

Place the halibut in a sauté pan and add enough hot water to come halfway up the sides of the fillet. Poach the fillet over medium heat, turning once, for 8 to 10 minutes, or until cooked through. Remove the halibut, flake with a fork, and set aside.

Melt 2 tablespoons of the butter in a nonstick pan set over medium high heat. Add the onion and garlic and sauté for 2 to 3 minutes, or until tender; do not let the mixture brown. Transfer to a mixing bowl and add the flaked halibut, bread crumbs, eggs, lemon zest, lemon juice, ginger, salt, and pepper. Mix thoroughly and chill in the refrigerator for 1 hour.

Remove the mixture and shape into 4 fish cakes. In a bowl, combine the flour and cayenne and coat the cakes with the mixture, shaking off any excess. Melt the remaining 3 tablespoons of butter in a nonstick pan set over medium-high heat and sauté the fish cakes for about 4 minutes on each side until golden brown and cooked through. Transfer to serving plates and serve with the tartar sauce.

grilled turkey sausage
with spiced cranberry relish and watercress salad

serves 4

This dish takes two traditional partners, turkey and cranberries, and transforms them into a light first-course appetizer. For more on cranberries, see page 139. The relish can be used with any poultry—and especially with Thanksgiving turkey—or pork. By all means add some hot sauce or fresh minced chile to the relish for some added zing. The sausage can be grilled rather than sautéed, if you prefer.

for the cranberry relish

Zest and juice of ½ orange

Zest and juice of ½ lime

1½ cups port

8 ounces fresh cranberries

½ small red onion, minced

1 clove garlic, minced

1 teaspoon peeled and minced fresh ginger

1 scallion, finely sliced (green and white parts)

1 cup (packed) light brown sugar

Salt and white pepper, to taste

Pinch of cinnamon

Pinch of nutmeg

To prepare the relish, set the orange and lime zest aside, and place the orange and lime juice in a saucepan. Add the port, cranberries, onion, garlic, ginger, scallion, sugar, salt, pepper, cinnamon, and nutmeg to the pan and cook over medium heat for 10 minutes, stirring occasionally. Stir in the reserved orange and lime zest and cook for 5 to 10 minutes longer, or until the mixture thickens. Remove the mixture from the heat and let it cool to room temperature.

To prepare the salad, place the oil and vinegar in a mixing bowl. Whisk together and season with salt and pepper. Add the watercress and toss until well coated.

for the salad

3 tablespoons olive oil

1 tablespoon balsamic vinegar

Salt and pepper, to taste

1 cup firmly packed watercress leaves

1 pound smoked turkey sausage links (or unsmoked), or chicken sausage

In a nonstick sauté pan set over high heat, sear the turkey sausage for about 8 minutes, turning so it browns on all sides and is cooked through. Slice the links on the bias. To serve, place the dressed watercress on 4 serving plates and lean the sliced links against the salad. Spoon the relish around the salad.

little havana
plantain-pork piononos

serves 4

Piononos are a classic Cuban-Floridian appetizer—plantain fritters filled with ground beef—that I have adapted using two other staples of the cuisine, pork and black beans. While filming the show on Little Havana, centered on the vibrant and colorful Calle Ocho in Miami, we took time off for a Saturday-night meal at a traditional Cuban diner that served food family-style. All the customers there were smartly dressed, and I was struck by how much everyone was relishing their food and the event of eating out. I wish dining out were treated with that much respect and enjoyment everywhere.

½ cup olive oil

2 large ripe plantains (dark yellow to brown), peeled and quartered lengthwise

8 ounces fresh pork sausage, skin removed

½ teaspoon ground cumin

¼ teaspoon cayenne pepper

1 can (15 ounces) cooked black beans, rinsed and drained

Salt and pepper, to taste

1 cup grated Monterey Jack cheese

Heat the oil in a large nonstick skillet set over medium-high heat. When it is almost smoking, add the plantain slices and cook for 1 or 2 minutes on each side, or until golden brown. Remove the plantain slices from the pan, being careful not to break them, and drain on paper towels. Let them cool.

Preheat the oven to 350° F.

Remove all but 1 tablespoon of the oil from the pan, add the sausage, and sauté over medium-high heat for about 10 minutes, or until golden brown. Add the cumin, cayenne, and black beans. Season with salt and pepper and cook for 5 minutes longer.

Gently form 2 plantain slices into a
ring about 4 inches across, overlapping the ends of each slice by 1 inch,
and secure each end with a toothpick
(alternatively, use a 4-inch ring mold).
Place the plantain rings in a large
baking dish without letting them
touch each other. Fill each ring with
the black bean and sausage mixture
and top with the cheese. Bake for 10
to 15 minutes, or until bubbling and
golden. Transfer the piononos to warm
serving plates.

tip This appetizer can also be made with baby
bananas, instead of plantains. In a cute
touch, the fritters are then called pioninos
(*ninos* being the word used for "little
bananas").

papaya and brie quesadillas with a
crabmeat and avocado salad

serves 4

Quesadillas have caught on in a big way—I think of them as the new century's version of the grilled cheese sandwich! Like sandwiches, quesadillas are a great medium for using leftovers and they are extremely versatile; the three essential ingredients are flour tortillas, cheese, and your imagination. This is a "Nuevo Latino" appetizer, celebrating the hot new fusion cuisine based in Florida that draws primarily on the culinary heritage and cooking styles of Latin America and the Caribbean. Nuevo Latino cuisine definitely has a tropical beat, and the papaya and avocado in this recipe set the tone. The delicious salad can be enjoyed on its own, without the quesadillas.

for the salad

¼ cup mayonnaise

1 tablespoon freshly squeezed lime juice

2 cloves garlic, finely minced

1 tablespoon chopped fresh cilantro leaves

½ teaspoon ground cumin

Salt and pepper, to taste

12 ounces lump crabmeat

2 Hass avocados, pitted, peeled, and diced

1 large tomato, cored and diced

To prepare the salad, spoon the mayonnaise into a mixing bowl and add the lime juice, garlic, cilantro, cumin, salt, and pepper. Stir to combine and fold in the crabmeat, avocados, and tomatoes. Keep refrigerated while preparing the quesadillas.

To prepare the quesadillas, heat the oil in a nonstick sauté pan or on a griddle set over medium-high heat. Mix the Brie, papaya, cilantro, salt, and pepper in a bowl. Lay 2 of the tortillas on a work surface and top evenly with the Brie mixture, spreading it out almost to the edges. Place the remaining tortillas over the filling and transfer to the sauté pan. Cook for about 4 minutes, or until the cheese starts to melt and the bottom

for the quesadillas

  1 tablespoon vegetable or olive oil

  5 ounces Brie cheese, diced

½ papaya, peeled, seeded, and thinly sliced crosswise

  2 tablespoons chopped fresh cilantro leaves

    Salt and pepper, to taste

  4 small (6- to 8-inch) flour tortillas

1½ cups firmly packed mixed salad greens

of the tortilla starts to brown. Using a large spatula, flip each quesadilla over and continue cooking until the cheese has melted, about 2 minutes. Remove and cut each quesadilla into quarters.

Place 2 quesadilla quarters on each serving plate. Arrange the mixed greens next to the quesadillas and top the greens with the crabmeat and avocado salad.

homemade corn dogs

Most people think of corn dogs as a popular Southern snack or food you'd find at the state fair or local carnival. But they are surprisingly easy to make at home and are a great hit at children's parties, the reason I featured them on my television show. Grown-up kids also enjoy corn dogs, and for them you can add some grown-up flavors such as jalapeño chile, cilantro, roasted bell peppers, or smoked sausage. You will need twelve wooden Popsicle sticks for this recipe (available at candy-making stores), and ideally, a small but tall-sided saucepan.

Vegetable oil, for deep-frying

⅓ cup cornmeal

½ cup flour

1½ teaspoons dried mustard powder

1 tablespoon sugar

1 teaspoon baking powder

½ teaspoon salt

½ teaspoon pepper

1 tablespoon vegetable shortening or butter, at room temperature

2 eggs, beaten

½ cup milk

12 hot dogs (skinless)

Pour about 6 inches of oil in a small, tall-sided saucepan, or enough to cover the hot dogs when held upright. Or you can use a larger saucepan, big enough to hold the hot dogs lying lengthwise, and enough oil to cover them. Heat the oil to 325°F., or until a drop of batter floats and sizzles.

Sift the cornmeal and flour into a bowl and mix in the mustard, sugar, baking powder, salt, and pepper. Using a hand mixer on slow, add the shortening and mix until well combined (it should be coarse and lumpy). In a separate bowl, combine the eggs and milk and pour into the dry ingredients. Stir the batter until smooth, then pour into a tall glass. Push about three quarters of a stick into each hot dog. Dip each hot dog into the glass to cover in batter. Cook 1 or 2 at a time in the hot oil for 5 or 6 minutes, or until golden brown. Repeat for the remaining corn dogs, refilling the glass with batter as necessary. Remove the corn dogs with tongs and drain on paper towels. Serve warm with mustard and ketchup.

Regardless of the score or statistics at any baseball game, you can always depend on an ample supply of the all-American comfort food. Like baseball, hot dogs are an institution in this country, but these ballpark stars have been in America for only a little more than 100 years. Even though they were not invented here, the evolution of the quaint European treat into today's popular concession is purely an American tale wagging the dog.

Hot dogs were first called frankfurters after the German city in which they were created more than 500 years ago. The sausages remained a hometown favorite until immigrants brought the handy snacks with them to America in the mid-1800s. German-American pushcart vendors gave their new countrymen their first taste of the sausages, which were sold without buns and wrapped in paper. In Chicago in 1893, the frankfurter was the taste sensation at the World's Columbian Exposition, which was catering to a crowd already clamoring for convenience food. At the Louisiana Purchase Exposition in 1904 (aka the St. Louis World's Fair), concessionaire Anton Feuchtwanger decided to dress up the dog by replacing the paper wrappers with white gloves so his patrons could enjoy their meal and keep their fingers clean, too. The concept was so popular that Anton's sales soared, but his profits dipped due to the expense of the gloves. Unwilling to revert to paper, Anton asked a baker to devise a roll to fit the sausages—and the hot dog bun was born.

In 1906, sports cartoonist Tad Dorgan playfully drew a picture of a dachshund lounging in a bun and labeled it "Hot Dog." The name stuck, and by the time Franklin D. Roosevelt publicly treated visiting heads of state to hot dogs, they were firmly established as America's favorite handheld food.

baked artichoke frittata with two cheeses

serves 4

A frittata is an Italian baked egg dish similar to an open-face omelet, and traditionally, frittatas are not flipped over. I fell in love with frittatas during a family vacation at a guesthouse on a farm in Tuscany. Although I am not usually a breakfast eater, the frittatas cooked for us regularly by the farmer's wife were hard to resist. As with omelets, you can add all sorts of vegetable, meat, or cheese fillings. I have kept this recipe, which is taken from my public radio show, pretty simple.

1 package (about 9 ounces) frozen artichoke hearts

6 eggs

½ cup half-and-half

¼ teaspoon salt

⅛ teaspoon pepper

⅛ teaspoon ground nutmeg

1 cup (about 4 ounces) shredded Fontina or Jack cheese

½ cup grated Parmesan cheese

Preheat the oven to 350° F.

Place the artichoke hearts in a saucepan of boiling water and blanch for 1 or 2 minutes, or until tender. Drain and spread the artichokes evenly in a well-greased, shallow 8- or 9-inch quiche dish or baking dish. In a mixing bowl, beat the eggs with the half-and-half, salt, pepper, and nutmeg. Stir in the shredded cheese and pour the mixture over the artichokes.

Transfer the baking dish to the oven and bake the frittata for about 20 minutes, or until the edges are lightly browned and the center feels firm when lightly pressed. Sprinkle evenly with the Parmesan cheese, return to the oven, and continue to bake for 5 to 8 minutes longer, or until puffy and lightly browned.

tip Graters are timesaving tools, but they can be a bother to clean. Save time by spraying your grater with nonstick cooking spray (or lightly coating it with vegetable oil) before you grate cheeses or citrus rinds.

creamed chipped beef with buttermilk biscuits

serves 4

In the Boston area with the TV show, we visited Peter Davis, executive chef at Henrietta's Table, located in the Charles Hotel in Cambridge. Peter has been honored by the James Beard Foundation as one of the best hotel chefs in the country, and his original recipes take a straightforward approach to classic New England cuisine. This recipe, which he prepared for our show on New England brunch, is a perfect example. Chipped beef is usually served in a béchamel sauce based on a flour-and-butter roux, but Peter's version is simpler, richer, and more elegant.

for the buttermilk biscuits

2 cups flour, sifted

1 tablespoon baking powder

½ teaspoon salt

½ cup (1 stick) butter

½ cup buttermilk

for the chipped beef

12 ounces chipped dried beef

1½ cups heavy cream

Preheat the oven to 450° F.

To prepare the biscuits, place the flour, baking powder, and salt in the bowl of an electric mixer fitted with a paddle attachment (alternatively, place in a mixing bowl and mix by hand). Add the butter and mix on low speed until granular in consistency. Add the buttermilk and mix to just form a soft dough. Turn out the dough onto a floured work surface and knead lightly. Roll out to a ½-inch thickness and cut into eight 3-inch biscuits. Transfer to an ungreased cookie sheet and bake for 12 to 15 minutes, or until golden brown. Transfer the biscuits to a rack to cool slightly.

While the biscuits are baking, place the chipped beef and cream in a saucepan and bring to a boil. Cook at a low boil for about 10 minutes, or until the cream is reduced by one third. Pour the chipped-beef mixture over the buttermilk biscuits, serving 2 biscuits per person.

tip

If you are sensitive to sodium, try to make sure the dried beef is not overly salty, which some brands tend to be. Dried beef is available at most delis, or in the refrigerated meat section of markets.

appetizers

97

marinated salmon skewers and caesar salad with soy dressing

serves 4

For one television episode, we visited the International Boston Seafood Show, the largest event of its kind in the country. I was struck by the quantity and variety of salmon on display, from such disparate parts of the world as Alaska, Chile, Norway, and the East Coast. There is also a large amount on the market these days that is farm raised. While river fishing for wild salmon in Alaska, I learned a lot about salmon, a subject close to my heart.

The nontraditional Caesar salad dressing in this recipe avoids raw eggs, and it goes well with the Asian-style salmon marinade. The salmon skewers can be pan-fried or broiled, rather than grilled, if you prefer.

for the salmon skewers

1 pound Alaskan salmon fillets, cut into ¾- to 1-inch cubes

Juice of ½ lemon

⅓ cup soy sauce

2 tablespoons white wine

¼ cup sugar

1 shallot, chopped

2 cloves garlic, chopped

1 tablespoon peeled and chopped fresh ginger

Soak 8 wooden skewers in water for 30 minutes to prevent them from burning up on the grill. Thread the salmon onto the skewers. Place the lemon juice, soy sauce, wine, sugar, shallot, garlic, and ginger in a blender or food processor and blend for 2 minutes, or until smooth. Transfer to a shallow dish and add the salmon, turning to coat. Marinate the skewers in the refrigerator, covered with plastic wrap, for 4 to 6 hours.

Preheat the oven to 350°F. and prepare the grill.

for the croutons

¼ cup olive oil

½ teaspoon granulated garlic

Salt and pepper, to taste

½ French baguette loaf, cut into ½-inch cubes

for the dressing

3 canned anchovy fillets, chopped

2 cloves garlic, chopped

½ teaspoon Dijon mustard

2 tablespoons grated Parmesan cheese

1 tablespoon freshly squeezed lemon juice

1 tablespoon soy sauce (preferably low-sodium)

½ cup olive oil

1 head of romaine lettuce, torn or cut into bite-size pieces

To prepare the croutons, mix the oil, garlic, salt, and pepper in a mixing bowl and add the bread. Toss to coat thoroughly and transfer to a cookie sheet. Bake for 12 minutes, or until crisp and golden. Remove and let cool.

To prepare the dressing, place the anchovies, garlic, mustard, cheese, lemon juice, and soy sauce in a blender and purée for 2 minutes, or until smooth. With the machine running, slowly pour in the olive oil in a steady stream until the dressing is completely emulsified. Place the romaine in a bowl and toss with the dressing.

Remove the skewers from the marinade, letting the marinade drip off. Grill the salmon over medium-high heat for 2 or 3 minutes on each side, or until cooked through. Place the dressed romaine on 4 serving plates and arrange the skewers crisscrossed on top. Scatter the croutons over the salad.

new england red flannel hash

serves 4

This distinctively regional recipe is another by Peter Davis, chef at Henrietta's Table at the Charles Hotel in Cambridge, Massachusetts. I'd never tried red flannel hash until I tasted Peter's, and I loved it so much I ordered it three mornings in a row—and I never eat breakfast! At his restaurant, he serves it with two eggs and hollandaise sauce. Traditionally, the hash used leftovers from another regional classic, the New England boiled dinner, with the addition of plenty of beets to give it color. For further authenticity, serve the hash with cornbread.

1 cup diced corned beef

1 cup cooked carrot

1 cup cooked onion

1 cup cooked parsnip

1 cup cooked potato

2 cups cooked beets

2 tablespoons vegetable oil, divided

Salt

8 eggs

tip

If you would like the hash to be perfectly round—a nice touch since you are topping it with an egg—use a ring mold to contain it. You can substitute turnip or rutabaga for the parsnip, carrot, or potato.

In a food processor, coarsely pulse the corned beef and cooked carrot, onion, parsnip, and potato until the mixture is ground medium-fine. Remove and transfer to a mixing bowl. Next, pulse the beets, mix together with the meat and vegetables and divide the mixture into 8 portions. Heat ½ tablespoon of the vegetable oil in a nonstick skillet or sauté pan and add one quarter of the hash mixture, spreading it evenly in the pan. Cook over medium heat for 3 to 4 minutes, or until the bottom turns brown and forms a crispy texture. Flip the hash over with a spatula and cook for 3 or 4 minutes on the second side. Repeat with the remaining oil and hash mixture.

While the hash is cooking, poach the eggs. Heat a saucepan of salted water. Gently break 2 eggs into a saucer and slide them into the pan. Cook at a low boil for 3½ to 4 minutes. Remove with a slotted spoon and repeat with the remaining eggs. Spoon portions of the hash onto 4 serving plates and top each with 2 poached eggs.

maine rock crab cakes with tartar sauce

serves 6

From the mid-Atlantic states up through New England, every chef in every restaurant worth its name has his or her own recipe for crab cakes. This one happens to belong to Peter Davis (see opposite). The Maine crab he uses is similar to blue crab, and his recipe is pretty traditional, with the addition of chopped asparagus. You can substitute chopped cooked spinach or artichoke hearts, roasted bell peppers, or sun-dried tomatoes, if you prefer.

for the tartar sauce

- 1 cup mayonnaise
- ¼ cup minced onion
- ¼ cup capers, drained
- ¼ cup minced dill pickle
- 3 tablespoons minced fresh flat-leaf parsley leaves
- 2 tablespoons freshly squeezed lemon juice

for the crab cakes

- 2½ tablespoons butter, divided
- 4 asparagus spears, trimmed and finely chopped
- 1½ pounds lump crabmeat
- 4 slices white sandwich bread, crust removed and finely diced
- 1 cup mayonnaise
- 3 tablespoons Dijon mustard
- 1 tablespoon crab-boil seasoning, such as Old Bay

To prepare the tartar sauce, place the mayonnaise, onion, capers, pickle, parsley, and lemon juice in a bowl and mix until well blended. Keep refrigerated.

Preheat the oven to 350° F.

To prepare the crab cakes, melt ½ tablespoon of the butter in a small nonstick sauté pan set over medium heat. Add the asparagus and sauté for 2 to 3 minutes, or until al dente. Transfer to a mixing bowl, add the crabmeat, bread, mayonnaise, mustard, and crab-boil seasoning and combine thoroughly. Flour your hands and form the mixture into 6 cakes. Melt the remaining 2 tablespoons of butter in a nonstick skillet large enough to hold all 6 cakes, and sauté the crab cakes over medium-high heat for about 4 minutes on each side, until browned. Transfer the skillet to the oven and bake for 15 minutes. Transfer the crab cakes to 6 serving plates and serve with the tartar sauce.

appetizers

caramelized onion and mushroom tart on mixed greens with balsamic vinaigrette

serves 8

This recipe was created by Rory Reno, executive chef of The Hotel Hershey in Hershey, Pennsylvania. The town is a worthy subject for a food show, as any chocolate lover will tell you, because it was founded in Pennsylvania dairy farm country by Milton Hershey, the entrepreneur who developed and popularized milk chocolate. He not only endowed Hershey School, a school for orphan boys that remains in the front ranks nationally, but he also established the Hotel Hershey as a first-class resort. The hotel is notable not just for its Spanish Colonial style and imported fixtures, but also for its unique Circular Dining Room. This was designed to Hershey's specifications so there would be no bad corner tables! Rory's menu, with its regional flair, certainly does it justice, as this quiche-like recipe proves.

for the vinaigrette

- 4 cups balsamic vinegar
- ½ cup rice wine vinegar
- ½ cup soy sauce
- 2 tablespoons (packed) light brown sugar
- ½ tablespoon minced garlic
- 1 tablespoon toasted (dark) sesame oil

To prepare the vinaigrette, place both vinegars, the soy sauce, sugar, garlic, and sesame oil in a saucepan and reduce over medium heat for about 20 minutes, or until it is reduced to a syrup and about 1 cup remains. Set the vinaigrette aside and let it cool.

Preheat the oven to 325° F.

for the tart

1 tablespoon butter

1 large onion, diced

3 ounces button mushrooms, stemmed and sliced (about 1¼ cups)

3 ounces shiitake mushrooms, stemmed and sliced (about 1¼ cups)

2 ounces portobello mushrooms, stemmed and sliced (about ⅞ cup)

Salt and pepper, to taste

2 eggs

2 cups heavy cream

2 ounces grated Swiss cheese (5 tablespoons)

1 ready-made 9-inch pie shell, thawed

4 cups mesclun salad mix or other mixed greens, washed

To prepare the tart, melt the butter in a sauté pan. Add the onion and cook over medium heat for 10 to 15 minutes, or until it starts to brown and caramelize. Add the button, shiitake, and portobello mushrooms, stir well, and season with salt and pepper. When the mushrooms are soft, about 5 minutes, remove from the heat and set aside to cool. In a mixing bowl, beat the eggs until fluffy and stir in the cream. Set aside. Spread the cooled mushroom mixture evenly inside the pie shell and top with the cheese. Pour the egg and cream mixture over the top and bake for 30 to 40 minutes, or until an inserted toothpick comes out clean. The tart should be set but still moist.

Mound the salad greens on serving plates. Cut the tart into 8 portions and arrange 1 slice on each plate with the greens. Drizzle the vinaigrette over and around the greens.

florida lobster and key west shrimp ceviche
with cayenne-spiced yuca chips

serves 6 to 8

The growing popularity of Nuevo Latino cooking (see page 92) and Florida's "New World Cuisine" has helped bring ceviches into the American mainstream. Ceviches—raw fish or seafood "cooked" in the acid of citrus juice and often mixed with diced vegetables—originated on the west coast of South America. There, they served the practical purpose for ancient civilizations of preserving fresh seafood for consumption by communities that were not located right on the coast. This recipe was created for our TV show on Miami by Frank Liberoni, executive chef of the Mayfair Grill restaurant in Coconut Grove's Mayfair Hotel. Start it well ahead of time, since the ceviche must marinate for twelve to twenty-four hours. Yuca (also called cassava) is a popular root vegetable in Nuevo Latino cooking.

for the ceviche

- 2 frozen lobster tails, about 8 ounces each, thawed

  Salt

- 1 pound extra-large shrimp (16 to 20), peeled, deveined, and cut in half lengthwise

- 1 red bell pepper, seeded and finely diced

- 1 green bell pepper, seeded and finely diced

- ½ cup freshly squeezed lemon juice

- ½ cup freshly squeezed lime juice

- ½ cup freshly squeezed orange juice

- ½ cup chopped fresh cilantro leaves

- 2 tablespoons olive oil

To prepare the ceviche, thread the lobster tails onto 2 long wooden skewers. Fill a bowl with water and ice. Bring a saucepan of salted water to a boil and add the lobster. Cover with a tight-fitting lid, turn down the heat to low, and poach the lobster for 5 or 6 minutes, or until cooked through. Transfer the lobster to the ice bath to stop the cooking process. Remove the meat from the shells by cutting the underneath membrane with scissors and slice the lobster meat. Transfer to a mixing bowl and add the raw shrimp, red and green bell pepper, lemon juice, lime juice, orange juice, cilantro, oil, salt, pepper, and Tabasco sauce. Combine thoroughly, cover the bowl, and marinate in the refrigerator for 12 to 24 hours, depending on the size of the shrimp.

Salt and pepper, to taste

Tabasco sauce, to taste

for the yuca chips

Vegetable oil, for deep-frying

2 medium yucas (about 12 ounces each), peeled, finely sliced, rinsed, and patted dry

1 teaspoon cayenne, or to taste

3 coconuts (optional), to serve

1 orange, peeled and sectioned, for garnish

1 lemon, peeled and sectioned, for garnish

To prepare the yuca chips, heat the oil in a deep-fryer or large saucepan to 350°F. Add the sliced yuca in batches; do not add too many at a time or the temperature of the oil will be too cool. Deep-fry the yuca slices for 3 or 4 minutes, or until golden. Remove with a slotted spoon and drain the chips on paper towels. Sprinkle with the cayenne and let cool.

If serving the ceviche in coconuts, cut the coconuts in half with the back of a heavy knife while rotating them. Drain off the coconut "milk" and pat the insides dry. Fill some individual serving bowls with crushed ice. Spoon the ceviche mixture into the coconut halves and set on the ice. Garnish with the citrus segments and serve with the yuca chips. (If not using coconuts, simply spoon the ceviche into large martini glasses or onto serving plates and garnish.)

maryland-style striped bass cakes with spinach salad

serves 4

The Chesapeake region of the East Coast is synonymous with all kinds of seafood, and the crab-boil seasoning and oyster crackers used in this recipe definitely give it that mid-Atlantic coastal feel. I also use the Maryland farm-raised sea bass (see page 205) in this recipe. Fish cakes are a great way to use up leftover potatoes, and the crumbled crackers, which are best ground in a food processor, make a coarser, drier crust than bread crumbs. If you compare this recipe to the halibut cake recipe on page 87 and the crab cake recipe on page 101, you can see how diverse and versatile these little appetizers can be.

for the bass cakes

- 1 cup bottled clam juice
- 12 to 16 ounces boneless, skinless striped bass fillet
- 2 tablespoons butter
- ½ onion, minced
- 1 red bell pepper, seeded and finely diced
- 2 sticks celery, finely diced
- 3 tablespoons flour
- 2 tablespoons grated Parmesan cheese
- ¼ cup sliced scallion (green part only)
- 1½ teaspoons crab-boil seasoning, such as Old Bay
- Salt and pepper, to taste
- 1 cup cooked and mashed potatoes
- ½ cup coarsely ground oyster crackers
- ½ cup canola oil

To prepare the cakes, heat the clam juice and 1 cup water in a saucepan and bring to a simmer. Add the fish, cover, and poach for 7 to 8 minutes. Remove the bass and let cool. Flake the fish with a fork; there should be about 2 cups.

Melt the butter in a large saucepan set over medium heat and add the onion, bell pepper, and celery. Sauté for 2 to 3 minutes, or until tender. Turn down the heat to the lowest setting and stir in the flour, cheese, scallion, and crab-boil seasoning. Add the salt and pepper and fold in the mashed potatoes. Fold in the poached bass and gently but thoroughly mix. Remove the pan from the heat.

for the salad

¼ cup olive oil

Juice of 2 lemons

Salt and pepper, to taste

2 cups packed spinach, washed and stemmed

When the fish mixture is cool enough to handle, lightly flour your hands and a work surface. Shape the mixture into four 3-inch fish cakes and coat well with the cracker crumbs. Heat the canola oil in a large sauté pan until almost smoking and add the fish cakes. Fry for about 3 or 4 minutes on each side, or until golden brown. Remove and drain on paper towels.

To prepare the salad, in a mixing bowl, whisk together the olive oil and lemon juice until well blended and season with salt and pepper. Toss the spinach in the dressing and top each cake with a mound of spinach.

tip Here's a helpful hint for keeping frozen leftovers tasty. If food is frozen in a container that is too large, it comes in contact with too much oxygen, which depletes the flavor. Choose containers that are roughly the same size as the volume of food you are freezing.

penn cove mussels with curry cream

serves 4

This is another recipe from Brian Scheehser at the Sorrento Hotel in Seattle (see page 61). It's a wonderfully simple dish that uses farm-raised West Coast mussels. Brian uses the Madras curry powder, which is a hot blend, but you can use a mild or medium blend according to your heat tolerance. Curry powders contain up to twenty different spices, and most contain chile, cumin, coriander, cardamom, cinnamon, cloves, fenugreek, turmeric, and fennel. They lose their pungency easily, so buy curry powder from a store with high turnover and once opened, keep it refrigerated or frozen in an airtight container.

2 cups heavy cream

1 cup fish stock, or bottled clam juice

1 tablespoon Madras curry powder, plus ½ teaspoon for garnish

Salt and pepper, to taste

4 pounds Penn Cove mussels, debearded and scrubbed

4 sprigs of fresh flat-leaf parsley, for garnish

Place the cream, stock, and 1 tablespoon of the curry powder in a saucepan and bring to a boil. Reduce the heat and cook at a low boil for 8 to 10 minutes, or until the liquid is reduced by two thirds and about 1 cup remains. Season with salt and pepper and add the mussels. Cook for about 8 minutes longer, or until the mussels have opened; throw away any mussels that do not open. Remove the mussels with a slotted spoon and transfer to 4 serving bowls with rims. Spoon the curry cream over the mussels and garnish around the rims of the bowls with the remaining ½ teaspoon of curry powder. Garnish the mussels with the parsley.

Bowls of steaming black mussels have been served in Europe for centuries, but in our country this delicious mollusk was ignored by all but the birds until a few decades ago. Until the late 1970s, the only menus in the United States featuring mussels were those in foreign restaurants. Americans have since developed a passion for this shellfish, which has always been available in abundant quantity on both the Atlantic and Pacific coasts.

Native Americans widely believed mussels to be poisonous because they were subject to contamination by a certain type of plankton. When Europeans colonized North America, they came here as mussel eaters but abandoned their taste for them once they moved in. Intent upon their survival, they followed the Indians' example and sated their shellfish cravings instead on America's plentiful supply of oysters and clams.

Today, all American mussels sold in restaurants or grocery stores are farm raised in carefully controlled waters, and they are one of the least expensive kinds of shellfish available. This kind of aquaculture is not new; in fact it has been a booming industry in Europe for a long time. The Irish entrepreneur who is credited with inventing the process of mussel farming stumbled into his vocation in 1235. After Patrick Walton was shipwrecked on a bleak region of French shore line, he stretched nets between stakes set out in shallow water in an attempt to snare seabirds for food. Instead, Walton noticed that a profusion of mussels had attached themselves to the stakes, and he altered his appetite to suit the situation. It also is said he invented a flat-bottomed boat called an acon, which he used to harvest his windfall crop. To this day, many mussels are farmed using similar stakes and collection boats.

foie gras, spinach, and portobello mushroom purses

serves 4

This elegant hors d'oeuvre recipe is adapted from a favorite canapé that I serve at the Rittenhouse Hotel. Most people think that foie gras is too expensive, but it's so rich that a little goes a long way. These days, most foie gras (including all that is produced in the United States) is duck liver, rather than goose liver. This makes the production process more humane because ducks do not need to be force-fed.

4 ounces foie gras, sliced about ½ inch thick

1 portobello mushroom (about 5 ounces), stemmed and diced

1 teaspoon minced garlic

1 teaspoon minced shallot

1½ cups loosely packed fresh spinach leaves, washed

Salt and pepper, to taste

2 sheets of phyllo dough, thawed

¾ cup clarified butter, warmed (see page 270)

Preheat the oven to 400° F.

Set a dry nonstick sauté pan over medium-high heat and when hot, sear the foie gras for 3 or 4 minutes on each side. Remove and drain on paper towels. Add the mushroom, garlic, and shallot to the pan and sauté for about 3 minutes, until soft. Add the spinach and toss until wilted, about 2 minutes. Transfer the mixture to a bowl. Dice the foie gras, add to the bowl, gently blend all the ingredients, and season with salt and pepper.

On a flat work surface, lay out a phyllo sheet with the shorter side facing you. Using a pastry brush, brush the sheet up to the edges with the clarified butter. Lay the second phyllo sheet on top and brush with the butter. Fold over the sheets toward you in half and cut across into 8 equal pieces. Working quickly, spoon one eighth of the foie gras mixture onto the middle of each piece of phyllo. Pull the sides up and together, twist, and pinch to form the shape of a purse or pouch.

Transfer the purses to a nonstick cookie sheet and brush the tops lightly with clarified butter. Bake the purses for 8 to 10 minutes, or until golden brown.

tip

If you're buying foie gras, then splurge on the frozen (raw) Grade A product available at gourmet food stores. The quality is far superior to the canned version.

fried plantain chips with shrimp and mango salsa

In Little Havana, the Cuban section of Miami, you will find tostones served as a popular snack. They are made by frying plantain slices, then mashing and flattening them, and refrying them. This hors d'oeuvre echoes that technique, and at the Rittenhouse Hotel, we top the chips with lobster, which is an option here. Use leftover salsa with fish, chicken, or plain tortilla chips.

for the salsa

4 ounces cooked extra-large shrimp (about 4 shrimp), peeled, deveined, and finely diced

½ ripe mango, peeled, pitted, and finely diced (about ¾ cup)

¼ cup red pepper, seeded and finely diced

¼ cup green pepper, seeded and finely diced

¼ red onion, finely diced

½ jalapeño chile, seeded and minced

1 teaspoon chopped fresh flat-leaf parsley leaves

1 teaspoon chopped fresh cilantro leaves

1 tablespoon freshly squeezed lime juice

1 tablespoon vegetable oil

1 teaspoon sugar (optional)

Salt and pepper, to taste

To prepare the salsa, place the shrimp, mango, bell peppers, onion, jalapeño, parsley, cilantro, lime juice, vegetable oil, sugar (if using), salt, and pepper in a mixing bowl. Combine thoroughly and let chill in the refrigerator for at least 30 minutes.

To prepare the chips, heat the oil in a saucepan until almost smoking (about 325° F.). Drop the plantain slices in the oil and fry for about 5 minutes, or until very light golden brown. Remove with a slotted spoon and drain on paper towels, leaving the oil heating in the pan. When the plantain slices are cool enough to handle, transfer them to a work surface. Using the side of a heavy chef's knife, or with your hand, press down on the plantain slices and flatten them out to make compact chips. Return the chips to the hot oil and fry for 3 or 4 minutes longer, or until golden brown. Remove the chips with a slotted spoon and drain on paper towels.

for the chips

1 cup vegetable oil

2 ripe plantains, peeled and cut crosswise into 8 slices each

4 fresh cilantro sprigs

Place the plantain chips on serving plates and top each one with 1 teaspoon of the salsa. Garnish with the cilantro sprigs.

tortilla chips with hot smoked honey-glazed salmon

serves 4

The Asian-style glaze for the salmon in this hors d'oeuvre recipe is a simpler version of the marinade for the salmon skewers on page 98. The assertively sweet and tangy flavors of the glaze really match the smokiness of the salmon well. The method used here for smoking makes a great alternative to the stovetop smoking technique described on page 46.

1 scallion (green part only)

¼ cup honey

2 tablespoons low-sodium soy sauce

½ cup finely chopped hickory wood chips

4 ounces salmon fillet

Salt and pepper, to taste

12 corn tortilla chips

1 teaspoon salmon roe, for garnish

Cut the scallion into 1-inch lengths and finely julienne. Place in a bowl of ice water and stir periodically until the scallions curl. When ready to serve, drain the scallions and dry on paper towels (the scallion curls will be used for garnish).

In a bowl, thoroughly combine the honey and soy sauce. Set aside. Line a sauté pan with aluminum foil, set over high heat, and add the wood chips. When the chips begin to smoke, lay another piece of aluminum foil over them and spray the foil with nonstick spray. Turn the heat down to medium, place the salmon on the foil, and season with salt and pepper. Cover the pan with a lid and smoke for 6 to 8 minutes, until just done. Remove the pan from the heat, but leave the lid on until the salmon has cooled.

Once it is cooled, remove the salmon from the pan and slice into 12 equal pieces. Spoon the honey-soy glaze on each slice and lay the slices on the tortilla chips. Garnish with scallion curls and the salmon roe. Serve 3 chips per person.

fingerling potatoes stuffed with curried coconut crab

serves 6

For the television show on hors d'oeuvres, I suggested holding a party and serving this recipe with the preceding two and the following one. If you are just serving these tasty morsels and no other food, plan on twelve hors d'oeuvres per person. For this recipe, the potatoes make a convenient and tasty means of holding the filling, but you could also use endive leaves, miniature pastry shells, or chips. An alternative filling would be the avocado-crabmeat mixture from page 92.

6 fingerling potatoes (about 9 ounces)

Salt, to taste

2 tablespoons shredded (desiccated) unsweetened coconut, for garnish

¼ cup mayonnaise

1 teaspoon medium curry powder

1 teaspoon chopped fresh flat-leaf parsley leaves

Pepper, to taste

4 ounces lump crabmeat

1 ounce black caviar, for garnish

Preheat the oven to 350°F. Place the potatoes in a saucepan of salted boiling water and cook until just tender, about 15 minutes. Let cool slightly. Cut the potatoes in half lengthwise and carefully scoop out some of the flesh, making them look like canoes. Spread the coconut on a cookie sheet and toast in the oven for about 8 minutes, or until lightly golden; do not let it brown. Remove it from the pan and let it cool.

In a bowl, mix together the mayonnaise, curry powder, parsley, salt, and pepper. Fold in the crabmeat and spoon the mixture into the potatoes. Garnish with the toasted coconut and caviar.

potato latkes
with apple compote

serves 4 to 6

Latkes are fried potato pancakes traditionally served on the Jewish holiday of Hanukkah. The oil in which they are cooked represents the miracle commemorated during these holy days. I do not pretend that my version, an hors d'oeuvre I serve at the Rittenhouse Hotel, is authentic, but it's simple to make and pairs really well with the fruit compote. Serve the latkes warm or at room temperature.

for the compote

1 teaspoon butter

½ onion, finely diced

1 Granny Smith apple, peeled, cored, and finely diced

1 tablespoon raisins or currants

1 tablespoon sugar

1 teaspoon ground cinnamon

for the latkes

1 russet potato (about 8 ounces), peeled and grated

1 egg, beaten

1 tablespoon flour

1 scallion, finely sliced (green part only)

Salt and pepper, to taste

2 to 3 tablespoons vegetable oil

¼ cup sour cream, for garnish (optional)

To prepare the compote, melt the butter in a saucepan set over medium-low heat and add the onion. Cook for 2 to 3 minutes, or until translucent. Add the apple and raisins and turn up the heat to medium-high. Add the sugar and 2 tablespoons water and reduce the mixture until it reaches a syrupy consistency, about 2 minutes. Add the cinnamon and remove the pan from the heat.

To prepare the latkes, place the grated potato in a colander and rinse under cold running water to remove the excess starch. Squeeze to remove the excess water. Place the egg, flour, scallion, salt, and pepper in a mixing bowl and whisk to form a batter. Stir in the potato, cover the bowl, and let the mixture rest in the refrigerator for about 30 minutes.

Heat 1 to 2 tablespoons of the vegetable oil in a large sauté pan set over medium-high heat and spoon in the batter, about 1 tablespoon for each latke. Repeat, cooking no more than 8 latkes at a time. Flatten the latkes slightly with a spatula to form pancakes. Cook on the first side for 3 or 4 minutes, or until golden brown, and then flip over. Add more oil if necessary, reduce the heat to medium, and cook until golden brown on the second side, 3 or 4 minutes longer. Remove the latkes from the pan and let cool on paper towels.

Transfer the latkes to serving plates and spoon some of the compote on top of each one. Garnish with the sour cream, if desired.

meat

Texas Grilled Brisket with Roasted Fingerling Potato Salad

Tex-Mex Beef and Cheese Enchiladas

Burgundy Barbecued Steaks with Crumbled Gorgonzola

Sautéed Veal Chops with Fennel, Chestnuts, and Pearl Onions

Chestnuts

Asian Veal Burgers with Cilantro-Roasted Corn

Braised Veal Osso Buco with Red Wine and Vegetables

Brother Hank's Barbecued Pork Ribs

Roasted Pork Loin with Honey-Orange Glaze

Honey

Cabernet Pork Chops with Portobello Mushrooms

Grilled Pepper Pork Chops with Mango-Corn Salsa

Sautéed Nuevo Latino Pork Loin Chops with Guava Sauce

Guavas

Ham, Crab, and Mixed Cheese Macaroni

Mother's Day Individual Sausage and Egg Casseroles

Grilled Center-Cut Pork Chops with Cranberry Stuffing

Cranberries

Irish-American Stew with Lamb and Beef

Jeff Sahib's Lamb Curry

Roasted Lamb Loin with Fresh Sauerkraut

Cabbage

Grilled Leg of Lamb with Spicy Merlot Basting Sauce

Rosemary-Citrus Lamb Roast

Greek-Style Roasted Leg of Lamb

Everyone seems to have been talking about the demise of red meat over the past fifteen years, and although demand comes and goes in small waves, red meat is still very much with us. Americans consume less red meat than they used to, but that decline seems to have leveled off, if not reversed somewhat. Here we are at the beginning of the twenty-first century, and more steakhouses are opening than ever before. I reckon meat is here to stay.

I think most people have cut down their meat intake over the years by reducing portion size. I eat more fish and poultry than I used to when I was growing up, but like most people, there are times when I just crave a juicy steak, a tangy plate of barbecued ribs, or a meaty stew. Many meat dishes are comfort foods, and they will always be with us.

Maybe it's because I grew up in Texas with parents who are from the South, but there is more pork in this chapter than any other kind of meat. I like the fact that pork is bred lean these days, and it's a good value. It is easy to prepare, and when cooked properly, it adapts to other flavors without losing its own identity. I also love cooking with lamb, which is such a popular meat outside the United States. I think part of the reason that lamb is underrated is that consumers suspect that the meat has a "gamey" taste. That may have been true years ago when stronger-tasting mutton was still available, but these days, virtually all of the lamb sold in the United States is deliciously mild yet tasty. In the case of both pork and lamb, these meats just seemed to fit into the themes of the television show more often than others, but I make no apologies because I know you are going to enjoy the recipes.

texas grilled brisket with roasted fingerling potato salad

In the old days, brisket of beef, a cut from the side of the animal, was either "corned" or ground up for dog food. It is not a naturally tender cut, but once cooks began to appreciate just how successfully it could be barbecued, and how it could absorb the flavors of barbecue sauces, brisket never looked back. In fact, one of the distinguishing features of Texas barbecue is brisket; pork is the meat of choice in Carolina. You will need to keep adding charcoal to the grill on a regular basis if that is the fuel you use. I prefer lump charcoal, which contains no additives. Remember: Never add liquid starter fuel to a burning charcoal grill.

for the spice rub

2 tablespoons celery salt

2 tablespoons ground coriander

2 tablespoons garlic powder

2 tablespoons onion powder

1 tablespoon salt

1 tablespoon black pepper

1 tablespoon cayenne pepper

2 tablespoons (packed) light brown sugar

1 beef brisket (4 to 6 pounds)

Prepare the grill. To make the spice rub, place the celery salt, coriander, garlic powder, onion powder, salt, pepper, cayenne, and brown sugar in a mixing bowl and combine until well blended. Rub all over the brisket.

To prepare the basting sauce, melt the butter in a large saucepan set over medium heat. Add the onion and garlic and sauté for 3 to 4 minutes, or until soft. Add the wine, honey, vinegar, Worcestershire sauce, chili powder, salt, and pepper, and bring to a boil. Turn down the heat and simmer for 8 to 10 minutes, or until thickened. Grill the brisket over indirect medium heat for 3 hours, basting every 20 minutes with the basting sauce. Meanwhile, preheat the oven to 375° F. Wrap the brisket in foil, baste one more time, and finish in the oven for 1½ to 2 hours longer, or until fork tender.

for the basting sauce

2 tablespoons butter

1 small to medium onion, finely diced

6 cloves garlic, minced

1½ cups Merlot wine

2 tablespoons honey

⅓ cup cider vinegar

1 tablespoon Worcestershire sauce

1 teaspoon pure red chili powder

Salt and pepper, to taste

for the potato salad and vinaigrette

1½ pounds fingerling potatoes, cut in half

4 cloves garlic, unpeeled

½ red onion, julienned

¼ red bell pepper, seeded and julienned

¼ green bell pepper, seeded and julienned

2 tablespoons chopped fresh flat-leaf parsley leaves

½ cup sherry vinegar

1 cup olive oil

Salt and pepper, to taste

1 teaspoon chopped fresh lemon thyme leaves, or thyme

While the brisket is in the oven, prepare the potato salad. Wrap the potatoes and garlic cloves in 4 foil packets and place over direct heat. Grill for about 30 minutes, or until tender. Unwrap the packets and transfer the potatoes to a mixing bowl. Add the onion, bell peppers, and parsley and mix together. Squeeze the roasted garlic out of the peels into another mixing bowl, add the vinegar, and slowly whisk in the oil. Season with salt and pepper, and add to the potato salad. Sprinkle in the lemon thyme, toss together, and serve warm or at room temperature.

Transfer the brisket to a cutting board, unwrap, and let sit for 15 minutes. Trim the excess fat and slice against the grain. Serve with the potato salad.

tip I have tested finishing brisket both on the grill and in the oven, and best results were achieved with the latter method (as in this recipe). The meat just never got quite as tender or succulent when cooked exclusively on the grill.

tex-mex beef
and cheese enchiladas

serves 4

These are enchiladas in the traditional style, with the cheese inside the tortillas and the meat sauce poured over. A true Texan, especially from San Antonio where we filmed this show, will tell you that any other arrangement is an adulteration! This is one of the two staple enchiladas in Tex-Mex cooking; the other is chicken and green chile enchiladas with a dollop of sour cream on top. This is a mildly spiced recipe that you can liven up if you wish by adding minced jalapeño chiles to the cheese mixture.

for the enchilada sauce

½ cup pure red chili powder

3 cups Beef Stock (page 267)

2 slices bacon, chopped

1 pound ground beef

1 onion, finely diced

3 cloves garlic, minced

1 teaspoon ground cumin

½ teaspoon ground dried oregano

To prepare the sauce, place the chili powder and beef stock in a blender and purée until smooth and completely blended. Set aside. Place the bacon in a large sauté pan set over medium-high heat and cook until crisp, about 4 minutes. Transfer the bacon to paper towels and drain most of the fat, leaving 1 or 2 tablespoons in the pan. Add the beef, onion, and garlic and cook, stirring occasionally, for 8 to 10 minutes, or until the meat is brown. Strain off any excess fat. Add the cumin, oregano, the stock and chili powder mixture, and the reserved bacon and cook for 30 minutes, reducing the liquid by one third. Keep warm.

for the enchiladas

1½ pounds Cheddar cheese, grated (about 6½ cups)

½ large onion, diced

¼ cup canola oil

12 corn tortillas (about 6 inches across)

1 tomato, chopped

2 jalapeño chiles, seeded, ribs removed, and minced

2 tablespoons chopped fresh cilantro leaves

Preheat the oven to 350°F. To prepare the enchiladas, blend the Cheddar cheese and onion in a mixing bowl. Heat the oil in a sauté pan set over medium heat and when hot, dip the tortillas into the oil and then into the warm sauce mixture. Transfer to a work surface and evenly fill with the cheese mixture. Roll up the tortillas and place in an ovenproof baking dish. Pour the remaining sauce over the enchiladas and bake in the oven for 12 to 15 minutes, or until the cheese is melted and the sauce is hot and bubbly. Remove from the oven and transfer to 4 warm serving plates. Top evenly with the tomatoes, jalapeños, and cilantro

burgundy barbecued steaks with crumbled gorgonzola

serves 4

It may be traditional to marinate beef in red wine, but adding soy sauce? Actually, it complements the wine very well, and it has just enough saltiness to accentuate all the other flavors. This is one of the shortest and simplest recipes in the book; I created it for my radio show. Be sure to use a good-quality blue cheese. Stilton is a fine substitute for gorgonzola, but crumbled American blue cheese does not melt quite as well. Serve with herbed mashed potatoes, asparagus, or a mixed salad, if you wish.

4 boneless beef strip loin steaks,
   8 to 10 ounces each

1½ cups red Burgundy wine

1 onion, finely diced

½ cup soy sauce

½ teaspoon pepper

½ cup finely crumbled Gorgonzola cheese

Place the steaks in a large resealable plastic bag. In a mixing bowl, combine the wine with the onion, soy sauce, and pepper and pour the mixture into the bag. Carefully press the air out of the bag and close securely. Turn the bag a few times to evenly coat the steak with the marinade and then refrigerate for about 4 hours.

Prepare the grill. Remove the steaks from the marinade, letting any excess liquid drip off. Place on the grill 4 to 5 inches above the coals and cook over medium-high heat for 5 or 6 minutes on each side for medium, or to the desired degree of doneness. Sprinkle the cheese evenly over the top of the steaks during the last few seconds of cooking. Remove the steaks to a cutting board, let them rest for 5 minutes, and slice them across the grain into thin slices.

sautéed veal chops with
fennel, chestnuts, and pearl onions

serves 4

This rich and satisfying dish comes from Laurent Manrique, executive chef at the Campton Place Hotel in San Francisco (see page 22). It is exactly the kind of comforting and intensely flavorful dish that I crave sometimes in the middle of winter, and it would make a stellar meal during the holiday season. Some of the ingredients, such as the chestnuts, veal jus, and duck fat, reveal Laurent's southwestern French heritage. They are available from gourmet food stores or the mail-order source on page 271.

8 ounces vacuum-packed shelled chestnuts (about 1¼ cups)

½ cup (1 stick) butter, divided

1-pound fennel bulb, julienned (3 to 4 cups)

2 tablespoons sugar

2 tablespoons duck fat or clarified butter

4 bone-in veal rib chops (about 12 ounces each)

1 tablespoon fennel seeds

1 cup frozen pearl onions

1 cup veal jus (reduced veal stock)

Salt and pepper, to taste

3 tablespoons chopped fresh dill

1 teaspoon olive oil

Preheat the oven to 300°F. Place the chestnuts in a roasting pan and roast for 6 minutes. Set aside.

Heat ¼ cup (½ stick) of the butter in a sauté pan. Add the fennel bulb and sugar and sauté over medium heat until the fennel darkens and caramelizes, 12 to 15 minutes. Set aside.

Turn up the oven to 400°F. Heat the duck fat in a large cast-iron (or heavy ovenproof) skillet or sauté pan and when hot, add the veal chops. Sauté over medium-high heat for about 5 minutes on each side. Add the caramelized fennel, roasted chestnuts, fennel seeds, and pearl onions. Transfer to the oven and cook for 12 minutes for medium-rare to medium. Remove the chops and keep warm, covered. Add the veal jus to the skillet and season with salt and pepper. Add the dill and olive oil and stir until heated through. Serve the veal chops on 4 warm serving plates together with the fennel-chestnut mixture.

meat

125

chestnuts

"Chestnuts roasting on an open fire, Jack Frost nipping at your nose . . ." Mel Tormé nostalgically conjured up all the sensual splendors of the season when he wrote "The Christmas Song" in 1946. In those days, vendors stoking open charcoal braziers lured customers on busy city streets with the toasty aroma of roasted chestnuts. Even though those nut vendors are pretty much a thing of the past, Americans (due in part to that perennial song) still cherish the notion of roasting chestnuts during the winter holidays.

In Colonial times, the American chestnut was one of the most common trees on the continent. It regularly grew to heights over 100 feet, flourishing as far north as Maine and all the way south to Georgia. It was the predominant tree of the Appalachian Mountains. In the fall, people gathered chestnuts as a cash crop, and nuts that were not sold or consumed were dried and stored for the rest of the year; livestock were fattened on leftovers from the harvest. In 1904 a forester at the New York Zoological Park noticed that the facility's native chestnut trees were dying as a result of a strange fungus. The disease, which was traced to an exhibit of Japanese chestnuts at the park, quickly spread. By the mid-1930s, more than nine million acres of American chestnut trees had been destroyed.

Ever since the blight erased almost all the native chestnuts, the majority of the chestnuts we see on the market are imported and therefore somewhat expensive. In addition, unlike most nuts, the shelf life of the chestnut is quite short—just a few weeks. But chestnuts seem to herald the festive cooking of the winter season, and as a bonus to holiday dieting woes, they are relatively low in fat and high in fiber. American plant breeders have been attempting to create a disease-resistant hybrid by crossing our trees with a variety from China. Early efforts to rejuvenate the native species have proved futile, but scientists are hopeful that a breeding project by the American Chestnut Foundation will make it possible within 30 to 50 years for the American chestnut to flourish in the wild once again.

asian veal burgers with cilantro-roasted corn

serves 4

If you are a burger, or even a cob of juicy sweet corn, then July Fourth is your big day. For our television show on Independence Day, I decided to cook some less conventional types of burger, made with veal, turkey (see page 179), and salmon. This particular recipe was inspired by some of my kitchen staff who are Thai. They sometimes prepare a staff meal consisting of flavored veal dumplings dropped into a soup with rice noodles, lemongrass, ginger, and other Asian seasonings, and I have adapted the concept of those dumplings for my burgers.

for the corn

4 ears of fresh sweet corn, in the husk

½ cup (1 stick) butter, melted

1 teaspoon finely chopped fresh cilantro leaves

for the burgers

1¼ pounds lean ground veal

2 tablespoons hoisin sauce

¼ cup barbecue sauce

½ tablespoon white sesame seeds

½ tablespoon black sesame seeds

1 tablespoon Chinese five-spice powder

tip To speed up the job of removing corn silk, hold each ear under running water and use a spare, clean toothbrush to brush gently back and forth against the corn. The silk comes off quickly and even the strands lodged between the kernels wash away.

Prepare the grill. Place the corn in a stockpot, cover with water, and weight down with a lid or plate. Soak for at least 30 minutes. Remove the corn from the water and peel back the husks carefully. Remove the corn silks, brushing up and down the corn with a clean toothbrush. Brush the kernels with the melted butter and sprinkle with the cilantro. Carefully rewrap the husks around the corn, place on the grill, and cover with the lid. Grill for about 10 minutes, turning once or twice. Remove from the grill, then remove the husks and brush again with butter.

Meanwhile, place the veal, hoisin sauce, barbecue sauce, sesame seeds, and five-spice powder in a mixing bowl and combine thoroughly. Divide the mixture into 4 equal balls. Flatten the balls and shape into burgers ½ inch to ¾ inch thick. Transfer to the grill and cook over medium-high heat for about 5 minutes on each side, turning over just once. Serve the burgers with the grilled corn.

braised veal osso buco
with red wine and vegetables

serves 4

Contrary to what many people think, osso buco (which means "hollow bones" in Italian) is not a complicated dish, even if the ingredient list seems long. Whether it's veal, lamb, or pork, I am a big fan of slow-cooked shank meat. Some cooks will tell you that hind shanks are preferable, and they are meatier and larger. But you will not be able to tell any difference in quality if you use the front shank and cook it properly. Serve with any type of risotto, rice, barley, or couscous, if desired.

4 veal shanks (12 to 14 ounces each)

Salt and pepper, to taste

1 cup flour

½ cup clarified butter (see page 270)

24 small pearl onions, peeled

1 tablespoon minced garlic

1 stalk celery, cut on the bias into 1-inch pieces

1 pound portobello mushrooms, stemmed and thickly sliced

2 carrots, diced

1 can (14 ounces) crushed tomatoes

3 cups red wine

4 cups Beef Stock (page 267)

5 sprigs of fresh flat-leaf parsley

3 tablespoons chopped fresh flat-leaf parsley leaves

1 teaspoon dried thyme

1 teaspoon dried sage

1 teaspoon dried oregano

2 bay leaves

Season the veal shanks with salt and pepper and dredge them in the flour, shaking off the excess (reserve the remaining flour). Heat the butter in a large, deep frying pan or saucepan set over medium heat. Add the veal shanks and brown them on all sides, about 10 minutes. Remove the shanks and place them on a platter.

Add the pearl onions, garlic, celery, mushrooms, and carrots to the pan and sauté for about 5 minutes. Add the tomatoes and cook for 5 minutes longer. Sprinkle in 2 tablespoons of the flour and stir it into the vegetable mixture. Add the wine and deglaze the pan. Return the veal to the pan and add the beef stock, parsley sprigs, chopped parsley, thyme, sage, oregano, and bay leaves. Cover the pan, turn down the heat to low, and simmer for about 2 hours, adding more stock or water if necessary; the osso buco is done when the meat falls from the bone. Ladle the meat and vegetables into large soup bowls.

brother hank's barbecued pork ribs

Although the larger spare ribs are the best-selling type of pork rib, baby back ribs are meatier and more tender. This makes them ideal for grilling, as they cook more quickly and do not dry out as easily. Spare ribs are best smoked slowly over lower heat, which is a more difficult technique. Growing up, I ate lots (and I mean lots) of ribs, but for whatever reason they were always the meaty country-style ribs.

Great side dishes for these ribs are Cilantro-Roasted Corn (page 127) and Roasted Fingerling Potato Salad (page 120). This is a recipe that I created with my older brother, Hank (see page 174).

for the barbecue sauce

- 1 cup tomato ketchup
- ¼ cup cider vinegar
- ¼ cup Dijon mustard
- Juice and zest of 1 lemon
- 1 onion, diced
- 3 cloves garlic, minced
- 1 teaspoon pure red chili powder
- 1 teaspoon hot sauce (or to taste)
- ¼ teaspoon liquid smoke
- 2 tablespoons honey
- 1½ tablespoons Worcestershire sauce

for the ribs

- 4 pounds baby back pork ribs
- ¼ cup salt
- 1 tablespoon pepper

Prepare the grill.

To prepare the sauce, place the ketchup, vinegar, mustard, lemon juice and zest, onion, garlic, chili powder, hot sauce, liquid smoke, honey, and Worcestershire sauce in a saucepan and stir to thoroughly combine. Bring to a boil, turn down the heat to low, and simmer for 30 minutes, stirring occasionally. Reserve some of the sauce separately to serve at the table, and the rest just for brushing.

To prepare the ribs, season them with the salt and pepper and place bone-side down on the grill over indirect medium heat. Close the lid and cook for 1 hour. Brush the ribs with the sauce and grill for 15 minutes longer. Brush them again and grill for 15 more minutes, or until done. Cut into single or double ribs and transfer to a serving platter. Serve family-style, with the reserved sauce on the side.

roasted pork loin with honey-orange glaze

Pork loin is a very lean cut to begin with, which is why I prefer to buy it with a little fat left on for extra succulence. The complex tones of the glaze help make up for the loin's lack of inherent assertive flavor. The combination of soy sauce, orange juice, and honey is typically Asian, and the other glaze ingredients make an interesting mix. Substitute pork tenderloin if you wish, but as with pork loin, take care not to overcook it or the meat will dry out and be tough. Serve with mashed potatoes, orzo, or rice with pine nuts if you like.

for the glaze

1 cup freshly squeezed orange juice

½ cup honey

½ cup dry Marsala wine

2½ tablespoons soy sauce

½ teaspoon ground cumin

½ teaspoon celery salt

for the pork

1 large onion, chopped

2 pounds boneless pork loin, trimmed

4 cloves garlic, minced

Salt and pepper, to taste

1 tablespoon clarified butter (see page 270)

Preheat the oven to 400° F.

To prepare the glaze, place the orange juice, honey, Marsala, soy sauce, cumin, and celery salt in a saucepan and mix well. Warm over medium heat; do not boil. Reserve about 1 cup of the glaze separately and use just for brushing; set the rest aside for serving.

To prepare the pork, line a large baking dish with foil and scatter the onions evenly. Place the pork loin on top of the onions and rub the loin with the minced garlic. Season with salt and pepper and then rub with the butter. Transfer to the oven and roast for 30 minutes. Baste the pork loin with the honey and orange glaze. Continue cooking for 40 minutes longer, or until the internal temperature reaches 160° F. for medium doneness, basting with the glaze every 10 minutes.

Remove the pork from the oven and cut into slices. Serve with the onion from the pan and the remaining glaze.

"The only reason bees make honey is so that I can eat it," mused Winnie the Pooh, the ultimate honey connoisseur. Actually, bees make honey as nourishment for themselves, but they have been reluctantly sharing it ever since the rest of us got a taste. Perhaps it was a bear or some other animal that first led people to try honey thousands of years ago. Early cave drawings in Spain show a man raiding a bee's nest, and the practice of beekeeping has been around since 2500 B.C. For centuries, honey was the only available sweetening agent, but it was even more prized in early years as a medicine. Aside from aiding digestion, honey was believed to reduce fever, cure acne, and eliminate insomnia.

The Romans were the first to cook with honey, combining it with everything from radishes to garlic. Use of the sweetener spread through Europe, and by the Middle Ages every nobleman kept a hive on his estate. The largest suppliers of honey to the public were monasteries where bees were raised to produce wax for sacred candles. When King Henry VIII abolished the monasteries in his kingdom, England was plunged into a honey shortage.

The kind of honey we eat today was unknown in the Americas when the Europeans first arrived. A native American bee did exist, but it produced inferior honey that did not impress the Colonists. European bees were soon imported, and by the 1800s they had visited flowers across the continent. The many varieties of honey derive from the diversity of blossoms supplying the nectar. Every local farmer's market boasts its own specialty, and honey is the buzzword in creative cooking as well as healthy eating.

cabernet pork chops with portobello mushrooms

serves 4

This simple dish that I created for the show about cooking with wine is a variation on smothered pork chops. It may seem as though there is a lot of liquid in the pan to begin with, but it reduces considerably. All the flavors work very well together and can be used in just the same way with veal chops. If you prefer shiitakes or creminis (baby portobellos) to the larger portobellos, substitute them, or if you're feeling extravagant, chanterelles provide an elegant touch.

- 2 tablespoons olive oil
- 4 pork loin chops, ¾ to 1 inch thick (about 8 ounces each)
- Salt and pepper, to taste
- 2 cloves garlic, minced
- 2 teaspoons minced fresh rosemary leaves
- 1 tablespoon minced fresh oregano leaves
- 2 portobello mushrooms (5 to 6 ounces each), stemmed and sliced
- 1 cup Cabernet Sauvignon wine
- 1 cup tomato sauce
- 2 red bell peppers, seeded and cut into ¼-inch strips
- 1 large onion, sliced
- 4 sprigs of fresh rosemary, for garnish

Heat the oil in a large nonstick sauté pan. Season the pork chops with salt and pepper and sear over medium-high heat for about 2 minutes on each side, or until browned. Remove the chops and set aside. Pour off all but 1 tablespoon of the oil and add the garlic, rosemary, oregano, and mushrooms. Stir together for a few seconds, add the wine, and bring to a boil. Add the tomato sauce, return the pork chops to the pan, and bring to a simmer. Sprinkle the bell peppers and onion into the mixture, cover the pan, and cook at a very light simmer for 1 hour; do not boil.

Remove the chops and keep warm. Bring the sauce to a boil and reduce by one half or until thickened, about 5 minutes. Transfer the chops to serving plates and spoon the sauce over the pork. Garnish with the rosemary.

grilled pepper pork chops with mango-corn salsa

serves 4

Pork and fruit are one of the classic flavor combinations in cuisines around the world, and pork paired with mango is a traditional presentation in the Caribbean and Mexico's Yucatán region. This dish is perfect for weekend entertaining in summertime, and the salsa works just as well with grilled chicken, tuna, or swordfish. Leave the jalapeño seeds in the salsa if you want to make it hotter. Add a side of mashed potatoes, Spanish rice, or grilled vegetables if you like.

for the salsa

1 ripe mango, peeled, pitted, and diced

½ cup seeded and finely diced green bell pepper

½ cup fresh corn kernels (from 1 ear of corn)

⅓ cup finely diced red onion

1 tablespoon freshly squeezed lime juice

1 tablespoon chopped fresh cilantro leaves

1 jalapeño or serrano chile, seeded and minced

for the pork

4 boneless center-cut pork chops, ¾-inch thick (about 6 ounces each)

Juice of 1 lime

Salt, to taste

2 tablespoons coarsely cracked pepper

To prepare the salsa, place the mango, bell pepper, corn, onion, lime juice, cilantro, and chile in a mixing bowl and combine thoroughly. Let sit for 30 minutes at room temperature for the flavors to marry (refrigerate if keeping longer).

Prepare the grill.

To prepare the pork, brush both sides of the pork chops with the lime juice and season with salt. Press the pepper onto both sides of the chops and grill the chops over medium-high heat for 5 to 7 minutes on each side, until medium, or to the desired doneness. Transfer to serving plates and top with the salsa.

tip

If you don't have a grill brush handy at your next barbecue, use a piece of crumpled foil as a scouring pad when cleaning your outdoor grill rack.

meat

sautéed nuevo latino pork loin chops with guava sauce

serves 4

The "New Latin" cooking pioneered in Florida by chefs such as Norman Van Aken, Allan Susser, and Doug Rodriguez (now in New York City) has become popular in other cities, especially those on the East Coast with a significant Latin population. In these larger cities, the availability of familiar ingredients has brought the style of cooking to a wider and appreciative audience. Guava is one of the lush, tropical flavors used in Nuevo Latino, and in this recipe, it once again illustrates the affinity of pork for fruit. For more on Nuevo Latino cooking, see page 92. This dish is wonderful served with black beans and rice and garnished with scallion stems.

8 boneless pork loin chops (about 3 ounces each)

Salt and pepper, to taste

1½ tablespoons olive oil

½ red onion, finely diced

2 cloves garlic, minced

1 cup dark rum

1 cup guava nectar or guava juice

1 tablespoon freshly squeezed lime juice

1 tablespoon honey

¼ cup thinly sliced scallions (green parts only)

2 tablespoons chopped fresh cilantro leaves

Season the pork with salt and pepper. Heat the oil in a large sauté pan and sauté the pork over medium-high heat for about 4 minutes on each side, or until golden brown and cooked through. Remove the pork and keep it warm. Turn down the heat to medium, add the red onion and garlic to the pan, and sauté for about 3 minutes, until tender. Add the rum and carefully ignite, taking care not to burn your house down (watch loose clothes and long hair). When the flames have died down, add the guava nectar, lime juice, and honey and deglaze the pan. Bring to a boil and reduce the liquid by half, about 5 minutes. Stir in the scallions and cilantro, return the pork to the pan, and cook for 2 minutes longer. Transfer the pork to warm serving plates and serve with the guava sauce.

jim coleman's flavors

134

Archaeological evidence suggests that societies in Peru were farming guavas as early as 800 B.C. The compact, shrub-like plant spread northward and was flourishing in the West Indies by the time European explorers arrived there. Like the papaya, the guava was transported back to areas of trade in Asia and India, where it became very popular.

In the world's subtropical areas, more than 150 species of guava grow in various sizes and shapes. The most commonly sold are yellow, oval fruits about two inches in diameter. They should be eaten very ripe, which is evident when the fruit gives freely to pressure. The guava's flavor has been compared to a cross between strawberry and pineapple, and luscious as it is, the scratchy texture of the guava's numerous tiny seeds disconcert some diners. In order for people to enjoy the sweet-tart taste of the fruit without worrying about the seeds, most guavas are sold in the form of preserves, jellies, paste, or juice.

Some semi-seedless varieties have been developed, but they are not cost efficient because they have to be propagated through grafting. Left on their own, seeded guavas are so prolific that they have become a pest plant in some areas. They seem unbothered by insects and plant diseases, and they pass their vitality along to humans in the form of a vitamin C level higher than that found even in citrus fruits.

ham, crab, and mixed cheese macaroni

Filming a show in Seattle, I was inspired to include Dungeness crabmeat with the ham in this distinctly upscale rendition of macaroni and cheese. This is a simple dish and relatively economical, so I encourage you to use a good-quality ham such as Smithfield. Do not use canned or pressed ham. Other options for the cheese are Brie, Camembert, Fontina, goat cheese, or a good melting cheese of your choice. A good crusty bread goes really well with this dish.

3 tablespoons butter

1 onion, finely diced

3 cloves garlic, minced

3 tablespoons flour

½ cup milk

2½ cups grated mixed cheeses (preferably Cheddar, mozzarella, and Swiss)

¾ cup diced smoked ham, such as Virginia, Serrano, or Tasso

1 tablespoon chopped fresh flat-leaf parsley leaves

1 tablespoon chopped fresh oregano leaves

1 tablespoon chopped fresh basil leaves

2 scallions, finely sliced (green part only)

4 cups cooked elbow macaroni

¾ cup Dungeness crabmeat (or lump crabmeat)

Salt and pepper, to taste

Preheat the oven to 350°F. Melt the butter in a large nonstick saucepan set over medium heat. Add the butter and sauté the onions and garlic for 3 or 4 minutes, or until soft. Add the flour and stir continuously for 4 or 5 minutes to form a roux. Stir in the milk and cook the sauce for 10 minutes, stirring often. Add the cheese, ham, parsley, oregano, basil, and scallions, and stir until the mixture is well blended. Stir in the cooked macaroni and crabmeat, season with salt and pepper, and then transfer the mixture to a large (about 8 × 10-inch) nonstick baking dish that has been sprayed with nonstick spray.

Transfer the baking dish to the oven, cover, and bake for 20 minutes. Uncover the baking dish and cook for 15 to 20 minutes longer, or until the top is browned.

mother's day individual sausage and egg casseroles

serves 4

Created for a specific day, and for a special someone, this elegant yet easy presentation also makes a great brunch dish for entertaining a number of guests. Suitable accompaniments are fruit salad, pastries, and toasted bagels or muffins. It can be prepared and refrigerated up to a day ahead of time, and then baked whenever you're ready. You can use the filling from your favorite link sausages for this recipe, with the casings removed.

8 ounces uncooked sausage meat

1 tomato, chopped

6 eggs

½ cup flour

½ teaspoon baking powder

Salt and pepper, to taste

1 clove garlic, finely minced

½ cup fresh corn kernels (from 1 ear corn)

1 cup sour cream

¾ cup cottage cheese

1¼ cups grated Cheddar cheese

1¼ cups grated Monterey Jack cheese

Preheat the oven to 375° F. Place the sausage in a dry nonstick skillet set over medium-high heat and cook, stirring often, for 10 to 12 minutes, or until browned. Drain off the excess fat and stir in the tomato. Remove from the heat.

Whisk the eggs in a mixing bowl and add the flour, baking powder, salt, pepper, garlic, corn, sour cream, and cottage cheese. Mix together until well blended. Stir in the Cheddar and Jack cheese and the cooked sausage mixture.

Spray four 1-cup ramekins with nonstick spray and evenly distribute the mixture among them. Place on a cookie sheet or in a roasting pan and bake for 30 to 35 minutes, or until set and golden brown.

meat

grilled center-cut pork chops with cranberry stuffing

serves 4

I always know when one of the dishes I have created for the television show is something extra special. As soon as we've finished filming, the crew will descend ravenously, and in no time the plate is clean. That was the fate that befell this dish featuring cranberries; it certainly looks marvelously inviting when the stuffed chop is cut open. The stuffing can be used with roasted chicken, and with either turkey or chicken in roulade form. Wilted garlic spinach and sautéed kale both make colorful, contrasting accompaniments. An alternative to grilling the pork chops is to roast them at 375°F. for 15 to 20 minutes.

for the stuffing

1½ cups fresh cranberries

⅓ cup butter

1 clove garlic, minced

1 shallot, finely minced

¼ cup (packed) light brown sugar

1 tablespoon minced fresh thyme leaves

1 teaspoon dried sage

Salt and pepper, to taste

Pinch of cinnamon

4 cups coarse day-old bread crumbs (about ½ family-size loaf)

for the pork

4 boneless center-cut pork loin chops (6 to 8 ounces each)

1½ teaspoons celery salt

1½ teaspoons ground dried thyme

1 teaspoon pepper

Prepare the grill. To prepare the stuffing, place the cranberries in a food processor and pulse until roughly chopped. Melt the butter in a saucepan set over medium-high heat, add the garlic and shallot, and sauté for 2 to 3 minutes, or until soft. Add the sugar, thyme, sage, salt, pepper, and cinnamon and stir to combine. Add the bread crumbs and chopped cranberries. If the cranberries are moist, cook until the liquid just evaporates; if they are dry, cook with a little water or chicken stock. Cook until warmed through.

Using a sharp knife, cut each pork chop along the side horizontally to form a pocket; take care not to cut all the way through the meat. Fill the pockets with as much stuffing as you can, and secure the pockets with toothpicks. Season the chops with celery salt, thyme, and pepper and transfer to the grill. Grill over medium direct heat until the chops are cooked to medium, 5 or 6 minutes on each side, or to the desired doneness.

Cranberries are one of only a few fruits that originated in North America. Centuries before Europeans began to sample American foods, native Indian tribes had been gathering cranberries to eat. They were enjoyed fresh in season, but many of the berries were dried to provide sustenance during the harsh winter months, and they served as a reliable food source as the people moved from place to place. Some Indians believed cranberries had healing powers, and the fruit was also used to brew poultices for wounds.

European settlers found the berries too sour on their own and added sweeteners like maple syrup or sugar when they started the tradition of making cranberry sauce for meat. Like the Indians, New England sailors believed that cranberries were a curative and stowed plenty on board as they took to the sea. Cranberries are in fact packed with vitamin C and citric acid, which, in addition to preventing the sailors from contracting scurvy, also helped preserve the fruit for long voyages. The cranberry was the first North American fruit to find its way into European markets, where it was sold as "Cape Cod Bell Berries." It became a profitable commodity in England and Germany.

Today Massachusetts is the world's leading cranberry producer, followed by New Jersey and Wisconsin. Cranberries grow on vines on lowland farms and generations of cranberry growers have perfected the art of their cultivation. When it is time to harvest the fruit in the fall, the croplands are flooded to create cranberry bogs. Large pontoon boats equipped with beaters comb the crimson dappled ponds, knocking the berries from the vines. The floating cranberries are then lassoed with thick plastic roping and pulled to the edge of the bogs, where they are suctioned into trucks. They are drained and hauled to processing plants, where more than a third of the $200 million annual crop is made into juice. During the fall and early winter, fresh cranberries line the country's produce shelves, offering a special American treat for our holiday fare.

irish-american stew with lamb and beef

Traditional Irish stew is made with equal parts lamb stewing meat and mutton shank, together with potatoes and vegetables. Mutton—the meat of sheep over two years old—is rarely available these days, so I have substituted beef instead to give the stew a similar, meaty flavor. I think that's an appropriate compromise given that we filmed our show about Irish cooking in Chicago, one of several American cities with a large Irish-American community, and smack in the middle of cattle country. Witnessing the Chicago River turned green in honor of St. Patrick's Day was definitely one of the highlights of the series for me!

12 ounces lamb stew meat, cubed

12 ounces beef chuck, cubed

⅓ cup flour

Salt and pepper, to taste

¼ cup olive oil

3 carrots, diced

2 russet potatoes (about 1 pound), peeled and diced

2 stalks celery, diced

1 onion, diced

2 tomatoes, diced

1½ cups Beef Stock (page 267), plus more if needed

1½ tablespoons chopped fresh thyme leaves

1½ tablespoons chopped fresh oregano leaves

2 bay leaves

½ cup red wine (optional)

Place the lamb and beef in a mixing bowl, sprinkle with the flour, and season with salt and pepper. Toss to completely coat the meat. Place the oil in a large saucepan set over medium-high heat and add the meat mixture. Stirring frequently for 2 to 3 minutes, brown the meat on all sides. (Do it in batches if your pan is not large enough to prevent overcrowding and steaming.) Add the carrots, potatoes, celery, onion, and tomatoes, stir well, and cook for 2 minutes longer. Add the beef stock, thyme, oregano, and bay leaves and turn down the heat to low. Cook at a very light simmer for 2 to 3 hours, or until the meat is tender. Adjust the seasonings and add some of the wine, or additional beef stock, if the stew becomes too thick. Serve in individual bowls.

tip Use parsnips or turnips in addition to (or instead of) the carrots and potatoes.

jeff sahib's lamb curry

serves 4

Let me state straightaway that this recipe does not pretend to be a traditional lamb curry. Instead, Jeff McKay, my Irish-American sous-chef at the Rittenhouse Hotel, created it, and he has never been mistaken for Indian. That said, the basic curry flavors are all here, and the finished dish is superb. Cooking the curry in the oven for the last half hour controls the heat distribution better, and it helps the flavor of the yogurt permeate the lamb more thoroughly than it would if it was cooked on the stovetop. The yogurt also breaks up less when cooked this way. Serve with the fragrant Indian basmati rice.

1 large onion, chopped

3 cloves garlic, chopped

¼ cup sliced almonds

2 tablespoons ground coriander

Salt and pepper, to taste

1½ pounds lamb stew meat, cut into ½-inch cubes

2 tablespoons clarified butter (see page 270)

⅔ cup Chicken Stock (page 266)

⅔ cup plain yogurt

⅔ cup heavy cream

Pinch of saffron

1 teaspoon medium curry powder

1 teaspoon paprika

Juice of 1 lemon

1 tablespoon chopped fresh cilantro leaves

4 cups hot cooked basmati rice, to serve

4 sprigs of fresh cilantro, for garnish

Place the onion, garlic, almonds, coriander, salt, and pepper in a food processor and purée to a fine paste. Transfer to a mixing bowl, add the lamb, and mix thoroughly. Transfer to a resealable plastic bag, seal tightly, and let the meat marinate in the refrigerator for 2 to 4 hours.

Preheat the oven to 325° F. Heat the clarified butter in a large ovenproof (and preferably nonstick) casserole and sauté the meat on all sides over medium-high heat for 4 to 5 minutes. Add the stock and bring to a boil. Turn down the heat to medium-low, cover, and simmer for 15 to 20 minutes. Remove the lid and continue cooking, stirring occasionally, until the liquid has evaporated, about 10 minutes longer. Stir in the yogurt and cook for 2 or 3 minutes. Add the cream, saffron, curry powder, paprika, lemon juice, and chopped cilantro. Cover the pan and transfer to the oven. Cook for 30 minutes, or until the lamb is tender. Serve over a bed of rice and garnish with the cilantro sprigs.

roasted lamb loin with fresh sauerkraut

serves 4

Sauerkraut is thought of as quintessentially German, and while that nation made the dish world-famous, it is originally a Chinese dish (see sidebar, opposite). True sauerkraut is aged, and the fermentation process gives the cabbage its sour, tangy flavor, so the fresh version presented here is a slight misnomer. It's still delicious, though. Try it too with grilled pork tenderloin. Lamb and fennel are natural partners, and sheep will happily graze on the plant if it grows in their pastures.

for the lamb

4 lamb loins (about 4 ounces each)

1 tablespoon ground fennel seed

1 tablespoon olive oil

for the sauerkraut

5 cups shredded red cabbage

1 cup white wine vinegar

1 tablespoon caraway seeds

1 tablespoon whole fennel seeds

1 tablespoon sugar

32 cooked asparagus spears (see page 61)

Preheat the oven to 400° F.

To prepare the lamb, thoroughly dust the lamb with the ground fennel seed. Heat the olive oil in an ovenproof sauté pan and when hot, sear the lamb over high heat on all sides for 4 or 5 minutes, or until brown. Transfer the pan to the oven and roast for 8 to 10 minutes, or until medium-rare to medium.

Meanwhile, prepare the sauerkraut. Place the cabbage, vinegar, caraway and fennel seeds, and sugar in a saucepan and bring to a simmer over medium heat. Cook for 8 to 10 minutes, or until the cabbage is tender.

Place the sauerkraut in a mound in the center of each serving plate. Arrange 8 spears of asparagus around the sauerkraut on each plate. Slice each lamb loin and arrange the slices on top of the asparagus around the sauerkraut.

tip Lamb loin is more readily available commercially than in supermarkets. If you have trouble finding it, simply buy a rack of lamb and cut the loin "eye" away from the bones, or ask a butcher to do it for you.

When prehistoric meal planners gathered vegetables for their families, cabbage was one of their top choices. It grew wild in all European coastal areas, making it a dependable source of nutrition on the Neolithic menu. Cabbage was first cultivated in Rome about 2,500 years ago. Aside from its culinary properties, the Romans were convinced that cabbage prevented intoxication if served while consuming alcohol. This characteristic considerably elevated the status of the lowly vegetable, which had had the reputation of peasant's fare.

Fresh cabbage was usually in supply throughout the year, but it would spoil on long journeys. The Chinese provided a culinary solution to this problem by concocting the first preserved cabbage using wine. The dish was so appealing to Genghis Khan that after he conquered China, he took the recipe with him as he plundered Eastern Europe. The dish's popularity spread across the continent and made its biggest impact on the Germans, who substituted salt for the wine, and sauerkraut was born.

Travelers learned that the dish was not only handy to pack for trips, but seemed to prevent sickness as well. In 1772, Captain James Cook ordered 25,000 pounds to take on his second great voyage to explore the Pacific. In fact, cabbage packs a very high vitamin-C level, and Cook's foresight prevented his crew from contracting scurvy. This was not the first time cabbage had been hailed as a health food. The ancient Greeks believed eating cabbage was the secret of long life, and in Medieval France cabbage was thought to assist fertility. In many parts of the world, cabbage was effectively used in poultices to heal wounds. Modern studies confirm that this abundant food is rich in vitamins and a leading ingredient in a cancer-preventing diet.

cabbage

grilled leg of lamb with spicy merlot basting sauce

serves 8 to 12

An Easter tradition in my family was enjoying roast lamb for dinner. The aroma of the meat cooking in the oven still evokes childhood memories. In other parts of Texas, and especially in the Hispanic community, kid goat (cabrito) is the meat of choice at Eastertime. In this recipe, which I created for our San Antonio Easter show, I used lamb, which is more easily available than goat, but I used a marinade and a wine and spice baste similar to those used for traditional cabrito. Instead of grilling, the lamb can be roasted in the oven at 350°F. for 1½ to 2 hours, basting often. Serve with roasted potatoes and asparagus.

for the lamb

1 boneless leg of lamb (6 to 8 pounds), untied

¼ cup cider vinegar

2 tablespoons kosher salt

for the basting sauce

1½ cups Merlot wine

1 tablespoon salt

1 tablespoon pepper

1 tablespoon garlic powder

1 tablespoon onion powder

1 teaspoon ground cumin

2 teaspoons ground coriander

2 teaspoons hot sauce

To prepare the lamb, place the leg of lamb in a large mixing bowl with 1 cup of water, the vinegar, and the salt. Marinate, covered, in the refrigerator for 4 to 6 hours, turning occasionally.

Prepare the grill.

To prepare the sauce, place the wine, salt, pepper, garlic powder, onion powder, cumin, coriander, and hot sauce in a blender and blend the ingredients until well incorporated.

Remove the lamb from the marinade and transfer to the grill. Grill over indirect medium-high heat for about 2 hours, basting every 15 to 20 minutes with the sauce. (The internal temperature of the leg of lamb should reach 135°F. for medium-rare.) Let the lamb rest for 15 minutes before carving.

rosemary-citrus lamb roast

serves 4

This chapter contains several examples of pork matched with fruit, but citrus and lamb are equally well paired. This is especially true of lamb leg meat because the refreshing, tangy qualities of lime (in this case) cut the rich flavor so well. The rosemary and red wine in this straightforward recipe are also ingredients that are used with lamb in many cuisines. A vegetable couscous would be the ideal side dish here, since the combination of flavors in this recipe is distinctly Mediterranean. Note that the lamb should marinate overnight.

1 tablespoon minced lime zest

1 tablespoon freshly squeezed lime juice

1 tablespoon chopped fresh rosemary leaves

Salt and pepper, to taste

2½ pounds boneless center cut leg of lamb

⅓ cup red wine

2 cups plain yogurt

½ cup Beef Stock (page 267)

In a bowl, combine the lime zest and juice with the rosemary, salt, and pepper. Completely rub all over the lamb. Place the lamb in a baking dish, cover, and marinate in the refrigerator overnight, turning occasionally.

Preheat the oven to 400° F.

Line a roasting pan with foil and place a cooking rack on top of the foil. Place the meat on top of the rack and roast for 45 to 55 minutes for medium-rare, or to the desired doneness.

Transfer the lamb to a cutting board and let it sit for 10 minutes. Meanwhile, add the wine to the foil-lined roasting pan and deglaze. Transfer the liquid to a saucepan and reduce it to a glaze, about 4 or 5 minutes. In a mixing bowl, whisk together the yogurt and stock. Whisk the mixture into the glaze and season with salt and pepper. Carve the lamb and arrange the slices on serving plates. Spoon the sauce over the lamb.

greek-style roasted leg of lamb

It would be hard to do a show on Greek cooking without presenting a lamb recipe. Greece is one of many countries around the world in which lamb is the most popular meat. This is a rustic dish that I have adapted from an old, traditional recipe, and it contains the classic combination of lamb, oregano, thyme, garlic, olive oil, and lemon—ingredients that form the core of Greek cuisine. The potatoes that are cooked under the meat are out of this world. You almost have to try this recipe just to taste them!

1 leg of lamb, bone in (about 12 pounds)

4 cloves garlic, peeled and halved lengthwise

Salt and pepper, to taste

1½ tablespoons dried oregano, divided

1½ tablespoons dried thyme, divided

¼ cup olive oil

Juice of 1 lemon

4 russet potatoes (about 2 pounds), peeled and quartered lengthwise

2 cups Chicken Stock (page 266)

Preheat the oven to 450° F.

Using a sharp knife, make 8 deep cuts into the leg and place the pieces of garlic in these slits. Season the lamb with salt, pepper, and 1 tablespoon each of the oregano and thyme. Place the lamb leg in a large roasting pan and rub it with the olive oil and lemon juice. Lift the lamb and scatter the potato wedges underneath. Place the lamb back on top of the potatoes and pour the stock around. Season again with salt, pepper, and the remaining ½ tablespoon each of oregano and thyme.

Transfer the pan to the oven and roast for 20 minutes. Reduce the oven temperature to 325° F. and roast for 1 hour longer. Remove the roasting pan from the oven, lift up the lamb, and remove the potatoes to a bowl and cover. Turn the lamb over, return it to the oven, and roast it for about 1 hour longer for medium-rare. (The internal temperature of the lamb should reach 135° F.) Transfer the lamb to a cutting board and let it rest for 15 to 20 minutes before slicing. Meanwhile, rewarm the potatoes in the oven. Slice the lamb, transfer to serving plates, and serve with the potatoes. Spoon over the pan juices.

tip Another great thing about this dish is that you will have plenty of leftover lamb for sandwiches and other uses.

poultry&fowl

Grilled Jerk Chicken on Black-Eyed Pea Cakes

Black-Eyed Peas

Chicken with Mushrooms and Champagne Sauce

Korean-Style Chicken with Kimchi

Poached Chicken with Farm Vegetables

Thyme

Roasted Butterflied Chicken with Rosemary,
    Thyme, and Roasted Shallots

Jasmine Tea–Smoked Chicken

Savannah Chicken with Asparagus and Parmesan

Coq au Vin (Traditional Chicken and Red Wine)

Redeye Chicken Thighs Stuffed with Herb Brie
    and Serrano Ham

Cuban Fricassee of Chicken

Chicken Tenders with Mushrooms and Madeira over Pasta

Madeira

Chicken Breasts with Artichokes, Snow Peas,
    and Vermouth

Skillet-Roasted Poussins with Corn Bread Stuffing

Barbecued Spice-Rubbed Chicken with Chickeria
    Barbecue Sauce

Holiday Turkey and Oven-Roasted Yams with Honey Glaze

Turkey

Turkey Burgers with Warm German Potato-Herb Salad

Lapsang Souchong Tea–Glazed Duck

Wok-Braised Savory Duck

Candy Coleman's Baked Pheasant

Pan-Roasted Pheasant Breast with Braised Apples
    and Cabbage

Chicken is one of my favorite meats to cook as well as eat because it's endlessly adaptable and versatile. There are so many ways to prepare it, and it can be presented in a wide variety of forms—whether individual parts or the whole bird. If there's one dish that is guaranteed to make me happy, it's fried chicken. I have not included a recipe for it here (there's one in my last book), but it was such a big part of my childhood. Most weekends, my parents would drive us from Dallas to our weekend home in Oklahoma, a trip that would take about four hours. Because my brothers and sisters all liked different cuts of chicken and my parents were savvy at preventing any squabbling, we each had our traveling meal neatly packed in a shoebox. This usually consisted of two or three pieces of fried chicken, a peanut butter and jelly sandwich, and a cookie. I would be just itching to open my shoebox before we left the Dallas city limits, and for sure I'd have cleaned out my shoebox first. This usually meant that when my more disciplined siblings opened theirs two hours later, I would be sitting there suffering! Despite that, chicken was an icon of our weekend trips and I have loved it ever since.

Chicken is one of the few truly international constants when it comes to food. Many diverse cultures consume little red meat—China and Cuba, for example—but I can't think of many that don't have chicken as a significant part of their diet, and I'm not aware of any cultures that have a religious taboo on the meat. For the public television series, recreating easy-to-make recipes from different parts of the world often means that I'm cooking chicken—it's almost a "default" meat.

Turkey is also a favorite because it is a healthful meat (like chicken) that's usually enjoyed at festive times and during holidays. Most people only think of it as an option at those times, but I encourage you to cook it "out of season." It's a great budget stretcher and it creates plenty of leftovers that can be used in lots of creative ways. This is particularly helpful with today's busy lifestyles. I enjoy duck too, because it has a red meat quality in terms of texture and flavor, yet it is different enough and stands in its own category. It's definitely underused and underrated. Like pheasant, it can be prepared without too much trouble to make an elegant meal that everyone will remember.

grilled jerk chicken on black-eyed pea cakes

serves 4

Between the revelry and resolutions, the beginning of the New Year in the United States is frequently heralded with a dish of black-eyed peas (which, botanically, are beans). They have a reputation for bringing good luck throughout the year and are traditionally served in Hoppin' John, a Southern specialty combining black-eyed peas with rice and pork. The custom is purely American, but black-eyed peas have been a celebrated food in other parts of the world for centuries (see sidebar, page 152). These delicious bean cakes stand up really well to the spiciness of the chicken. For notes on jerk seasoning, see page 34.

for the chicken

- 4 boneless, skinless chicken breasts (6 to 8 ounces each)
- ¾ cup Jerk Marinade Rub (page 34)

for the cakes

- 1 can (14 ounces) black-eyed peas, rinsed and drained
- ½ green bell pepper, seeded and finely diced
- 1 tablespoon butter, melted
- 2 cloves garlic, minced
- ¼ cup plain dried bread crumbs
- 1 egg
- 2 teaspoons ground cumin
- ½ teaspoon ground allspice

To prepare the chicken, place the chicken on a plate and cover with the rub on both sides. Transfer to a resealable plastic bag and let it marinate in the refrigerator for at least 4 to 6 hours, and preferably, overnight.

To prepare the black-eyed pea cakes, purée half of the peas in a blender and then fold in the remaining peas. Transfer to a mixing bowl and add the bell pepper, butter, garlic, bread crumbs, egg, cumin, allspice, cilantro, salt, and pepper. Divide the mixture into 4 balls and flatten them to form patties. Dust with the cornmeal on each side and chill in the refrigerator for about 1 hour, until firm.

1 tablespoon chopped fresh cilantro
   leaves

   Salt and pepper, to taste

½ cup yellow cornmeal

3 tablespoons olive oil

Prepare the grill. Preheat the oven to 200°F. Heat the olive oil in a large nonstick sauté pan set over medium heat. Add the black-eyed pea cakes and sauté for 3 to 4 minutes on each side. Keep warm in the oven.

Remove the chicken breasts from the plastic bag and grill over direct medium-high heat for about 5 minutes on each side, or until cooked through. Let the chicken rest briefly, then slice and serve over the warm black-eyed pea cakes.

black-eyed peas

The black-eyed pea (sometimes called the cowpea) is actually a bean, and historians disagree as to whether it originated in Asia or Africa. In China, a climbing variation of the black-eyed pea is referred to as the yard-long bean and the huge immature pods are eaten whole like green beans. Short plants that form smaller pods produce the more familiar type of black-eyed peas that are eaten hulled. In India, black-eyed peas are sometimes used in dhal, a dish that is often served with curry (see page 29). The early Greeks and Romans ate black-eyed peas during the Classical era, but perhaps because they can only be cultivated in hot climates, the tradition was mostly lost. Growing conditions were perfect for the legume in Africa, where it has been incorporated into many of the continent's regional dishes. West Africans are particularly fond of black-eyed peas and use them to make soup and also a type of pea meal that is formed into balls or doughnuts and fried in oil.

African slaves brought black-eyed peas to the Western Hemisphere, planting them first in Haiti, where they continue to be one of the island's main food crops. They became a mainstay for Jamaicans and Cubans, whose popular black-eyed-pea fritters called *bollos* are reminiscent of the West African preparation.

James Oglethorpe introduced the black-eyed pea to Georgia in 1734, and it was soon cultivated all over the American South, where it was primarily produced to feed livestock. Yet the peas always found a way into the kitchen and were even a favorite of Thomas Jefferson, who grew them in his garden and counted the days until the fresh crop could be harvested. The black-eyed pea became an intrinsic part of the region's cuisine and continues to be a fixture in soul food that is enjoyed throughout the nation.

coq au vin
(page 164)

poached
chicken with
farm vegetables
(page 156)

chilean sea bass
with a ragout
of smoked
vegetables
and spinach
(page 204)

grilled
salmon with
strawberry-
cucumber
salsa
(page 208)

chicken with mushrooms and champagne sauce

Traveling with the television show to France and spending a little time in a region like Champagne has certainly increased my appreciation of what a wine from that region can bring to a dish like this. I also learned how the chalky soil of the region and unique topography make French champagne something special. We visited some of the champagne producers around Rheims and Épernay, including Moët & Chandon, and it was fun to taste some of the vintages while matching them with different foods. I created this recipe in the same vein. The good news is that you can use leftover champagne that may have lost some of its fizz in this dish—or use this recipe as an excuse to pop the cork on a new bottle.

3 tablespoons butter

4 boneless, skinless chicken breasts (6 to 8 ounces each)

Salt and pepper, to taste

½ onion, diced

3 cloves garlic, minced

2 shallots, finely chopped

6 ounces mushrooms, cleaned and sliced

¾ cup champagne

¾ cup heavy cream

tip

I recommend using a good-quality but not necessarily expensive champagne for this dish. My rule of thumb is as follows: If you wouldn't want to drink it, don't use it; and if you wouldn't want to share it, don't use it either.

Melt the butter in a large sauté pan set over medium-high heat. Season the chicken with salt and pepper and add to the pan. Sauté for 3 to 4 minutes on each side, or until lightly browned. Keeping the chicken in the pan, drain off any excess fat and add the onion, garlic, and shallots. Reduce the heat to medium-low and cook for 3 or 4 minutes, or until soft. Add the mushrooms and champagne, cover the pan, and simmer for 10 to 15 minutes, or until the chicken is cooked through. Remove the chicken and keep warm. Turn up the heat and reduce the cooking liquid until only 2 or 3 tablespoons remain, about 4 minutes. Add the cream and reduce by half, about 4 more minutes. Transfer the chicken to serving plates and spoon the vegetables and sauce over the chicken.

korean-style chicken with kimchi

serves 4

Korean cuisine, to paraphrase food writer Bruce Cost, is not timid. At the same time, the range of spices used is more limited than in most other Asian cuisines. Ginger, garlic, and dried chile are those most favored, so this recipe is pretty typical. We were fortunate enough to have Daniel Oh, a Los Angeles restaurateur, demonstrate the method for the spicy condiment kimchi for our show on Korean cooking. His special twist was to use a stock rather than water, which got the fermentation process under way faster. Properly stored in the refrigerator, kimchi will last up to three weeks. This dish has a terrific aroma while it's cooking. Note that the marinade also works wonderfully well with chicken wings. This recipe must be started the day before serving.

for the kimchi

- 1 pound Napa cabbage, cut into 2-inch slices
- 6 tablespoons salt
- 4 scallions, finely sliced (green and white parts)
- 1 tablespoon peeled and minced fresh ginger
- 2 cloves garlic, minced
- 1 tablespoon sugar
- 2 tablespoons paprika
- 2 teaspoons cayenne pepper
- 2 cups Chicken Stock (page 266)

To prepare the kimchi, place the cabbage in a nonreactive bowl and sprinkle with the salt. Let the cabbage sit at room temperature for 2 hours. Transfer the cabbage to a colander and rinse off the salt. Return to a clean nonreactive mixing bowl and mix in the scallions, ginger, garlic, sugar, paprika, cayenne, and stock. Cover tightly and refrigerate for at least 24 hours before serving. To store, transfer to airtight glass jars or containers and keep refrigerated.

To prepare the chicken, place the garlic, soy sauce, sesame oil, ginger, sugar, vinegar, pepper flakes, sesame seeds, and pepper in a mixing bowl and whisk together. Transfer to a large resealable plastic bag and add the chicken, turning to coat. Seal the bag and marinate in the refrigerator overnight.

for the chicken

6 cloves garlic, minced

½ cup soy sauce

¼ cup toasted (dark) sesame oil

2 teaspoons peeled and minced fresh ginger

3 tablespoons sugar

2 tablespoons rice wine vinegar

2 teaspoons dried red pepper flakes

2 teaspoons white sesame seeds

1 teaspoon pepper

4 large bone-in, skinless chicken breasts, wings attached (about 8 or 9 ounces each)

2 scallions, sliced (green parts only)

Preheat the oven to 375° F. Line a roasting pan with foil and place a cooking rack on the foil. Remove the chicken from the marinade and place on the rack. Put in the oven and roast for 50 minutes to 1 hour, until cooked through. Transfer the chicken to serving plates, spoon some of the kimchi next to the chicken, and garnish with the scallions.

tip Typically, kimchi is made with cabbage, but it does not have to be. Daniel Oh showed us examples using long beans, daikon radish, squash, and any number of other vegetables. This kimchi recipe makes 4 cups. It's worth making this amount and keeping the rest as a condiment for other dishes (see page 17).

poached chicken with farm vegetables

I created this heart-healthy, easy-to-prepare recipe to showcase some of the wonderful vegetables grown by Chino Farms (see page 4). Buy the best-quality produce you can—and organically grown if possible— because this dish sets off the flavors of the vegetables to the best possible advantage. Daikon is a type of elongated Asian radish with a crisp, sweet, and spicy flavor that is often grated and used as garnish in Japan, and also pickled. For notes on celeriac, see page 22. Alternative root vegetables you can use here include turnips, salsify, rutabaga, and Jerusalem artichokes.

1 tablespoon olive oil

1 onion, roughly diced

4 cloves garlic, finely minced

1 leek, white part only, washed and cut into 1-inch slices

1 cup peeled and cubed celeriac (1-inch cubes)

1 carrot, cut into 1-inch slices

½ daikon, peeled and cut into 1-inch slices

1½ cups Chicken Stock (page 266)

2 tablespoons chopped fresh flat-leaf parsley leaves

2 tablespoons chopped fresh thyme leaves

Salt and white pepper, to taste

4 boneless, skinless chicken breasts (about 6 ounces each)

8 sprigs of fresh thyme

Heat the oil in a large nonstick high-sided sauté pan or large saucepan set over medium-high heat. Add the onion, garlic, leek, celeriac, carrot, and daikon and sauté for 4 to 5 minutes, or until the onions and leeks are softened. Add the stock, parsley, thyme, salt, and pepper, and bring to a boil. Add the chicken, reduce the heat to medium-low, cover, and poach for 12 to 15 minutes, or until the chicken is cooked through.

Remove the chicken from the pan and keep warm. Turn up the heat to high and reduce the cooking liquid by half, about 6 minutes. The celeriac and carrots should be soft; if not, cook a little longer. Transfer the chicken breasts to serving plates and spoon the vegetables and sauce over the chicken. Garnish with the thyme sprigs.

thyme

"When in doubt, use thyme," is an old kitchen adage that hints at the herb's versatility. Almost any savory dish is enhanced by this slightly pungent, aromatic herb. It is one of the key ingredients in a bouquet garni, the famous French herbal mixture that acts like a magic potion in soups, stocks, and stews. Grilled and roasted meats, fish, or vegetables; salad dressings; omelets; breads; and pilafs are bumped to a higher level of flavor once the essence of thyme mingles with each particular preparation. Some recipes, such as New England clam chowder and shrimp Creole, would definitely suffer without it. Yet as indispensable as thyme has become to the cook, its culinary uses are relatively new.

For centuries thyme was valued almost everywhere but the kitchen. The bushy perennial was initially used by the Sumerians and later the Egyptians, who found it ideal for embalming the dead. Hippocrates was the first to document it as a healing herb, and his fellow Greeks also used thyme as a burnt offering to the gods. Romans believed the fragrant plant promoted bravery, and their military legions carried it throughout Europe as they broadened their empire. Thyme remained a symbol of courage in the Middle Ages and was frequently embroidered on the flags of knights. It was often used in incantations, and was believed to lure fairies and prevent the plague. Throughout the ages it was thought to ease dementia, melancholy, and epilepsy, and as late as World War One its oil was incorporated into antiseptics and mouthwash.

Thyme is a key ingredient in the liqueur Benedictine, and thyme honey has always been prized for its exceptional flavor. At some point French cooks noticed that lambs and rabbits that grazed on the herb made particularly tasty meals. Thyme finally found its way onto tables throughout Europe and North America, where diners can ponder its other attributes with every delicious bite.

roasted butterflied chicken with rosemary, thyme, and roasted shallots

serves 4

Sometimes, I think I live to cook chicken in every way possible, the same way the characters discuss preparing shrimp in the movie Forrest Gump. Butterflying is the method of cutting ingredients such as chicken (or larger cuts of meat or shrimp) down the middle and almost in half, but leaving the two parts attached. These halves are then opened out, like a butterfly (or book), so that the meat can be cooked more easily and quickly. This recipe demonstrates how well fresh herbs can infuse chicken, and the aroma of the roasting bird alone makes it worth making.

4 large shallots, peeled

2 tablespoons olive oil

Salt and pepper, to taste

¼ cup chopped fresh thyme leaves

¼ cup chopped fresh rosemary leaves

1 chicken (3 to 3½ pounds), washed and cleaned

Preheat the oven to 325°F. Place the shallots in a small baking dish and toss with the olive oil. Season with salt and pepper. Transfer to the oven and roast for about 1 hour, or until the shallots are lightly brown and soft. Put the roasted shallots in a mixing bowl and begin to mash. Add the thyme and rosemary and continue mashing to form a consistent paste. Season with more salt and pepper if necessary.

Turn the oven up to 425°F. With a heavy knife, split the chicken down through the backbone (the nonbreast side) and into the cavity. Using your hands, pull the sides of the chicken outward, keeping the bird in one piece, and flatten evenly with your hands (or use a heavy skillet or pan). Season the underside of the butterflied chicken with salt and pepper.

Slide your fingers underneath the skin of the chicken to separate it from the meat as much as you can. Rub the paste under the skin and over the meat. Rub any remaining paste over the skin of the chicken.

Place the chicken on a rack set inside a large roasting pan and transfer to the oven. Roast for 50 minutes to 1 hour, or until cooked through and the internal temperature reaches 165° F. Remove the chicken from the oven and let it rest for 10 minutes before slicing.

tip Butterflying is a great way to roast whole chicken because with this technique, the thigh and leg meat take about the same length of time to cook as the breast. Normally, the leg meat of chicken tends to be overcooked by the time the breast meat is done.

jasmine tea–smoked chicken

serves 4

Tea smoking is a technique that I picked up while working for a year in China. The idea is to flavor (and sometimes color) food as well as to cook it, and the method is typically used with poultry (see also the duck recipe on page 180). Steaming the chicken first over jasmine tea gives it a more subtle, infused flavor, compared to smoking it for longer on the stovetop. This recipe is similar to one that I prepare at the Rittenhouse Hotel, and it's a popular menu item. Serve with jasmine rice or noodles.

3 tablespoons salt

2 tablespoons Szechwan peppercorns

1 chicken (3 to 3½ pounds)

1 cup jasmine tea leaves, divided

1 tablespoon toasted (dark) sesame oil

½ cup (packed) light brown sugar

Place the salt and peppercorns in a sauté pan set over medium heat and toast for 4 minutes, until fragrant. Transfer to a spice grinder or blender and grind. Spread the salt and pepper mixture over the outside of the chicken and inside the cavity. Cover the chicken with plastic wrap and marinate it in the refrigerator overnight.

Add ½ cup of the jasmine tea leaves to a large saucepan of boiling water fitted with a bamboo or vegetable basket or colander and add the chicken. Steam for 40 minutes. Remove the chicken and pat it dry with paper towels.

Rub the chicken with the sesame oil. Using a heavy-duty disposable aluminum roasting pan, sprinkle the bottom with the brown sugar and remaining ½ cup of tea leaves. Place a cooking rack over the mixture and set the chicken on the rack, breast-side up. Place the pan on the stovetop over high heat and when the sugar

jim coleman's flavors

160

begins to caramelize and the tea begins to smolder, cover the pan and chicken with aluminum foil. Continue to smoke the chicken for 15 minutes. Remove the pan from the heat, remove the foil lid, and let the chicken stand for 30 minutes. Carve the chicken and serve with rice or noodles.

tip It's a good idea to keep the kitchen well ventilated when smoking any food with this method.

savannah chicken with asparagus and parmesan

serves 4

The city of Savannah, on the Georgia coast, was once the toast of the Old South, like Charleston and New Orleans. It seems to have changed very little over the last couple of centuries, and visitors will find a lot of ante-bellum architecture and character. For our television show from there, I adapted a recipe from an old fund-raiser cookbook that I own, dating from turn-of-the-century Savannah. The original version of this recipe, contributed by a restaurant that had already closed by the time the book was published, used a whole chicken. Mine uses chicken breasts instead and cuts down the cooking time for the vegetables considerably!

6 tablespoons butter, divided

4 boneless, skinless chicken breasts (6 to 8 ounces each)

Salt and pepper, to taste

16 asparagus spears, trimmed

3 scallions, thinly sliced (white and green parts)

1 shallot, minced

2 cloves garlic, minced

2 tablespoons flour

½ cup Chicken Stock (page 266)

1 cup heavy cream

¼ cup dry white wine

1 tablespoon chopped fresh tarragon leaves

Melt 3 tablespoons of the butter in a large sauté pan set over medium-high heat. Season the chicken breasts with salt and pepper and add to the pan. Sauté for 3 or 4 minutes on each side, or until lightly browned. Remove the chicken and set aside. Fill a bowl with water and ice. Bring a saucepan of lightly salted water to a boil and blanch the asparagus for 3 or 4 minutes. Transfer to the ice bath to stop the cooking process, drain, and set aside.

Preheat the oven to 375° F. Melt the remaining 3 tablespoons of butter in a saucepan set over medium heat and add the scallions, shallot, and garlic. Sauté for 2 to 3 minutes. Stir in the flour, season with salt and pepper, and cook for 4 or 5 minutes longer while stirring. Add the stock, bring to a simmer, and return the chicken to

1 tablespoon chopped fresh flat-leaf parsley leaves

½ cup grated Parmesan cheese, divided

the pan. Cook for about 15 minutes, until just done. Lower the heat and whisk in the cream until the mixture is thick and smooth. Add the wine and bring to a boil. Add the tarragon and parsley and remove the pan from the heat. Stir in ¼ cup of the cheese and thoroughly combine.

In a large baking dish, lay 4 spears of asparagus parallel to one another and top with a chicken breast. Make 3 more similar piles, using the remaining asparagus and chicken. Spoon the sauce evenly over each pile and sprinkle with the remaining ¼ cup of cheese. Transfer to the oven and bake for 15 minutes. Serve on warm serving plates.

coq au vin
traditional chicken and red wine

serves 4

For our television show on French cooking, I wanted to present a menu of traditional favorites, and this is one of the all-time classics. We filmed on location in Burgundy, a region with a reputation for fine food and wine. Coq au Vin is a specialty of the region. I taste-tested several versions while we were there and concluded that in addition to the quality of the chicken, it was the richness and complexity of the cooking liquid that ultimately determined the success of the dish. Be sure to use a good-quality wine; a bottle of "plonk" will result in an indifferent dish, at best.

8 ounces bacon, cut into ½-inch strips

20 frozen pearl onions, thawed

12 ounces button mushrooms, cleaned and quartered

2 tablespoons olive oil

1 chicken (3 to 4 pounds), cut into 8 serving pieces

Salt and pepper, to taste

1 onion, diced

3 shallots, finely diced

5 cloves garlic, minced

2 teaspoons tomato paste

¼ cup flour

2 cups dry red wine

1½ cups Beef Stock (page 267)

2 tablespoons chopped fresh thyme leaves

2 tablespoons chopped fresh flat-leaf parsley leaves

Preheat the oven to 325° F.

In a large ovenproof casserole, sauté the bacon over medium-high heat for about 4 minutes. Remove with a slotted spoon and set aside on paper towels. Add the pearl onions and mushrooms to the rendered bacon fat and cook for 5 to 8 minutes, or until lightly browned. Using a slotted spoon, remove and drain on paper towels. Add the olive oil to the casserole. Season the chicken with salt and pepper and sauté for 3 or 4 minutes on each side, or until golden brown. Remove the chicken and set aside. Add the onion, shallots, garlic, and tomato paste to the casserole and cook for 2 or 3 minutes. Stir in the flour and cook for about 5 minutes to make a roux. Add the wine, stock, thyme, and parsley and bring to a boil. Stir constantly until the mixture thickens. Return the reserved pearl onions, mushrooms, and bacon along with the chicken to the pan, cover, and transfer to the oven. Braise for 1 hour, or until the chicken is tender.

redeye chicken thighs stuffed with herb brie and serrano ham

serves 4

This recipe, devised for my show on coffee, combines the classic redeye gravy (made with brewed coffee and traditionally served with ham steak) and chicken stuffed with Brie. You can prepare this dish with chicken breasts, but the darker thigh meat provides a slightly more assertive flavor and holds up better to some of the other ingredients. An ideal side dish here would be mashed sweet potatoes.

4 boneless, skinless chicken thighs

Salt and pepper, to taste

7 ounces herbed Brie cheese, diced

4 ounces Serrano or Tasso ham, julienned

3 tablespoons olive oil

2 cloves garlic, minced

1 shallot, minced

½ cup red wine

½ cup brewed double-strength black coffee

3 tablespoons honey

1 teaspoon chopped fresh oregano

1 tablespoon chopped fresh flat-leaf parsley leaves

Juice and zest of 1 lime

1½ tablespoons flour

Preheat the oven to 375° F. Season the inside of the chicken thighs with salt and pepper. Fill the thighs evenly with the Brie and ham, fold the meat over the filling, and secure with toothpicks. Heat a dry nonstick ovenproof sauté pan or cast-iron skillet and add the chicken. Sear on all sides over medium-high heat until browned, 3 or 4 minutes on each side. Transfer the pan to the oven and roast for 15 to 18 minutes, or until cooked through.

Meanwhile, heat the oil in a saucepan, add the garlic and shallot, and sauté over medium heat. Add the wine, coffee, honey, oregano, parsley, and lime zest and juice, and bring to a boil. Reduce the liquid by one third, about 8 minutes. In a cup, mix together the flour and 1½ tablespoons water until smooth and stir into the reduced mixture until the gravy thickens. Return to a simmer and adjust the seasonings.

Cut each chicken thigh on the bias into 3 slices. Spoon the sauce over and around the chicken.

poultry & fowl

cuban fricassee
of chicken

Green olives, capers, and raisins are common ingredients to many tradi-tional Cuban dishes, including more than one fricassee-style dish I tried on location in Miami's Little Havana neighborhood. I was surprised at first to find capers in several different dishes, as they are the flower buds from a prickly shrub native to the Mediterranean, but on reflection, their use can be attributed to the cuisine's Spanish heritage. The other overwhelming impression that I took away from my visit to Little Havana is just how much of Cuban cooking involves chicken and pork.

for the chicken

2 tablespoons olive oil

8 large boneless, skinless chicken thighs (about 3 pounds)

3 tablespoons butter

1 onion, finely diced

1 red bell pepper, seeded and finely diced

3 tomatoes, diced

4 cloves garlic, minced

2 russet potatoes (about 1 pound), peeled and diced

1 cup Chicken Stock (page 266)

1 cup dry white wine

1 teaspoon dried oregano

½ teaspoon cayenne pepper

1 teaspoon ground cumin

Salt and pepper, to taste

To prepare the chicken, heat the oil in a large nonstick sauté pan. Add the chicken thighs and sauté over medium-high heat for 5 to 7 minutes, or until browned on all sides. Meanwhile, melt the butter in a large saucepan set over medium-high heat, add the onion and bell pepper, and sauté for 3 minutes. Add the tomatoes and garlic and cook for 3 minutes longer. Add the browned chicken, potatoes, stock, wine, oregano, cayenne, cumin, salt, and pepper. Bring to a boil, turn down the heat to a simmer, and cover the pan. Cook for 20 minutes, or until the chicken is tender. Add the olives, peas, capers, and raisins and simmer for 5 to 10 minutes longer.

⅓ cup pitted green olives, sliced

⅓ cup frozen peas, thawed

2 tablespoons capers, drained and rinsed

¼ cup raisins

for the rice

1 cup long-grain white rice

Salt, to taste

While the chicken is cooking, prepare the rice. Place the rice, 2 cups water, and the salt in a saucepan and bring to a boil. Turn down the heat, cover, and simmer for 20 minutes, or until all the liquid is absorbed and the rice is tender. Fluff the rice with a fork and spoon onto warm serving plates. Spoon the chicken mixture over the rice.

tip Olives are preserved in brine, but once a bottle is opened oxygen causes a bacterial film to gradually form at the surface. To maximize their freshness, pour a thin layer of cooking oil over the brine to keep out the oxygen.

chicken tenders with mushrooms and madeira over pasta

serves 4

I received a lot of positive feedback from interested listeners after my radio show devoted to cultivated "wild" mushrooms. Guests on the show —growers and experts—discussed new techniques for raising mushrooms using a specialized sawdust-based growing medium. It is an exacting process, and wild mushroom growers are as much scientists as farmers. Soon, you will be able to buy logs that need watering once a week and that will yield a dozen shiitake mushrooms every week for months. I tried one and it really worked—you heard it here first!

16 ounces dried penne pasta

1 cup pearl onions

1 pound chicken tenders

1 cup stemmed and sliced portobello mushrooms

1 cup stemmed and sliced shiitake mushrooms

1 cup stemmed and sliced cremini mushrooms (baby portobellos)

1 cup stemmed and sliced button mushrooms, or wild mushrooms

2 tablespoons minced garlic

½ cup plus 2 tablespoons dry Madeira

2 cups Chicken Stock (page 266)

2 tablespoons minced fresh flat-leaf parsley leaves

2 tablespoons minced fresh rosemary leaves

Bring a saucepan of salted water to a boil. Add the pasta and boil for 9 minutes, or until al dente. Drain and set aside. Blanch the pearl onions in a saucepan of boiling water for 3 to 4 minutes. Drain, peel, and set aside.

Coat a large nonstick sauté pan with cooking spray. Place the pan over medium-high heat, add the chicken, and sear for 2 to 3 minutes, stirring frequently. Add all of the mushrooms and sauté for 4 minutes, stirring often. Add the pearl onions and the garlic and turn up the heat to high. Sauté until all the liquid has evaporated, stirring so the ingredients do not stick to the pan.

2 tablespoons minced fresh sage
   leaves

2 tablespoons cornstarch

2 tablespoons finely sliced scallions
   (white and green parts)

Deglaze the pan with ½ cup of the Madeira, taking care because the Madeira may ignite. Add the stock, bring to a boil, and reduce for 2 minutes. Lower the heat to medium-low and stir in the parsley, rosemary, and sage. Mix together the cornstarch and the remaining 2 tablespoons of Madeira in a cup and pour into the pan, stirring until the mixture thickens. Add the cooked pasta, toss together, and heat thoroughly until the pasta is well coated. Scatter the scallions over the dish and serve.

tip All Madeira wine is categorized as sweet. Pale and smooth varieties, such as the slightly dry Sercial, make a delicious light apéritif. At the other end of the spectrum, tawny, rich blends like Malmsey are best used as an after-dinner drink.

madeira

The Madeira Islands lie about seven hundred miles southwest of Portugal and were claimed by that country soon after they were discovered in the early 1400s. The mountainous islands were covered with dense forests (*madeira* means "wood" in Portuguese), and early colonists were instructed by the king to burn them down to make the land tillable. The resulting soil, which was a mixture of the ashes, centuries of leaf mulch, and volcanic residue, was incredibly fertile. One of the first crops to be planted on the new farmland was grapes, which would form the basis of one of the world's most famous wine traditions. By the end of the fifteenth century, Madeira wines were an important Portuguese trading commodity.

When sailing ships began to export barrels of Madeira's vintage, they frequently crisscrossed the equator transporting their goods. It was discovered that the warm tropical climate actually improved the flavor of the wine, and thereafter the islands' winemakers began to cure their product in hothouses called *estufas*. Although the wines traveled well, Madeira vintners fortified them with brandy to further ensure their longevity and in so doing created the unique character of the beverage.

Madeira became the most popular wine in colonial America, where it was commonly served as a cocktail before dining. It seeped into American history when it was used for a toast after the signing of the Declaration of Independence, at George Washington's inauguration, and to celebrate the dedication of Washington, D.C., as the nation's capital. After a blight at the end of the nineteenth century destroyed almost all of the islands' vines, Madeira devotees in America and throughout the world had to make do with other libations. Fortunately the wines of Madeira have made a comeback in the last few decades and are winning over a new generation of enthusiasts.

chicken breasts with
artichokes, snow peas, and vermouth

serves 4

Here is another simple dish from my radio show. Artichokes, snow peas, and pistachios are among my favorite individual ingredients, so putting them together seemed like a great idea. This recipe can be made just as easily with swordfish or halibut as with chicken.

1 cup Chicken Stock (page 266)

4 boneless, skinless chicken breasts (6 to 8 ounces each)

Salt and pepper, to taste

4 tablespoons butter, divided

2 tablespoons minced shallots

½ cup dry vermouth

4 teaspoons chopped fresh basil leaves

2 cooked frozen artichoke bottoms (see page 96), sliced

1 cup snow peas

⅓ cup pistachio nuts, roughly chopped

Place the stock in a saucepan, bring to a boil, and reduce by half, about 6 minutes. Set aside. Using the bottom of a heavy skillet, flatten the chicken breasts slightly and season with salt and pepper. Heat 2 tablespoons of the butter in a sauté pan and add the chicken. Sauté over medium-high heat for about 3 minutes on each side, or until just cooked through. Transfer the chicken with a slotted spoon to a warm plate, cover with foil, and keep warm. Add the shallots to the sauté pan and cook over medium heat for 2 or 3 minutes, stirring often. Stir in the reduced stock, vermouth, and basil, increase the heat to medium-high, and reduce the sauce to ¾ cup, 6 to 8 minutes. Meanwhile, warm the artichoke slices in a steamer or vegetable basket over simmering water. Blanch the snow peas in boiling water for 2 or 3 minutes, then drain and refresh under cold running water to stop the cooking process. Strain the sauce into a clean saucepan and reheat gently. Over low heat, gradually swirl in the remaining 2 tablespoons of butter.

Place the chicken on warm serving plates and arrange the artichokes, snow peas, and nuts around it. Drizzle the plates with the sauce.

poultry & fowl

skillet-roasted poussins with corn bread stuffing

serves 4

Small birds such as dove and quail are popular fare in Texas and the South, and in this recipe from San Antonio's La Mansión del Rio Hotel, chef Scott Cohen provides a recipe for poussin, the French word for small, immature chickens. They are small enough to almost be a finger food, like quail, and Scott uses a demi-glace baste and sauce to provide some intensity for the delicately flavored birds. You can substitute two miniature Cornish game hens for the poussins if need be. The corn bread stuffing and skillet cooking make this a distinctively Texan dish.

for the corn bread stuffing

8 ounces yellow corn bread, diced (about 2 cups)

1½ teaspoons butter

¼ cup diced celery

¼ cup diced carrots

¼ cup diced wild mushrooms

2 tablespoons chopped fresh sage leaves

Salt and pepper, to taste

½ cup Chicken Stock (page 266)

for the glaze

¼ cup Chicken Stock (page 266)

½ cup demi-glace

4 poussins (about 1 pound each), boned, or 2 Cornish game hens (about 1¼ pounds each)

Preheat the oven to 350° F.

To prepare the stuffing, place the corn bread in a mixing bowl. Melt the butter in a skillet set over medium heat and add the celery and carrots. Turn down the heat to low and cook gently until the vegetables are translucent and tender, 5 or 6 minutes. Add the mushrooms and continue to sweat the vegetables for 4 or 5 minutes longer without browning them. Transfer the vegetables to the mixing bowl, gently mix in the sage, and season with salt and pepper. Transfer the mixture to a buttered 8-inch square baking dish. Pour the chicken stock over the stuffing and bake in the oven for 30 minutes. Remove from the oven and set aside to cool.

To prepare the glaze, heat the stock and demi-glace in a small saucepan. Set aside half for basting and keep the other half warm for the sauce.

Turn up the oven temperature to 450°F. Stuff each poussin with about ¾ cup of the cooled stuffing. Line a roasting pan with foil and set a cooking rack on the foil. Transfer the poussins to the rack and brush with the basting glaze. Roast in the oven for 20 minutes, or until cooked through and golden brown. While the poussins are roasting, brush 2 or 3 times more with the basting glaze.

Transfer the poussins to warm serving plates. Remove the stuffing and serve on the side. Spoon the warm reserved sauce next to the poussins and stuffing.

tip Demi-glace is a delectable sauce that results from the combination of a rich brown sauce, beef stock, and Madeira or sherry wine. A mail-order source is given on page 271, but if you go to the trouble to make it, you don't want to waste a drop. Make a double batch and freeze what you don't use right away in ice-cube trays until solid. Empty the cubes into plastic sealable freezer bags until needed. One cube equals approximately enough sauce for one serving.

barbecued spice-rubbed chicken with chickeria barbecue sauce

serves 4

My older brother, Hank, and I owned an upscale fajita and barbecue restaurant together in Dallas for a while in the early 1980s. We had thoroughly researched our subject all over Texas and northern Mexico, and if we had not been a little ahead of our time when it came to fajitas, my career might have taken a completely different path! This recipe, taken from my weekly public radio show, includes a version of our signature "chickeria" barbecue sauce, which proved so popular that it even made the food magazines of that era. Corn, coleslaw, or potato salad would make a terrific optional side dish.

for the barbecue sauce

½ cup bottled chili sauce

2 tablespoons Dijon mustard

2 tablespoons soy sauce

2 tablespoons Tabasco sauce or Pickapeppa sauce

3 tablespoons (packed) light brown sugar

3 tablespoons minced garlic

2 teaspoons white pepper

Juice of ½ lemon

Prepare the grill.

To prepare the barbecue sauce, mix together the chili sauce, mustard, soy sauce, Tabasco sauce, sugar, garlic, pepper, and lemon juice in a saucepan and bring to a boil. Turn down the heat to medium-low and, stirring occasionally, cook for 8 to 10 minutes, or until the flavors are thoroughly blended.

Meanwhile, prepare the spice rub. Combine the garlic powder, chili powder, paprika, onion powder, sugar, oregano, black pepper, white pepper, and cayenne in a mixing bowl.

for the spice rub

2½ teaspoons garlic powder

2 teaspoons pure red chili powder

2 teaspoons paprika

2 teaspoons onion powder

2 teaspoons (packed) light brown sugar

1 teaspoon ground dried oregano

1 teaspoon black pepper

1 teaspoon white pepper

½ teaspoon cayenne pepper

4 boneless, skinless chicken breasts
(6 to 8 ounces each)

Rub the chicken breasts all over with the spice rub. Place the chicken on the grill and cook over direct medium-high heat for 5 minutes. Turn the breasts over and cook for 2 minutes longer. Brush the chicken with some of the barbecue sauce and continue grilling for 2 to 3 minutes, or until cooked through. Remove the chicken breasts from the grill and let them sit for a few minutes before serving.

holiday turkey and oven-roasted yams with honey glaze

serves 6 to 8

Over the five years that A Chef's Table *has been on the air, I have covered a lot of ground when it comes to Thanksgiving dinner. The technique I use here for flavoring the meat underneath the skin is similar to that used in the chicken recipe on page 158, and the reason for it is that poultry skin is relatively impervious. This means that applying flavorings directly on the skin is somewhat inefficient in comparison. The yam recipe comes from the* Flavors of America *show I did on Thanksgiving, and I hope you will be glad to hear that it does not include marshmallows (I hate that combination!). Spiced Cranberry Relish (page 88) makes a perfect accompaniment for this dish.*

for the turkey

1 turkey (about 12 pounds)

2 tablespoons chopped fresh thyme leaves (stems reserved)

2 tablespoons chopped fresh rosemary leaves (stems reserved)

2 tablespoons chopped fresh sage leaves (stems reserved)

2 tablespoons minced garlic

2 tablespoons minced shallots

Pepper, to taste

3 lemons

Preheat the oven to 350° F. Wash the turkey inside and out with cold water and pat dry with paper towels. Place the turkey in a roasting pan and pull 3 or 4 inches of the skin away from the meat at the neck of the bird. In a bowl, mix together the thyme, rosemary, sage, garlic, and shallots. Using your hands, and without tearing the skin, rub the herb mixture onto the meat under the skin. Use any herb mixture that is left to coat the top of the turkey. Squeeze the juice of 1 lemon over the entire turkey. Prick the remaining 2 lemons with a fork and place them with the reserved herb stems into the cavity of the turkey. Transfer to the oven and cook for 3 hours, or until the juice runs clear when the turkey is pierced with the sharp point of a knife at the base of the leg. Remove the turkey and let it

for the yams and glaze

3½ pounds yams, peeled and cut into 1-inch cubes (about 9½ cups)

2 tablespoons olive oil

Salt and pepper, to taste

½ cup honey

2 tablespoons Grand Marnier

2 tablespoons (packed) light brown sugar

¼ teaspoon ground cinnamon

¼ teaspoon ground nutmeg

rest on a cutting board for 10 to 15 minutes before carving.

About 30 minutes before the turkey is finished roasting, place the yams in a large roasting pan and sprinkle with the oil. Season with salt and pepper and toss well. Transfer to the oven and roast for 25 minutes. Meanwhile, place the honey, Grand Marnier, sugar, cinnamon, and nutmeg in a nonstick saucepan and bring to a simmer. Cook for 3 or 4 minutes and remove from the heat. Remove the yams from the oven, drizzle with the glaze, and toss well. Return to the oven and roast for about 10 minutes longer, or until the yams are glazed and tender.

tip One common mistake people make when they roast a turkey or chicken is not waiting long enough to carve it after pulling it from the oven. If you slice into the bird too soon, most of the juices will run out and your meat will be unnecessarily dry. Allow turkey one minute per pound to rest before carving, and give a chicken about 2½ minutes per pound.

turkey

Benjamin Franklin considered the turkey to be a "true original of America," and be jokingly campaigned for it to become our national bird instead of the bald eagle (which he considered to be of bad moral character). Franklin's account of the turkey's heritage was correct, but in a broader sense than he assumed. The America that turkeys first called home was much farther south than Franklin's Philadelphia. In fact, by the time the great statesman was championing the turkey, the bird had hitchhiked around the globe and had found its way back to America for the second time.

Turkeys are indigenous to the mountains of the central plateau of Mexico, and by 200 B.C. they were one of the first animals in this hemisphere to be domesticated. More than a thousand turkeys a day were sold in busy Aztec markets, and Mayans used parts of the birds in sacred ceremonies. Spanish and Portuguese explorers were impressed with the birds and introduced them to Europe in the early sixteenth century. Turkish traders were instrumental in marketing the American birds along with other fowl, and in England they assumed the name of their purveyors. Meanwhile, the wild turkey population spread to North America, where they thrived on the abundant vegetation and became a dietary staple for Native American tribes. When hungry European settlers arrived, they were relieved to discover a food source already familiar in their homelands.

Although the Pilgrims dined upon wild turkey, it was the domesticated White Holland turkey imported back to America from Europe that became the foundation for this country's turkey industry. Commercial turkey breeding took off in the 1800s after the wild turkey population was almost eliminated by hunters. For years turkeys were consumed mainly during the winter holidays, partly due to the time and trouble entailed in cooking the big birds. Turkey parts are now sold more frequently than the whole bird, allowing consumers to gobble this low-fat supermarket bargain year round.

turkey burgers with warm german potato-herb salad

serves 4

If you are entertaining a crowd for July Fourth (or any other occasion), it makes a nice change to offer your guests different kinds of burgers. These turkey burgers and the veal burgers on page 127 might just make your guests think twice about the ubiquitous and ever-popular hamburger. My family actually prefers turkey burgers to hamburgers, so I am ahead of the game. These burgers get their zip from the addictive chipotle chiles, which are smoked jalapeños canned with a spicy tomato and vinegar-based stew (available in the Mexican section of supermarkets). Try the Fingerling Potato Salad (page 120) or the Cilantro-Roasted Corn (page 127) instead of the German potato salad, if you prefer.

Warm German Potato-Herb Salad
(page 38)

for the burgers

1½ pounds ground turkey

1 scallion, finely sliced (green and white parts)

1 canned chipotle chile in adobo sauce, minced

1½ tablespoons chopped fresh cilantro leaves

1 tablespoon Worcestershire sauce

4 focaccia buns or rolls

Prepare the grill. Prepare the salad.

To prepare the burgers, place the turkey, scallion, chipotle, cilantro, and Worcestershire sauce in a mixing bowl and combine thoroughly. Divide the mixture into 4 equal balls. Flatten the balls with your hand and shape into burgers ½ inch to ¾ inch thick. Transfer to the grill and cook over direct medium-high heat for about 7 minutes on each side, or until medium-well done, turning over just once. Serve the burgers with the potato salad.

tip As much as I love Thanksgiving, I hate trying to devise ways to use the rest of the turkey. For a successful holiday dinner and one or two great days of leftovers, buy a turkey that averages one pound for each person you are serving.

poultry & fowl

179

lapsang souchong tea–glazed duck

serves 4

The flavor of duck meat and smoke were made for each other, and it's likely a combination that goes back millennia. While the technique of smoking the duck with tea is similar to that of the chicken smoked with jasmine tea on page 160, the cooking method is a little different, and the results are quite dissimilar. Lapsang souchong is a black Chinese tea from the Fujian province with a woodsy, smoky flavor; it's made by slowly drying the leaves over pine fires. The duck takes on its assertive tones beautifully. Serve with polenta or grits.

4 Lapsang souchong tea bags

1 cup light corn syrup

⅓ cup (packed) light brown sugar

½ teaspoon ground cinnamon

¼ teaspoon ground allspice

4 duck breasts (about 8 ounces each)

Salt and pepper, to taste

tip

Although this tip does not apply to this particular recipe, it does pertain to duck. Save your cardboard egg containers and use them as a roasting rack. By absorbing a lot of grease while working as a rack, they are perfect for whole duck or other fatty meats.

Preheat the oven to 350°F. Place 1 cup of water in a saucepan and bring to a boil. Remove from the heat, add the tea bags, and let steep for 5 minutes. Squeeze out the tea bags and discard. Add the corn syrup, sugar, cinnamon, and allspice, stir well, and return the mixture to a boil. Remove from the heat immediately and let cool.

Score the skin side of the duck breasts with a sharp knife. Add the duck breasts, skin-side down, to a nonstick sauté pan set over high heat and sear for 4 or 5 minutes. Turn over and sear for 1 minute longer. Line a roasting pan with foil and place a cooking rack on the foil. Place the duck breasts skin-side up on the rack and season with salt and pepper. Pour half of the tea mixture over the duck. Transfer the pan to the oven and roast for 10 to 12 minutes for medium-rare, basting a couple of times with the remaining half of the tea mixture. Remove the duck from the pan and let it rest for 5 minutes before slicing.

wok-braised savory duck

It's not often you use a wok for prolonged cooking, but this traditional Chinese recipe gives a range of great flavors. Some people dislike duck because they think it's too fatty, but wok braising solves that particular issue. When I included this recipe on my weekly radio show, I mentioned that duck or goose was most likely the bird enjoyed at the first Thanksgiving dinners, as there were no wild turkeys in the Plymouth area at that time (I can guarantee that there were no woks, either). Serve with long-grain white rice.

2½ tablespoons peanut oil

1 duck (3 to 3½ pounds), cut into 8 pieces

3 scallions, cut into thirds (green and white parts)

2 cloves garlic, crushed

2 thin slices peeled fresh ginger

1 cup soy sauce

2 tablespoons dry sherry

2 tablespoons (packed) light brown sugar

1 teaspoon salt

1 tablespoon cornstarch

Place a wok or deep frying pan over medium-high heat and add the oil. Quickly stir-fry the duck pieces until they are golden brown, about 5 minutes. Drain off any excess fat, add the scallions, garlic, and ginger, and stir-fry for 2 minutes longer. In a bowl, combine the soy sauce, sherry, sugar, and salt. Add this mixture to the wok and mix well. Add 2 cups of water and bring the mixture to a boil. Reduce the heat, cover the wok, and simmer for 1½ to 2 hours. Remove the duck and transfer to serving plates. Mix the cornstarch with 2 tablespoons of water, stir into the wok, and blend thoroughly. Spoon the sauce over the duck and serve with long-grain white rice.

candy coleman's
baked pheasant

Farm-raised pheasants and their cousins that roam the wild are almost two different birds, and one of my radio shows was devoted to the topic. The former, who lead a comparatively easy life, are, on average, double the weight of wild pheasants, and they are much less lean. This means they do not need barding—the addition of bacon or other fat laid over the breast meat while roasting to prevent it from drying out. This is my wife's recipe for wild pheasant. She grew up in a family of enthusiastic outdoorsmen that ate a lot of game. If using farm-raised pheasant, you will need only one five-pound bird. Roasted potatoes or broccoli raab make great side dishes.

2 wild pheasants, cleaned and dressed (about 2½ pounds each)

Salt and pepper, to taste

2 large onions, chopped, divided

3 stalks celery, chopped, divided

6 strips of bacon

3 cups Beef Stock (page 267)

½ teaspoon dried marjoram

Preheat the oven to 300° F. Season the pheasants inside and out with salt and pepper. Place half of the chopped onion and celery into the cavities of the birds and lay 3 strips of bacon across the breast of each bird. Place the pheasants, breast-side up, on a rack in a large roasting pan. Add the stock and marjoram to the pan, and scatter the remaining onion and celery around the birds.

Transfer the pan to the oven and roast for approximately 3 hours, basting every 20 minutes. Remove the pheasants and let cool for 5 to 10 minutes before carving.

pan-roasted pheasant breast with braised apples and cabbage

serves 4

This recipe, which is a variation on a dish I sometimes serve at the Rittenhouse Hotel, uses farm-raised pheasant (unlike the previous recipe). It is a comforting, filling dish of strong flavors that has a late-fall or winter feel. It also reminds me of central European cuisine, which is appropriate as that is where pheasant originated. This is a dish of several natural flavor combinations: apples and raisins, cabbage and honey, apples and mixed spices, and pheasant with fruit.

4 farm-raised skinless pheasant breasts (8 or 9 ounces each)

1 tablespoon minced garlic

1 teaspoon pepper

1 tablespoon olive oil

4 Red Delicious apples, peeled, cored, and diced

¼ cup black raisins

¼ cup golden raisins

2 cups sliced white cabbage

2 cups sliced red cabbage

1½ cups apple juice

¼ cup honey

1 tablespoon ground cinnamon

1 tablespoon ground cloves

Pinch of mace

Preheat the oven to 375° F. Rub the pheasant breasts with the garlic and pepper. Heat the olive oil in a nonstick sauté pan and when the pan is hot, add the pheasant. Sear over medium-high heat for 3 to 4 minutes per side, or until golden brown; be careful not to burn the garlic. Remove the breasts from the pan and set aside.

Combine the apples, black and golden raisins, white and red cabbage, apple juice, honey, cinnamon, cloves, and mace in a mixing bowl. Transfer to a small roasting pan and place the pheasant breasts on top. Roast in the oven for 10 to 12 minutes, or until the breasts are cooked through. Remove from the oven, let sit for 5 minutes, and finely slice the pheasant breasts. Fan the slices on serving plates and spoon the apple and cabbage mixture on top. Spoon some of the pan juices over each serving.

poultry & fowl

fish&seafood

"Year of the Dragon" Seared Sea Scallops with Lobster Sauce

Scallops with an Orange and Watercress Salad

Scallops

Fettuccine with Artichokes, Shrimp, and Pancetta

Grilled Shrimp with Corn Bread and Grits Dressing

Atlantic Oyster Loaf with Red Onions, Tomatoes, and Greens

Roasted Maine Lobster with Crabmeat Stuffing

Lowcountry Seafood Steampot with Charleston Red Rice

Big Jim's Chinatown Seafood Clay Pot

Valentine's Day Red Snapper Fillet with Red Grapes

Snapper

Avocado Snapper

Avocados

Fish Tacos Coleman's Way

Chilean Sea Bass with a Ragout of Smoked Vegetables and Spinach

Sautéed Striped Bass with Basil Rose Sauce

Grilled Black Bass with Mango and Papaya Salsa

Flounder with Mushrooms

Grilled Salmon with Strawberry-Cucumber Salsa

Seattle Salmon Provençal Style

Pan-Fried Alaskan Salmon and Halibut with Honeyed Apples

Horseradish-Crusted Halibut on Wilted Spinach with Beet Relish and
    Matchstick Potatoes

Alaskan Halibut with Tagliatelle of Vegetables and American Caviar

American Caviar

Home-Cured Grilled Cod with Dill Sauce

One of my goals on *Flavors of America* is to demystify seafood as much as possible. While most people will order fish and seafood when they dine out without thinking twice about it, they will hesitate to cook it at home. This is largely because of unfamiliarity with fish, especially compared to meat. Only recently has fish and seafood become so widely available. Many people find seafood intimidating because there is so much different product on the market, and many home cooks are unsure how to handle and cook it. However, the issues are not complicated, and once people learn a little about the subject and gain some confidence about cooking it, there's no looking back.

Fish and shellfish have a lot going for them. They are healthful—low in fat but with healthful natural oils; they offer good value for money; they are full of flavor; and they are among the easiest and quickest foods to cook. One of the most common mistakes that home cooks make is to overcook seafood. Another is to cook it in a pan that is too cool. Shellfish especially should be seared in a hot pan set over medium-high or high heat. Otherwise, the natural juices are released and the shellfish just boils in them, resulting in a gummy, pasty texture.

Demand for seafood all over the world has been so great that the industry is faced with a real problem of overfishing. One symptom of the smaller catches is the reduction in fish size, especially for species such as cod and sea bass. With ever smaller fish being harvested, normal breeding cycles are interrupted, leading to a vicious cycle of depletion. Although this situation shows signs of being gradually remedied through government regulation, there is no doubt that fish farming is a trend of the future.

In filming *Flavors of America*, I was fortunate to spend time with many fishermen and seafood harvesters and growers. Learning about the process that brings clams or lobsters or salmon to the plate is an eye-opening experience, and I now have an even healthier respect for the dedicated individuals who harvest the bounty of the oceans. It's a tough life, and a rewarding one, but it should never be taken for granted.

"year of the dragon" seared sea scallops with lobster sauce

serves 4

Following a vegetable first course for a Chinese New Year celebration (see page 8), it is traditional to serve a seafood main course. We filmed the festivities in Philadelphia's Chinatown marking the Year of the Dragon. Chinese lobster sauce never contains lobster; its color makes it look as though it does. Instead, lobster sauce typically contains ground pork, but I've substituted turkey to make it a little lighter. Serve with white rice.

2 tablespoons fermented black beans

1 pound large sea scallops (about 16 to 20)

2 tablespoons dry sherry

1 cup Chicken Stock (page 266)

1 tablespoon low-sodium soy sauce

1 teaspoon toasted (dark) sesame oil

¼ teaspoon sugar

Pinch of dried red pepper flakes

¼ cup olive oil

3 cloves garlic, finely minced

1 teaspoon peeled and minced fresh ginger

4 ounces ground turkey

1½ tablespoons cornstarch

1 egg, beaten

Soak the fermented black beans in a bowl of cold water for 5 minutes. Drain and chop the beans fine. Mix the scallops with the sherry in a bowl and let sit for 5 minutes. Place the stock, soy sauce, sesame oil, sugar, and red pepper flakes in a bowl and set aside. Heat the olive oil in a wok or sauté pan set over high heat. Remove the scallops from the bowl with tongs (reserve the sherry liquid). When the oil is very hot and almost smoking, add the scallops to the wok and sear on each side for 30 seconds. Remove the scallops and drain on paper towels. Add the garlic, ginger, and black beans to the hot pan and stir until well blended. Add the turkey and stir-fry for 5 to 6 minutes, or until cooked through. Stir in the reserved soy sauce mixture and the reserved sherry liquid and bring to a boil. In a cup, mix the cornstarch with 3 tablespoons of water and stir into the sauce. Cover the wok and simmer for 2 minutes, or until thickened. Stir in the beaten egg, return the scallops to the wok, and warm through.

scallops with an orange and watercress salad

serves 4

On Flavors of America, this dish was presented as an appetizer, but with a few more scallops it makes a wonderful lunch entrée or light dinner. The inspiration for the dish came from a visit to Atlantic City for the New Jersey Seafood Festival, held each year in early June. The richness of the scallops is contrasted by the peppery watercress and the tangy citrus —a combination that you can also try with shrimp.

2 oranges, peeled and sectioned

2 scallions, sliced (white and green parts)

1½ tablespoons freshly squeezed lime juice

1 tablespoon freshly squeezed orange juice

1 tablespoon chopped fresh mint leaves

Salt and pepper, to taste

4 tablespoons olive oil, divided

1 large bunch of watercress, washed and ends trimmed

1½ pounds sea scallops (24 to 28)

In a small mixing bowl, mix together the orange sections, scallions, lime juice, orange juice, mint, salt, and pepper. Whisk in 2 tablespoons of the olive oil. Add the watercress and toss well.

Heat the remaining 2 tablespoons of oil in a sauté pan set over medium-high heat. Season the scallops with salt and pepper and sear for about 2 minutes on each side, or until medium to medium-well done. Mound the watercress in the center of serving plates and arrange 6 or 7 scallops around the perimeter.

tip If you are buying scallops in packages, rather than in loose form, make sure there is little or no liquid in the packages. Also make sure the tendons have already been removed from the scallops.

fish & seafood

187

Most shellfish are passive creatures, living out their lives moored to rocks or other stationary hosts. Not so the lively scallop, which by repeatedly snapping together its twin shells makes leaping journeys across the ocean floor. This crafty mollusk takes flight when it perceives danger, avoiding the many underwater predators, such as sea stars, that find scallops as tasty as humans do. Its attractive ridged shells are designed for this kind of mobility; they are much lighter than those of other bivalves, and the ribbed texture gives them added durability as they bounce along the bottom of the sea.

Scallop shells have long been prized for their beauty and symbolism. Cultures around the world have used them for motifs in jewelry, architecture, and art—such as Botticelli's famous *Birth of Venus* in which the goddess springs forth from a scallop shell. In the Middle Ages, scallops became the symbol of Christian pilgrims who visited the grave of Saint James. The burial shrine was located at Santiago de Compostela in Spanish Galicia, which in those days was one of the few places scallops were seriously fished. The travelers would return home with scallop shells in their hats to prove they had made the journey. In France the scallop took on the name of the saint and is still called Saint Jacques.

The scallop family contains more than three hundred species found throughout the waters of the Atlantic, Pacific, and Mediterranean. In the United States consumers are usually offered one of two varieties, and both are invariably sold already shelled. Plump American sea scallops are the larger and most plentiful type found in fish markets. The meat, which is the powerful adductor muscle that controls the shell, measures about 1½ inches in diameter. Their tiny cousins, referred to as bay scallops because they are found in shallow coastal waters, are preferred by many who consider them sweeter and more tender.

fettuccine with artichokes, shrimp, and pancetta

serves 4

The combination of flavors in this recipe, based on California artichokes, is wonderfully complementary. For this recipe, I used fresh sun-dried tomatoes that were flexible enough that they did not need to be rehydrated in warm water; if the ones you use are drier, soak them for 10 minutes and drain before chopping.

Salt

1 pound dried fettuccine

1 cup diced pancetta

1 pound extra-large shrimp (16 to 20), peeled and deveined

¼ cup (½ stick) butter

1 shallot, minced

3 cloves garlic, minced

1⅓ cups Chicken Stock (page 266)

¼ cup chopped sun-dried tomatoes

1½ cups frozen artichoke halves, thawed (or fresh baby artichokes, cleaned and blanched)

¼ cup grated Parmesan cheese

Pepper, to taste

¼ cup chopped black olives

2 tablespoons chopped fresh basil leaves

Bring a saucepan of salted water to a boil and add the fettuccine. Cook according to the directions on the package, drain, and set aside. Meanwhile, place the pancetta in a dry non-stick sauté pan and cook over medium-high heat until the fat is rendered, 5 or 6 minutes. Add the shrimp and sauté for about 4 minutes on each side. Remove the shrimp and pancetta and set aside. Add the butter to the pan, and when melted, add the shallot and garlic. Sauté over medium heat for 2 minutes. Add the stock and sun-dried tomatoes, turn up the heat to high, and bring to a boil. Add the cooked fettuccine and toss well to coat. Add the reserved cooked shrimp and the artichokes and toss together. Cook for 2 to 3 minutes, add the cheese, and season with salt and pepper. Sprinkle with the olives and basil and toss.

tip Pancetta is a type of Italian unsmoked, salt-cured bacon that's often used in sauces and pastas. You can substitute any bacon as long as it's not too smoky.

fish & seafood

189

grilled shrimp with corn bread and grits dressing

serves 4

For our trip to Charleston, we just had to pair shrimp and grits, two trademarks found on menus all over the city. Just to give a different spin on the combination, I used the grits in a corn bread dressing that's also loaded with colorful sautéed vegetables. The dressing also goes really well with chicken or pork chops. For an extra flavor dimension, use one of the barbecue sauce recipes from this book (or your favorite recipe) and baste the shrimp as it grills (or broils, if preferred). Cook the grits or polenta according to the directions on the package.

for the shrimp

2 tablespoons Worcestershire sauce

1 tablespoon honey

3 tablespoons freshly squeezed orange juice

2 teaspoons Dijon mustard

20 to 24 extra-large shrimp (1¼ to 1½ pounds), peeled and deveined

To prepare the shrimp, place the Worcestershire sauce, honey, orange juice, and mustard in a mixing bowl and combine. Transfer to a resealable plastic bag, add the shrimp, seal tightly, and turn to coat. Marinate the shrimp in the refrigerator for 1 hour.

Prepare the grill and soak 4 long bamboo skewers in water for at least 30 minutes to prevent them from burning up on the grill. Preheat the oven to 350° F.

To prepare the dressing, melt the 3 tablespoons of butter in a large sauté pan set over medium-high heat. Add the bell pepper, onion, celery, and garlic and sauté for 2 or 3 minutes. Transfer to a large mixing bowl and add the corn bread, diced bread, cracker crumbs, grits, stock, melted butter, eggs, sage, and thyme. Season with salt and pepper and thoroughly

for the dressing

3 tablespoons butter

1 red bell pepper, seeded and finely diced

1 small onion, diced

2 stalks celery, diced

2 cloves garlic, minced

5 cups crumbled corn bread (or corn bread muffins)

1 cup diced day-old bread

1 cup coarse cracker crumbs

1½ cups cooked grits or polenta

2 cups Chicken Stock (page 266)

¼ cup (½ stick) butter, melted

4 eggs, beaten

2 teaspoons dried sage

2 teaspoons dried thyme

Salt and pepper, to taste

combine the ingredients. Transfer to an 8 × 10-inch baking pan and bake in the oven for 30 minutes, or until firm.

A few minutes before the dressing is cooked, thread 5 marinated shrimp on each skewer and grill over direct medium heat for 2 to 3 minutes on each side, or until cooked through. Spoon a heaping mound of the dressing in the center of 4 warm serving plates. Remove the shrimp from the skewers and arrange around the dressing.

atlantic oyster loaf with red onions, tomatoes, and greens

serves 4

I am a huge fan of oysters, dating from my childhood in Texas, when my family would take vacations in New Orleans and I was introduced to my first oyster po'boy sandwich. If po'boys are literally the poor man's sand-wich, then this is the rich man's po'boy! The combination of ingredients works even without the bread if you'd like to transform the recipe into a salad or appetizer. Atlantic oysters are generally larger than their Pacific counterparts, and if you choose farm-raised oysters, the old axiom about an "r" in the month no longer applies.

1 long baguette loaf or country loaf

¼ cup (½ stick) butter, softened

⅓ cup flour

½ teaspoon salt

½ teaspoon pepper

2 eggs, beaten

¼ cup milk

1 cup yellow cornmeal

2 pints (4 cups) shucked Atlantic oysters such as Wellfleets or Bluepoints, drained in a colander

Canola oil, for frying

1 red onion, thinly sliced into rings

1 tablespoon chili sauce

1 tablespoon rice wine vinegar

1 tablespoon olive oil

Preheat the oven to 425°F. Cut off lengthwise the top quarter of the bread and remove enough of the bread from the center of the loaf to leave a depth and thickness of ½ inch. Spread the butter inside the loaf and toast in the oven for 10 to 15 minutes, or until golden brown.

In a mixing bowl, combine the flour, salt, and pepper. In a separate bowl, mix together the eggs and milk. Spread the cornmeal on a plate. Dredge the oysters first in the flour, then in the milk mixture, and finally in the cornmeal. Pour enough canola oil into a sauté pan to come ½ inch up the sides and when the oil is hot, pan-fry the oysters over medium-high heat for 2 to 3 minutes on each side, or until golden brown. Remove with a slotted spoon and drain on paper towels.

1 cup mixed baby lettuce greens

2 tomatoes, cored and thinly sliced

1 lemon, unpeeled, washed, and thinly sliced

Add another 1 inch of the canola oil to the pan, dredge the onion rings in the flour mixture, and fry for 2 to 3 minutes, or until golden brown. Remove with a slotted spoon and drain on paper towels.

In a mixing bowl, combine the chili sauce, vinegar, and olive oil. Add the mixed greens and toss to coat thoroughly. Fill the toasted loaf with the oysters and top with the mixed greens, sliced tomatoes, and fried onions. Garnish with the lemon slices.

roasted maine lobster
with crabmeat stuffing

serves 4

I created this elegant dish after spending a day on Joe Driebeek's lobster boat, out of Marshfield, Massachusetts, north of Boston. This experience gave me a real appreciation of what it takes to put lobsters on the table: It's a whole lot of hard work. Jim grew up in a fishing town before leaving to pursue a career in the world of business. Later, he returned to his roots, and he's one of those fortunate individuals who really and truly loves his job. I think of Jim as a steward of the sea and a fisherman who appreciates the importance of ocean ecology, and as a chef, I always appreciate growers, harvesters, and suppliers whose integrity can be trusted. A simple salad makes this a perfect meal.

for the stuffing

2 pounds crabmeat, preferably backfin

1 shallot, minced

2 teaspoons chopped fresh flat-leaf parsley leaves

1 tablespoon mayonnaise

1 tablespoon Dijon mustard

3 tablespoons plain dried bread crumbs

2 eggs, beaten

Juice of 1/2 lemon

1/4 teaspoon Worcestershire sauce

Preheat the oven to 425° F. To prepare the stuffing, place the crabmeat, shallot, parsley, mayonnaise, mustard, bread crumbs, eggs, lemon juice, and Worcestershire sauce in a mixing bowl. Blend together, being careful not to break up the crabmeat. Keep refrigerated.

Split the lobsters in half (lengthwise, from between the eyes to the tail) and remove the stomach sack. Using the back (handle-end) of a heavy knife blade, crack the lobster claws (this will ensure they cook evenly with the meat). Evenly stuff the crabmeat mixture into the cavities of the lobster (including the head). Sprinkle the butter, paprika, and lemon juice all over the lobster and transfer to a baking sheet, shell-side down.

for the lobster

4 live lobsters (1 to 1¼ pounds each)

1 cup (2 sticks) butter, diced

2 teaspoons paprika

Juice of 1 lemon

Melted butter, to serve (optional)

Lemon wedges, to serve (optional)

Roast in the oven for about 15 minutes, or until cooked through. Serve, if desired, with melted butter and lemon wedges.

tip Backfin meat from blue crabs is cheaper than lump crabmeat, but it has more flavor. Use whatever kind of good-quality fresh crabmeat is available.

lowcountry seafood steampot with charleston red rice

serves 4

The marshland area around Charleston, South Carolina, is known as Lowcountry, and the region has a distinctive cuisine all its own that has been influenced over the centuries not only by local ingredients (especially seafood), but also by the contrasting traditions and cooking styles of African-American and European settlers. Some of the ingredients are specific to the Lowcountry, but of course you should use whichever varieties you can find locally. Note that the clams, oysters, and mussels are in the shell, while the scallops are shucked and the shrimp peeled.

for the rice

- 6 strips of bacon (preferably applewood smoked), diced
- 1 onion, diced
- 1 cup Carolina long-grain rice
- 1 can (14 ounces) chopped tomatoes
- ½ cup minced Tasso ham
- Salt and pepper, to taste
- ¼ cup chopped fresh flat-leaf parsley leaves

To prepare the rice, place the bacon in a dry saucepan and sauté over medium-high heat until crisp. Remove the bacon and drain on paper towels, leaving at least 2 tablespoons of bacon fat in the pan. Add the onion and sauté for 2 to 3 minutes, or until soft. Stir in the rice until it is well coated and cook for 2 to 3 minutes, or until it turns opaque, making sure not to brown it. Add the tomatoes, ½ cup of water, the Tasso, salt, and pepper. Bring to a boil and then turn down the heat to a simmer. Cover the pan and cook for about 20 minutes, or until the rice is tender and the liquid has been absorbed. Add the reserved bacon and the parsley and toss together.

While the rice is cooking, prepare the seafood. Place the lemon juice, ¾ cup of water, crab-boil seasoning, onion, and tomatoes in a stockpot and bring to a boil. Line the bottom of a steamer

for the seafood

Juice of 1 lemon

1 teaspoon crab-boil seasoning (such as Old Bay)

1 onion, cut into large dice

2 tomatoes, quartered

3 new potatoes, cut in half

8 Folly River clams, scrubbed

8 John's Island oysters, scrubbed

8 Shem Creek mussels, debearded and scrubbed

8 ounces kielbasa sausage (or other smoked "rope" sausage), cut into 4 pieces

2 ears sweet corn, husked and cut in half crosswise

8 ounces extra-large Creek shrimp (8 to 10), peeled and deveined

8 ounces shucked Calico scallops, or sea scallops

1 small tomato, seeds and pulp removed, finely diced, for garnish

8 long fresh chives, for garnish

basket (deep enough to just touch the liquid in the stockpot) with the potatoes. Stack the clams and oysters on top of the potatoes. Drop the basket in the pot and cover with a lid. Simmer for about 5 minutes and then drop in the mussels, sausage, and corn. Simmer for 8 to 10 minutes longer, or until the clams are just starting to open. Add the shrimp and scallops, simmer for 5 or 6 more minutes, until just done, and remove the basket.

Fluff the rice and spoon into warm wide-rimmed serving bowls. Arrange the seafood over the rice, dividing it evenly, and pour the remaining liquid from the stockpot over the seafood. Stand the corn vertically in the rice and garnish the edge of each bowl with the finely diced tomato and chives.

tip The terrain in the Lowcountry is ideal for growing rice—the first plantations dedicated to the crop were established in this area—and red rice is another traditional Charleston dish. Tasso is a double-smoked, spice-rubbed Cajun ham. Substitute any high-quality ham, preferably one that is well seasoned.

big jim's chinatown seafood clay pot

serves 4

In China, at the market food stalls, you are likely to see clay kilns with holes all over them set over a fire. Little bowls of meat and broth fit neatly over the holes to keep warm. I was reminded of this when Flavors of America *went to San Francisco's Chinatown. Clay-pot cooking is an ancient tradition in China, and this dish re-creates the flavors, if not the exact technique.*

for the seasoning mixture

2 cups Chicken Stock (page 266)

1 tablespoon (packed) light brown sugar

3 tablespoons soy sauce

1 tablespoon rice wine vinegar

2 tablespoons balsamic vinegar

for the seafood

6 dried black Chinese mushrooms

3 tablespoons corn oil

4 scallions, cut into 2-inch slices (white and green parts)

4 slices fresh peeled ginger, about ¼ inch thick, quartered

4 cloves garlic, minced

1 large carrot, finely sliced

3 pounds boneless, skinless fish fillets, such as grouper or halibut, cut into chunks

12 ounces extra-large shrimp (10 to 12 shrimp), peeled and deveined

6 ounces sea scallops

8 ounces Napa cabbage, cut into bite-size pieces

To prepare the seasoning mixture, place the stock, sugar, soy sauce, rice wine vinegar, and balsamic vinegar in a mixing bowl and stir well to combine. Set aside.

Soak the Chinese mushrooms in a bowl of warm water for 30 minutes. Drain, stem, slice, and set aside. In a large sauté pan, heat the corn oil and sauté the scallions, ginger, and garlic over medium-high heat for 2 minutes. Add the carrot, fish, shrimp, and scallops and sauté for 1 to 2 minutes. Add the reserved mushrooms and the cabbage and sauté for 5 minutes, stirring occasionally. Add the reserved seasoning mixture, cover, and cook for 15 minutes longer, or until all the seafood is cooked through. Transfer to large serving bowls.

tip For a stylish presentation, serve this at the table from a soup tureen with a matching lid, accompanied by steamed rice. For best results, use a nonoily fish such as sea bass, cod, swordfish, or halibut.

valentine's day
red snapper fillet
with red grapes

serves 4

When it comes to a Valentine's Day meal, I like to see red—the color of love—on the plate. As it's often a day when occasional cooks try to impress a loved one, I've kept the recipe light and simple, which has the added advantage of saving space for dessert—a must for Valentine's Day (see page 262). Serve this dish with a saffron risotto or steamed baby vegetables, and champagne, of course!

2 tablespoons olive oil

2 red snapper fillets (6 to 8 ounces each), skin on

2 cloves garlic, minced

2 tablespoons freshly squeezed lime juice

1½ cups freshly squeezed orange juice

¼ cup dry white wine

30 to 35 red seedless grapes

1 tablespoon chopped fresh cilantro leaves

Salt and pepper, to taste

1 tablespoon chopped fresh parsley leaves

2 tablespoons cornstarch

2 tablespoons soy sauce

Heat the oil in a nonstick pan set over medium-high heat. When hot, add the red snapper, skin-side down. To keep the fillets from curling, spray a piece of foil with nonstick spray and lay over the fish. Then lay a pan or weight on top of the foil. Sear for 4 minutes, or until the skin is crisp; remove the foil and weight, turn the fish over, and cook for 2 minutes longer. Add the garlic, lime juice, orange juice, and wine and bring to a boil. Reduce the heat to a simmer, gently turn the fish over, and cook for another 2 to 3 minutes, or until done. Remove the fish from the pan and keep warm.

Mash half of the grapes in a bowl and add to the pan with the cilantro, salt, pepper, and parsley. Turn up the heat to high and reduce the liquid by one third, about 5 minutes. In a cup, stir together the cornstarch and soy sauce and add to the pan. Stir until the sauce thickens and remove from the heat. Place the snapper on warm serving plates and top with the sauce and the remaining grapes.

snapper

Fish called snappers were probably named for their habit of snapping up smaller fry with their imposing jaws filled with canine-like teeth. Thirty-four of the more than two hundred snapper species are found in American waters, where they thrive in the warm currents off the coasts of Florida and the Carolinas and in the Gulf of Mexico. Several types of local snapper grace Hawaiian tables, including opakapaka (pink snapper), onaga (long-tailed Pacific red snapper), ehu (short-tailed Pacific red snapper), and uku (gray snapper).

Most snappers are deep-water fish that prefer to live next to reefs, making commercial fishing with large trawlers impossible. They are usually caught using hook and line by fishermen in small boats that can maneuver around their rocky hiding places. Snapper fish can tip the scales at forty or more pounds, but fish markets usually sell five- to ten-pounders that have already been filleted. Shoppers who want to make fish stock should ask for discarded snapper bones because they are rich in gelatin, which adds richness to the preparation.

Red snapper is one of the most popular varieties of the fish, and as such has had imposters sold using its name. Shoppers seeking red snapper should look for fillets with the rosy colored skin still attached. When smaller red snappers are sold whole, you can see that even the eyes of this attractive fish are a fiery red.

avocado snapper

serves 4

The creamy texture and rich flavor of ripe avocados make them a natural ingredient for sauces, and the color they provide is an added advantage. It's surprising to me that you don't see avocados used this way more often. This sauce recipe can be used for most fish, as well as chicken. Try serving it with pine-nut rice or rice with roasted red bell peppers.

¼ cup heavy cream

2 ripe avocados, peeled, pitted, and chopped

2 tablespoons freshly squeezed lime juice

2 cloves garlic, minced

2 tablespoons soy sauce

2 tablespoons Dijon mustard

Salt, to taste

Cayenne pepper, to taste

2 tablespoons olive oil

4 red snapper or striped bass fillets (6 to 8 ounces each)

Pepper, to taste

½ cup dry white wine, or more if needed

In a food processor or blender, combine the cream, avocados, lime juice, garlic, soy sauce, mustard, salt, and cayenne. Process until smooth and transfer to a bowl. Cover the surface of the mixture with plastic wrap and set aside.

Place the olive oil in a nonstick sauté pan set over medium-high heat. Season the snapper fillets with salt and pepper and when the oil is almost smoking, place the fillets in the pan skin side down. To keep the fillets from curling, spray a piece of foil with nonstick spray and lay over the fish. Then lay a pan or weight on top of the foil. Sear for 5 or 6 minutes, or until the skin is crisp; remove the foil and weight, turn the fish over, and cook for about 3 minutes longer. Remove the fish from the pan and keep warm.

Add the wine to the pan and deglaze with a wooden spoon or spatula. Pour in the avocado sauce and warm through; add a little more white wine if necessary to thin the sauce. Spoon the sauce onto warm serving plates and top with the snapper fillets, skin-side up.

tip As anyone who has made guacamole can tell you, brown guacamole is unappetizing. The same applies to this avocado sauce and other sauces such as pesto. To prevent discoloration, lay plastic wrap directly on the surface of the mixture to keep the air out. This method also works to prevent skin from forming on puddings and sauces.

fish & seafood

avocados

Guacamole is probably the best-known avocado recipe, but it is not a modern concoction. The Aztecs invented this perennial party food, preparing it much like we enjoy it today with tomatoes, chiles, and cilantro. The high percentage of fat and protein in avocados made them an important part of their diet, and Aztecs were the first to cultivate the fruit as early as 6,000 B.C. in the Tehuacán Valley of Mexico. Spanish explorers were delighted to discover the delicately flavored pear-shaped food, devising their own favorite preparations. Yet unlike other New World plants that Spanish missionaries helped to spread when they settled in North America, the avocado was left behind because it was considered an aphrodisiac.

It was not until 1848 that the first avocados were grown in California, and in 1871 the American avocado industry was launched in Santa Barbara. Avocado trees can annually bear as many as four hundred fruits, which can be picked year-round. Taking advantage of the state's perfect growing environment, farmers planted thousands of these prolific trees, and today California grows 95 percent of the nation's avocado crop. Though many varieties are grown in the state, the Hass avocado is the top producer and the type most commonly found in supermarkets. A descendant of the Guatemalan variety, the Hass has a rough green skin that turns black when ripe.

In Florida, the avocado was first cultivated south of Miami by a horticulturist named Henry Perrine in 1833. Florida avocados resemble their California cousins, but like most relatives they flaunt their differences more than their family tree. The Florida or Caribbean avocado (also called the Fuerte) is larger than the West Coast version and has a smoother, green skin that does not blacken. Though they produce a comparatively smaller crop, Florida avocado growers tout their milder, sweeter-flavored fruits and publicize the much lower oil content to attract the weight-conscious among us.

fish tacos coleman's way

Fish is a popular filling for tacos in California and the Southwest, as well as in Mexico. For our show on tortillas, I spent some time with Ralph Rubio, a former "surfer dude" who now owns a chain of more than 100 restaurants (Rubio's Baja Grill) out west. In Mexico, fish tacos are always wrapped in corn tortillas, but Ralph uses flour tortillas because the soft corn used south of the border just isn't available here. Firm-fleshed fish works best for this recipe. Consider substituting such fish as halibut, sea bass, mako shark, or mahimahi, for example. My recipe calls for grilling, but the fish could also be broiled.

for the fish

Juice of 2 limes

2 tablespoons olive oil

Salt and pepper, to taste

2 swordfish steaks (about 8 ounces each and 1 inch thick)

for the tacos

½ cup sour cream

Juice of 1 lime

8 flour tortillas (6 inches across)

¾ cup grated Cheddar or Monterey Jack cheese (optional)

2 cups shredded green cabbage (about ¼ cabbage)

1 tomato, chopped

1 small onion, finely sliced

12 sprigs of fresh cilantro

Hot chili sauce, to taste

To prepare the fish, combine the lime juice, olive oil, salt, and pepper in a bowl and transfer to a large resealable plastic bag. Add the fish and seal tightly, turning to coat. Marinate in the refrigerator for 1 hour.

Prepare the grill. Remove the fish from the marinade and grill over direct medium-high heat for 5 or 6 minutes on each side, or until just done.

To assemble the tacos, whisk together the sour cream and lime juice in a bowl until well incorporated. Heat the tortillas on the grill for 5 to 10 seconds on each side until pliable. If using cheese, place the tortillas on a cookie sheet, sprinkle on the cheese, and place under the broiler for about 30 seconds, or until the cheese begins to melt. Slice the fish and place in the center of the tortillas. Add the cabbage, tomato, onion, cilantro, sour cream, and hot sauce, and fold over. Serve 2 tacos per person.

fish & seafood

chilean sea bass with a ragout of smoked vegetables and spinach

serves 4

Dr. Deborah Chud, author of Gourmet Prescription *(see page 46), is also known as* A Doctor in the Kitchen, *and this is one of the innovative low-carb, low-fat recipes she presented on* Flavors of America. *Smoked vegetables are an important part of her cooking, and they only take a matter of minutes in a stovetop smoker. You could slowly grill the leek and tomatoes in this recipe over soaked wood chips, but their flavor will be less intense.*

1 large leek, washed

4 plum tomatoes

1 tablespoon olive oil, divided

4 boneless, skinless Chilean sea bass fillets (about 6 ounces each)

Salt and pepper, to taste

2 tablespoons minced garlic

2 cups sliced shiitake mushroom caps

4 cups loosely packed washed, stemmed, and chopped fresh spinach

1 tablespoon chopped fresh thyme leaves

1 tablespoon freshly squeezed lime juice

Prepare a stovetop smoker with 1 tablespoon of hickory chips sprinkled with 1 tablespoon of water. Place the leek and tomatoes on the smoker rack and half-close the lid. Set the smoker on medium-high heat and when smoke first appears, close the lid. Smoke the vegetables for 8 to 10 minutes. Remove from the smoker and let cool. Slice the leek and dice the tomatoes.

Heat 1/2 tablespoon of the oil in a sauté pan set over medium-high heat. Season the sea bass with salt and pepper and add to the pan. Sauté the bass for about 4 minutes on each side, then remove and keep warm. Add the remaining 1/2 tablespoon of oil to the pan and sauté the garlic, mushrooms, and smoked leek for about 2 minutes. Add the smoked tomatoes and spinach and cook for 3 or 4 minutes, or until the spinach is wilted. Season with salt and pepper and add the thyme.

Spoon the vegetable mixture onto 4 serving plates and place the fish on top. Drizzle with the lime juice.

tip

A stovetop smoker simply consists of a rectangular deep dish with a rack and a tight-fitting lid. You add wood chips and wait for them to begin smoking when set over heat before closing the lid. Stovetop smokers are available at kitchen equipment stores.

jim coleman's flavors

sautéed striped bass
with basil rose sauce

serves 4

When we took Flavors of America *to visit Tony Mazzaccaro, the owner of High Rock Seafood in Maryland, to discuss farm-raising sea bass, I was surprised to discover that producing 100,000 pounds of bass a year is considered small-scale by industry standards. The fish are raised in salt-water—unlike other striped-bass farms in the country—and fed grass shrimp and saltwater minnows, which also contribute to their excellent flavor. Most of Tony's bass are sold to markets in New York City. As the title suggests, the sauce has an attractive rose-colored hue. Rice Florentine would be my first choice for a side dish here.*

2 red bell peppers, roasted, peeled, seeded, and chopped (see page 268)

1/4 cup pine nuts, toasted (see page 269)

2 cloves garlic, roughly chopped

1 small shallot, chopped

1 cup drained canned diced tomatoes

2 tablespoons freshly squeezed lime juice

1/4 cup heavy cream

Salt and pepper, to taste

2 tablespoons olive oil

4 striped bass fillets (6 to 8 ounces each)

1/4 cup minced fresh basil leaves

In a blender or food processor, combine the bell peppers, pine nuts, garlic, shallot, tomatoes, and lime juice, and purée until smooth. Transfer to a saucepan and bring to a boil over medium-high heat. Turn down the heat to a simmer and add the cream. Season with salt and pepper and keep warm while cooking the fish.

Place the oil in a large sauté pan set over medium-high heat. Season the bass fillets with salt and pepper, and when the oil is almost smoking, sear the fish for 3 to 4 minutes on each side, or until it is cooked through and flakes easily.

Stir the basil into the sauce. Spoon the sauce onto 4 warm serving plates and top with the fish.

tip Striped bass has a meaty texture and a clean, delicate flavor. Unlike most other fish, it's easy to handle on the grill.

fish & seafood

grilled black bass with mango and papaya salsa

serves 4

While filming for the show at the annual New Jersey Seafood Festival, I cooked this dish for 350 participants. I wanted to use a local fish, and black bass is abundant offshore from January through July. Whenever I attend the festival, held during June, there always seems to be a heat-wave, which is why I chose the cooling salsa accompaniment for the bass. You can serve the salsa with chicken or pork, and if you'd like it spicier, leave in the chile seeds.

for the salsa

2 ripe mangos, peeled, pitted, and diced

2 ripe papayas, peeled, seeded, and diced

½ red onion, finely diced

½ red bell pepper, seeded and finely diced

1 tablespoon chopped fresh cilantro leaves

1 tablespoon chopped fresh mint leaves

1½ tablespoons freshly squeezed lime juice

1 jalapeño chile, seeded and minced

   Salt and pepper, to taste

4 black bass fillets (about 8 ounces each)

To prepare the salsa, place the mangos, papayas, onion, bell pepper, cilantro, mint, lime juice, jalapeño, salt, and pepper in a mixing bowl and thoroughly combine. Marinate in the refrigerator for 2 to 3 hours to let the flavors marry.

Prepare the grill. Season the bass with salt and pepper and grill over direct medium-high heat for about 4 minutes on each side. Serve with the salsa.

flounder with mushrooms

A number of types of flatfish are grouped together and described as "flounder," including dabs, plaice, and sole. These bottom-dwelling fish are similar in having a delicate, mild flavor and a fine texture, and they are versatile as they take well to most cooking techniques. This simple recipe was featured on the television show about Polish cooking, and I adapted it from an old Polish cookbook in my collection. Roasted potatoes or rice make excellent choices as side dishes.

serves 4

4 skinless, boneless flounder fillets (6 to 8 ounces each)

1½ cups milk

1½ cups Chicken Stock (page 266), divided

¼ cup (½ stick) butter

2½ cups sliced mushrooms (about 10 ounces)

½ onion, chopped

⅓ cup flour

3 tablespoons chopped fresh flat-leaf parsley leaves

Salt and pepper, to taste

Tightly roll up the flounder fillets and place on two 6-inch wooden skewers (two fillets each). Heat the milk and ¾ cup of the chicken stock in a saucepan; do not boil. In another saucepan, bring the remaining ¾ cup of stock almost to a boil. Turn down the heat, add the skewered flounder to the stock, and barely simmer for 8 to 10 minutes, or until tender; do not boil. Remove the fish from the pan and keep it warm.

Add the stock in which the flounder cooked to the stock and milk mixture in the other saucepan and keep it warm. Place the butter, mushrooms, and onion in the empty saucepan and sauté for 3 to 4 minutes, or until the vegetables are soft. Add the flour and, stirring continuously, cook for 2 to 3 minutes longer. Add the reserved stock and milk mixture and bring to a boil, stirring constantly until thickened. Add the parsley and season with salt and pepper.

Remove the skewers from the flounder and arrange on serving plates. Ladle the vegetables and sauce over the flounder.

fish & seafood

207

grilled salmon
with strawberry-cucumber salsa

Salmon and strawberries make an unusual combination—but a successful one because the fish's richness is cut by the mild acidity of the fruit. The refreshing salsa, which can be served chilled or at room temperature, also tastes wonderful with pork. If you are making it ahead of time, add the strawberries just prior to serving, to preserve their texture.

for the salsa

½ English (seedless) cucumber, peeled and finely diced (about 1 cup)

½ red onion, peeled and diced

2 tablespoons chopped fresh cilantro leaves

¼ cup rice wine vinegar

2 cups fresh strawberries, hulled and diced

1 large jalapeño chile, seeded and minced

1 red bell pepper, seeded and diced

¼ teaspoon salt

1 teaspoon freshly squeezed lime juice

for the salmon

3 tablespoons melted butter

2 tablespoons soy sauce

2 cloves garlic, minced

1 tablespoon honey

Juice of 1 lime

4 boneless, skinless salmon fillets (6 to 8 ounces each)

To prepare the salsa, place the cucumber, onion, cilantro, vinegar, strawberries, jalapeño, bell pepper, salt, and lime juice in a mixing bowl and mix thoroughly. Set aside.

Prepare the grill. To prepare the salmon, place the butter, soy sauce, garlic, honey, and lime juice in a mixing bowl and thoroughly combine. Spray the salmon with nonstick spray and place on the grill over direct medium-high heat. Grill for 3 to 4 minutes on the first side, flip over, and brush evenly with the mixture. Grill for about 3 minutes on the second side for medium and transfer to serving plates. Serve with the salsa.

seattle salmon provençal style

serves 4

The fishmongers at Pike's Market in Seattle are famous for catching the attention of customers and luring them in by putting on a fish-throwing show. Whole salmon are heaved from one salesman to another, and considering they are slippery and weigh up to twenty pounds each, catching them is harder than it sounds. I know, because we spoofed the scene in our kitchen studio for the show about the market. Salmon remain prolific from the Northwest Coast up to Alaska, partly due to seasonal fishing restrictions that protect stocks.

3 tablespoons olive oil

4 boneless, skinless salmon fillets (about 8 ounces each)

1 onion, chopped

½ green bell pepper, seeded and chopped

10 button mushrooms, quartered

3 cloves garlic, minced

½ cup dry white wine

1 cup bottled clam juice

Pepper, to taste

3 tomatoes, cored and chopped

1 tablespoon flour

2 tablespoons butter, softened

Preheat the oven to 350° F. Heat the oil in a heavy ovenproof skillet or sauté pan set over medium-high heat. Add the salmon and cook for 1 to 2 minutes on each side, until browned. Add the onion, bell pepper, mushrooms, and garlic, and cook for 2 minutes longer. Add the wine and clam juice and season with pepper (the clam juice should provide enough saltiness). Cover the skillet and bake for 12 to 15 minutes.

Remove the skillet from the oven, remove the fish from the pan, and keep the fish warm. Transfer the skillet to the stovetop, bring the sauce to a boil over medium heat, and stir in the tomatoes. In a small bowl, blend the flour and butter together then whisk the mixture into the skillet to thicken the sauce. Place the salmon on warm serving plates and pour the sauce and vegetables over the fish.

fish & seafood

209

pan-fried alaskan salmon and halibut with honeyed apples

serves 4

Looking back, it does seem ironic that my trip to the International Boston Seafood Show (see page 98) focused on Alaskan salmon rather than seafood from the East Coast. Halibut is the second most important fish (after salmon) caught in the chilly Alaskan waters, and the contrasting flavors and textures of the two fish work well together on the same plate. If you have difficulty finding either one for this recipe, then go exclusively with the other. I deliberately chose an old Alaskan apple recipe for the side dish. Use another good cooking apple instead of the Granny Smiths, if you prefer.

for the apples

2 tablespoons butter

1 large shallot, diced

4 Granny Smith apples, peeled, cored, and thinly sliced

¼ cup honey

1 tablespoon chopped fresh tarragon leaves

To prepare the apples, melt the butter in a saucepan set over medium heat. Add the shallots and sauté for 1 minute. Add the apples and cook for 5 to 7 minutes, or until tender. Drizzle with the honey and tarragon, toss together to mix well, and keep on the lowest heat setting to keep warm.

To prepare the fish, heat the oil in a sauté pan set over medium-high heat until it is almost smoking. Place the flour on a plate and season with the garlic powder, salt, and pepper. Place the eggs in a shallow bowl and the bread crumbs on a separate plate. Dredge the salmon and halibut fillets in the flour, then dip in the egg, and finally, dredge in the bread crumbs to coat. Transfer to the sauté pan and cook for 3 to 4 minutes on each side, or until golden brown.

for the fish

¼ cup olive oil

2 cups flour, for dredging

1 tablespoon garlic powder

Salt and pepper, to taste

2 eggs, beaten

2 cups fine dried prepared bread crumbs

4 small salmon fillets (about 3 ounces each)

4 small halibut fillets (about 3 ounces each)

4 sprigs of fresh tarragon, for garnish

Place 1 salmon fillet and 1 halibut fillet on each serving plate and spoon the honeyed apples over the top. Garnish with the tarragon sprigs.

tip A nice alternative to prepared bread crumbs is panko, the Japanese style of coarse bread crumbs. Panko is usually available in the Asian section of supermarkets, and it gives a crunchy texture to foods coated with it.

horseradish-crusted halibut on wilted spinach with beet relish and matchstick potatoes

serves 4

An Alaskan fishing guide once told me, "Landing a two-hundred-pound halibut is like landing a garage door from the bottom of the ocean." Having caught one myself, I can tell you that's an accurate description.

Crusting fish with horseradish creates wonderful flavor and texture, and it works equally well with other fish such as salmon, or with pre-seared bone-in chicken breast. Carole Peck created this recipe, and it's one of the best-selling items at her Good News Cafe in Woodbury, Connecticut. The white fish, green spinach, red beets, and golden brown potatoes make for a beautifully colorful dish.

for the horseradish crust

- 2 egg yolks
- 2 tablespoons freshly squeezed lemon juice
- 1 cup vegetable oil
- Salt and pepper, to taste
- 2 tablespoons prepared horseradish
- ½ cup fine plain prepared bread crumbs

for the beet relish

- 3 small cooked beets (2 to 3 ounces each), peeled and chopped
- 1 tablespoon raspberry vinegar
- 1 teaspoon salt
- 1 teaspoon honey

To prepare the crust, place the egg yolks and lemon juice in a food processor. Using a steel blade, mix together and with the machine running, add the oil in a steady stream. Season with salt and pepper, add the horseradish, and then the bread crumbs. Process quickly and then transfer to a bowl. Cover and keep refrigerated until ready to use.

To prepare the relish, place the beets in a food processor and add the vinegar, salt, and honey. Using a metal blade, process for about 1 minute until finely chopped. Transfer to a bowl, cover, and keep refrigerated until ready to use.

Preheat the oven to 375° F. Using a mandoline slicer or a very sharp knife, slice the potatoes and cut into fine julienne. Transfer to a colander and rinse under cold running water.

for the potatoes

2 large Yukon Gold potatoes (1⅛ pounds total), peeled

Vegetable oil, for deep-frying

Salt and pepper, to taste

for the halibut

2 pounds boneless, skinless halibut

2 tablespoons vegetable oil

for the spinach

1 tablespoon vegetable oil

8 ounces spinach leaves, washed

1 clove garlic, minced

Salt and pepper, to taste

tip Halibut is the largest of all the flatfish, averaging 100 to 200 pounds (the record weight is 700 pounds). When buying halibut, look for bright white flesh.

Hold the potatoes in a bowl of cold water until the halibut is cooking. Drain the potatoes and pat them dry with paper towels. In a deep-fryer or large saucepan, heat the vegetable oil to 350°F., or until it is almost smoking. Add the potatoes and fry for 2 to 3 minutes, or until golden. Remove with a slotted spoon and drain on paper towels. Sprinkle with salt and pepper while hot.

To prepare the halibut, cut it into 4 equal portions. Heat the oil in an ovenproof skillet or sauté pan set over high heat, and when hot, add the halibut. Sear on the first side for about 3 minutes, or until browned around the edges. Turn the fish over and spread about ¼ inch of the horseradish crust on each fillet. Transfer the skillet to the oven and roast for 6 to 9 minutes, depending on the thickness of the fish.

While the fish is cooking, prepare the spinach. Heat the oil in a skillet or sauté pan set over high heat. When hot, add the spinach, garlic, salt, and pepper. Sauté for 3 or 4 minutes, or until wilted. Transfer the spinach to the center of each serving plate and top with the halibut. Arrange the matchstick potatoes on top of the fish and spoon the beet relish on both sides of the fish.

fish & seafood

alaskan halibut with
tagliatelle of vegetables and american caviar

Halibut is a popular fish in the Pacific Northwest, which is one reason why Brian Scheehser of Seattle's Sorrento Hotel (see page 61) chose it for this recipe. The "vegetable pasta" makes a colorful presentation. Tagliatelle is another term for flat, thin fettuccine, and using a mandoline slicer is the easiest and most efficient way to cut the vegetables thin enough. You can also cut the vegetables by hand—it will just take longer. An alternative serving suggestion is to cook tagliatelle pasta and to toss it with sautéed julienned vegetables.

for the beurre blanc sauce

1 shallot, minced

¼ cup dry white wine

2 tablespoons freshly squeezed lemon juice

2 tablespoons heavy cream

1 cup (2 sticks) chilled butter, cubed

Salt and pepper, to taste

for the tagliatelle of vegetables

2 zucchini squash (unpeeled)

2 yellow squash (unpeeled)

1 carrot

1 leek, white part only

2 tablespoons butter

To prepare the beurre blanc sauce, place the shallot, white wine, and lemon juice in a saucepan and reduce over medium heat until almost all the liquid is evaporated, about 4 minutes. Add the cream and reduce slightly. Add the butter in increments and whisk each addition into the sauce until incorporated. Season with salt and pepper. If the sauce seems "flat," add a little more lemon juice; if it seems too acidic, add a little more butter. Keep the sauce warm.

Preheat the oven to 350° F. To prepare the vegetables, use a mandoline slicer or a very sharp knife to cut the squash, carrot, and leek into long julienne (6 to 8 inches long), resembling tagliatelle pasta. Set aside.

for the halibut

4 Alaskan halibut fillets (about 8 ounces each)

   Salt and pepper, to taste

2 tablespoons vegetable oil

2 teaspoons white sturgeon caviar

2 teaspoons whitefish caviar

2 teaspoons salmon caviar

4 sprigs of fresh chervil, for garnish

Season the halibut with salt and pepper. Heat the oil in a large ovenproof skillet or sauté pan set over medium-high heat and add the halibut. Sear the fillets for 2 or 3 minutes, or until golden brown on the first side. Turn the fillets over and transfer the skillet to the oven. Roast for 8 to 10 minutes, or until the fillets are cooked through.

While the fish is cooking, heat the butter for the vegetables in a sauté pan and add the vegetables. Sauté over medium-high heat for 3 to 4 minutes, or until al dente.

Place the tagliatelle of vegetables in the center of each serving plate and top with the cooked halibut. Ladle a little of the beurre blanc sauce on top, and garnish with dollops of the caviar and the fresh chervil.

tip The caviar is available at gourmet or specialty food stores. By all means use 6 teaspoons of one type of caviar, if you prefer; the recipe also works fine without any caviar.

fish & seafood

american caviar

Anyone who has ever relished a tidbit of caviar would have been in paradise a century ago in America. Caviar was once so plentiful in this country that great scoops of the glistening "black pearls" were served free in nineteenth-century bars. Costing proprietors a mere ten cents per pound, it was far cheaper than salted peanuts but had the same thirst-inducing effect on happy customers.

Caviar is the eggs of sturgeon, a fish that from the earliest times thrived in American waters. Native American mothers used to wean their babies on sturgeon roe, and early settlers used the eggs as bait for other fish. The abundant fish became a mainstay in the diet of early Colonists, and it was so commonplace that children used to play football with the muzzles of the fish in the streets of New York. By the end of the nineteenth century, people began to take their caviar more seriously, and along with champagne, it became the ultimate celebratory food. As its popularity exploded, American caviar producers pressed to meet the demand; the United States was already the largest producer of caviar in the world, processing more than six hundred tons a year. Though American caviar was of high quality, Russian caviar had the loftier reputation. In a shrewd but less than ethical move, U.S. caviar fisheries began to ship most of their product to Europe and import it back again with Russian labels. The product was so wildly popular that the fisheries self-destructed by depleting the North American sturgeon population to near extinction.

In spite of these severe conditions, and in spite of the modern problem of pollution, the American sturgeon has managed to persevere with the help of conservation and fishing regulations. Today, American caviar is making a comeback through the cultivation of farm-raised sturgeon in the rivers of the Ozarks and the Pacific Northwest. In the past twenty-five years, American caviar production has again soared from about 5,000 to more than 75,000 pounds.

home-cured grilled cod with dill sauce

serves 4

Boston has always been an important center for the cod industry, and it made an interesting subject for our show on historic foods of the city. Drastic overfishing of the once-teeming St. George's Banks has meant that cod is no longer a mainstay for New England fishermen. Where fifty- to sixty-pound fish used to be the norm, ten-pounders are now considered large. Unfortunately, the same problem affects cod stocks worldwide. In this recipe, the cod is cured like salmon gravlax, but not all the way. This technique firms up the meat, making it less flaky. Otherwise, it is hard to grill cod.

for the cod

4 boneless, skinless cod fillets
    (about 8 ounces each)

½ cup sugar

¼ cup chopped fresh dill

¼ cup kosher salt

2 tablespoons pepper

    Vinegar for removing the seasonings

for the sauce

2 tablespoons butter

2 shallots, minced

1 clove garlic, minced

1 cup Chicken Stock (page 266)

1 cup heavy cream

2 tablespoons Dijon mustard

    Juice of 1 lemon

1 tablespoon chopped fresh dill

Place the cod in a baking dish. In a mixing bowl, thoroughly combine the sugar, dill, salt, and pepper and pour over the fillets. Transfer to the refrigerator and let cure for 4 to 5 hours, turning the fish once or twice.

Prepare the grill. To prepare the sauce, melt the butter in a large sauté pan set over medium-low heat. Add the shallots and garlic and sauté for 3 or 4 minutes. Add the stock and cream and reduce the liquid by half, about 8 minutes, making sure the cream does not boil over. Stir in the mustard and lemon juice and blend well. Add the dill and keep the sauce warm.

While the sauce is reducing, take the cod from the marinade and brush off the seasonings with a damp paper towel sprinkled with a little vinegar. Transfer the cod to the grill and grill over direct medium-high heat for 3 or 4 minutes on each side or until cooked through. Place on warm serving plates and spoon the sauce over.

fish & seafood

desserts

Irish Potato Pie with Irish Whiskey, Almonds, and Orange

Steamed Beijing Cake

Hot Banana Shortcake

Bananas

Mint Crepes with Strawberry Preserves and Mascarpone Cheese

Lime and Pistachio Pie

Galactoboureko (Greek Custard with Phyllo)

Phyllo

Dried Apricot Cheesecake

Chocolate Waffle and Strawberry Sundaes

Roasted Pears with Gorgonzola

Children's Party Special: Cookies and Berries with Chocolate–Peanut Butter Dip

Butter

Raspberry Tart

Georgia Peach Cobbler

Blueberry-Merlot Cobbler

Coffee and Walnut Cake

Mother's Day Pancake Soufflés

Cherries

Cabernet-Cherry Pudding

Apple Strudel Tart with Brandy Whipped Cream

Cranberry-Walnut Cake with Caramel Sauce

Butterscotch Cookie Ice Cream Sandwiches

Cuban Diplomat Bread Pudding

Boston Brown Betty

Pineapples

Miami Frozen Fantasy

Orange Flan

Blueberry and Chocolate Black-Bottom Pie

Old-Fashioned New England Indian Pudding

Bittersweet Chocolate Cupcakes

Carolina Rice Pudding with Benne Wafers

Almond Cake with Honey-Orange Glaze

Almonds

Coeur à la Crème with Berry Sauce

The nature of the *Flavors of America* program dictates that these desserts be short and sweet. Each dish for a particular course that I prepare on the show occupies an eight-minute segment, so there's no time to construct anything too elaborate or to get too fancy. Food shows that tell you about fantastic desserts that take hours to prepare off-screen annoy me too! So, in keeping with the other recipes in this book, the emphasis is on user-friendly dishes that can be made at home without too much trouble. These desserts are brought together from around the country and beyond, so they embrace a diversity of ingredients and styles.

A majority of the recipes in this chapter are pies, cobblers, cakes, and puddings that contain fruit. That's my personal preference; I am not a chocolate fiend, although of course I enjoy it in moderation. But I don't go for overly rich or sweet desserts, as I don't think that is the best way to end a meal. When planning desserts, I try to take stock of which fresh fruits are in season. If necessary, I will substitute alternative fruits where appropriate rather than use frozen fruit, which is convenient but often has a greater water content and never tastes quite the same. I recommend canned fruit only as a last resort, because the texture is inferior and the accompanying syrup is overly sweet.

If you are a cookie fan, you may notice that we have not included some of the recipes we made on the show. We could not fit everything into this chapter—we featured more desserts on the show than any other course—but the good news is that good cookie recipes are not hard to find.

irish potato pie
with irish whiskey, almonds, and orange

This recipe answers the question of whether the Irish used potatoes for just about everything! I adapted a simpler, blander recipe that I came across in an old Irish cookbook, and browsing through it, I concluded that the potato really was a multipurpose food. When you taste this rich, custardy pie, it is not at all obvious that it contains potatoes. Have fun quizzing your guests about the main ingredient.

1 russet potato (8 ounces), diced

Salt

6 large eggs, separated

½ cup (½ stick) butter, melted

½ cup ground almonds (about 3 ounces)

1 tablespoon orange extract

1 teaspoon vanilla extract

1½ cups sugar

3 tablespoons Irish whiskey

1 frozen ready-made 9-inch deep-dish pie shell, thawed

Whipped cream, to serve (optional)

Preheat the oven to 375°F. Place the potato in a saucepan of salted boiling water and cook for 15 to 20 minutes, or until soft. Meanwhile, in a bowl, whisk the egg whites until stiff peaks form. In a separate bowl, beat the yolks until fluffy and lemon colored. Set aside. When the potato is done, drain and transfer to a mixing bowl. Add the butter and mash by hand or with an electric mixer until smooth. Add the almonds, orange extract, vanilla extract, sugar, whiskey, and egg yolks to the potato mixture and blend. Gently fold in the egg whites and pour the mixture into the pie shell. Bake for 50 minutes to 1 hour, or until a toothpick inserted in the center comes out clean. Remove the pie from the oven, slice, and serve with whipped cream, if desired.

tip

Here's a tip to streamline your pie-crust recipe: Instead of dicing chilled butter with a knife, use a grater to shred it into the mixing bowl. It's faster, and makes it easier to combine with the flour.

steamed beijing cake

Dessert is not a tradition in China, where plain fruit is sometimes served at the end of a meal. A cake like this would be served with afternoon tea, as I discovered when I worked in China. It is certainly the perfect cake for dunking into tea or coffee. As a dessert, it's not particularly sweet, so you could add a little more sugar, or serve it with chocolate sauce or ice cream. I made this recipe for the television show on Chinese New Year.

4 eggs, separated

⅓ cup cold water

½ teaspoon vanilla extract

1 cup flour

¼ teaspoon ground cinnamon

¼ teaspoon baking powder

¼ cup sugar

Spray the bottom and sides of a round 8-inch cake pan with nonstick spray. Place a steamer basket in a large saucepan, add enough water to come 2 inches up the sides of the pan, and bring to a boil. (Alternatively, instead of a steamer basket, you can use a tall wire cooling rack or 3 pieces of foil wadded up so you can balance the cake tin on it above the level of the water.)

In a mixing bowl, whisk the egg whites until stiff peaks form. In another mixing bowl, add the cold water and vanilla to the yolks and whisk together. In another bowl, sift together the flour, cinnamon, baking powder, and sugar and then mix into the egg yolk mixture. Fold in the beaten egg whites to form a batter. Pour the batter into the prepared cake pan and place on the rack in the saucepan of boiling water. Cover the pan and steam for 25 minutes, or until a sharp knife or toothpick inserted in the center comes out clean.

Using oven mitts, remove the cake pan and place a plate over the top of it. Flip it over to remove the cake. Serve warm.

hot banana shortcake

It is not often that you get to use the grill to make dessert, but I created this recipe for our show from Texas on grilling. You can also cook this recipe in a sauté pan or under the broiler. In this recipe, bananas Foster meets strawberry shortcake; or think of it as bananas Foster but without the liquor and with the addition of pound cake! You can use a store-bought pound cake for this recipe, but if you have time to make a home-made pound cake, so much the better.

¼ cup (½ stick) butter

3 ripe bananas, peeled and quartered lengthwise, then cut in half crosswise

2 tablespoons freshly squeezed lemon juice

⅔ cup (packed) light brown sugar

¼ teaspoon ground cinnamon

4 slices pound cake (about 1 inch thick)

4 scoops vanilla ice cream

Prepare the grill.

Place the butter in a disposable aluminum pan, set it over medium heat on the grill, and melt the butter. Add the bananas and heat for 1 minute. Add the lemon juice, sugar, and cinnamon and coat the bananas, making sure the sugar is melted. Set aside. Place the slices of pound cake on the grill and quickly grill for a few seconds just until they are slightly warmed and grill marks appear. Transfer the pound cake to serving plates and top with the ice cream. Spoon the warm banana mixture over the top.

America's cheapest and most popular fruit was once considered an exotic luxury item, but the onset of refrigerated transportation in the 1920s made bananas available for everybody's breakfast. Demand for them soared, prompting U.S. fruit companies to establish plantations in tropical countries that became known as banana republics. The taste for the fruit continued to grow in America, and in this country we each eat an average of twenty-eight pounds of bananas a year.

Although we consume more bananas than any other country, Americans were among the last fans to jump on the banana boat. The banana has been around so long that some sources peg it, rather than the apple, as the fruit that Adam should have politely refused. In some cultures bananas were even called the fruit of paradise, and they have probably been cultivated for more than three thousand years. Ancient Arab traders took bananas to Egypt, and the fruit became a mainstay throughout Africa.

Portuguese navigators found them there in the 1400s, and they were responsible for introducing them to the New World. Today the countries of the Caribbean and Central and South America are the world's top bananas when it comes to producing the fruit. Along with their sunny flavor, they are supremely nutritious. Bananas are loaded with brain-boosting potassium and phosphorus, they have been shown to reduce the risk of strokes, and they can even help fight the blues because they contain serotonin.

mint crepes with strawberry preserves
and mascarpone cheese

serves 4

Using herbs to flavor these paper-thin pancakes sets up all kinds of possibilities for flavor combinations. As I described on the Flavors of America *show devoted to herbs, you can use the same principle to create savory crepes—for example, tarragon crepes for a filling of chicken and mushrooms. Mascarpone, made in the Italian region of Lombardy, is a rich, smooth, and creamy "cheese"—although no rennet is used, so it is technically more of a cream than a cheese. Mixing the mascarpone with cream cheese lightens the flavor and texture of the filling, which can be made with honey or the preserve of your choice.*

for the crepes

½ cup flour

2 eggs

1 tablespoon melted butter

Pinch of salt

2½ tablespoons chopped fresh mint
leaves

To prepare the crepes, place the flour, ½ cup plus 1 tablespoon water, the eggs, butter, and salt in a food processor and blend for about 10 seconds. Scrape down the sides of the container and blend for 20 seconds longer. Transfer the batter to a bowl and let it rest for 1 hour. Stir in the mint.

While the batter is resting, prepare the filling. Place the strawberry preserves, cream cheese, mascarpone, sugar, cinnamon, nutmeg, and vanilla in a mixing bowl and stir together until well blended.

Preheat the oven to 325°F. Spray a small (6- to 7-inch) skillet with nonstick spray and set over medium heat. Pour about 2 tablespoons of the batter into the pan (the bottom of the pan should be very thinly coated when it is

for the filling

9 tablespoons (½ cup plus
1 tablespoon) strawberry preserves

¼ cup cream cheese

¼ cup mascarpone cheese

1½ tablespoons sugar

½ teaspoon ground cinnamon

½ teaspoon ground nutmeg

¼ teaspoon vanilla extract

Ice cream or whipped cream, to serve

Sprigs of fresh mint, for garnish
(optional)

tilted to distribute the batter). Cook the crepe for 1 or 2 minutes, or until it no longer sticks to the pan. Flip it over and cook it for 30 seconds longer. Place 3 tablespoons of the filling in the center of the crepe, fold over to form a half-moon, and then fold over again. Transfer to a baking dish sprayed with nonstick spray and repeat for the remaining crepes and filling, overlapping the folded crepes slightly.

Bake the crepes for about 20 minutes, or until they are completely heated through. Serve with ice cream or whipped cream and garnish with mint sprigs, if desired.

tip If opting for whipped cream as a garnish, here's a simple tip for maximizing its fluffiness: Add 3 drops of lemon juice to 1 cup of whipping cream. It will whip up more volume in less time.

lime and pistachio pie

serves 8

The famous Key limes, of pie fame, are smaller versions of the widely available Mexican limes (also known as West Indian or bartender limes). These are the round, juicy limes found in most supermarkets that typically have a mottled green and yellow skin, and they are the type I use for this recipe. If you can find Key limes, by all means make an authentic Key lime pie. When I visited Herbie Yamamura in Homestead, Florida, to take a look around his lime orchards, he told me that Key limes were cultivated commercially on a wide scale in the Florida Keys until a hurricane destroyed the industry in the early 1900s. Unfortunately, Herbie suffered a similar setback with Hurricane Andrew (see page 40). Herbie invited us to try his recipe for homemade Key lime pie, which was unbelievably good. It inspired me to include this refreshing, easy-to-make unbaked pie on the show. Herbie swore us all to secrecy when it came to the special ingredient he used, but he released me from my promise for this book—it was Cool Whip!

for the pie crust

- 1 cup shelled pistachio nuts (about 3½ ounces), divided
- 1 cup finely crushed graham cracker crumbs
- 1 tablespoon sugar
- ⅓ cup melted butter

To prepare the pie crust, preheat the oven to 350°F. Place ½ cup of the pistachios in a food processor and grind. Transfer to a small bowl, add the cracker crumbs, sugar, and butter, and mix well. Evenly press into a 9-inch pie pan. Transfer to the oven and bake for 10 minutes.

To prepare the filling, place 2 tablespoons of the lime juice in a bowl and sprinkle the gelatin over the top. Let it stand for 15 minutes, or until the gelatin is softened. In a separate bowl, whisk together the egg yolks and condensed milk and when it is well blended, transfer the mixture to a saucepan. Whisk in the remaining ½ cup of lime juice and set the pan

for the filling

½ cup plus 2 tablespoons freshly squeezed lime juice

1½ teaspoons unflavored powdered gelatin

4 egg yolks

1 can (14 ounces) sweetened condensed milk

1½ teaspoons grated lime zest

½ teaspoon ground ginger

for the topping

1 cup heavy cream

1 tablespoon chopped fresh mint leaves

over medium heat, beating constantly to make sure the eggs do not cook. Cook for about 6 minutes, or until the mixture is warm to the touch. Remove the pan from the heat and add the gelatin mixture, lime zest, and ginger. Stir until the gelatin is dissolved. Pour into the prepared pie crust and refrigerate overnight, until set.

For the topping, whisk together the cream and mint in a mixing bowl until firm peaks form and spread over the pie. Roughly chop the remaining pistachio nuts and sprinkle over the top.

tip The other type of lime commonly sold in the United States is the Persian or Tahiti lime, which resembles a green lemon. Most people are surprised to learn that this variety is picked and sold unripe (if left to ripen on the tree, the fruit will turn yellow). In part because of this, the Persian lime is more acidic and less juicy than the Mexican lime.

galactoboureko
greek custard with phyllo

serves 6 to 8

If you are a lover of either baklava or custard, then you are in for a treat with this dessert. Like baklava, it contains buttery phyllo and a sweet syrup, but the creamy pudding-like custard really sets it apart. My version is based on a traditional Greek recipe, and one of the twists I added was to infuse the syrup with fresh rosemary. I experimented with oregano, the most widely used herb in Greek cooking, but it just did not work as well. Besides, the rosemary flavor worked best in this finale for the other Greek courses I had prepared on the Flavors of America *show (see recipes on pages 13 and 146).*

for the syrup

1 cup sugar

1 sprig of fresh rosemary

for the custard

6 egg yolks

¼ cup sugar

2 tablespoons cornstarch

3 cups warm milk

½ cup heavy cream

1½ teaspoons vanilla extract

To prepare the syrup, place the sugar and ½ cup water in a saucepan and bring to a boil. Let the syrup cool, add the rosemary sprig, and set aside to infuse for 30 minutes. Remove the rosemary.

Preheat the oven to 375° F.

To prepare the custard, whisk together the egg yolks and sugar in a mixing bowl until thick and pale yellow. Whisk in the cornstarch and milk. Transfer to a saucepan and cook over low heat until the mixture almost reaches a boil. Add the cream and vanilla.

Fold a phyllo sheet in half and place in an 8-inch square baking dish. Brush generously with some of the melted butter. Fold a second phyllo sheet in half, lay it on top of the first, and brush again with butter. Pour the custard mixture over the phyllo in the dish. Fold another phyllo sheet in

for the phyllo base

4 sheets of phyllo dough, thawed

½ cup (1 stick) butter, melted

half, place it on top of the custard, and brush with butter. Repeat for the remaining phyllo sheet. Transfer the dish to the oven and bake for 45 to 55 minutes, or until the top is golden in color. Remove from the oven and slowly pour the syrup over the top. You may not need all of the syrup; use enough so that it is absorbed but do not let the syrup stand on top or it will make the galactoboureko too soggy. Let the dessert cool completely before cutting.

phyllo

When the Turks first entered the history books in the seventh century, these central Asian tribes already had an impressive understanding of agriculture. Grains made up a large part of their diet, and their most popular recipe was a rustic predecessor to phyllo called *yufka.* The Turks would prepare this thin unleavened bread by folding it many times with butter or other fillings tucked between the layers, then cook it over a grass fire on an iron sheet.

Yufka began to evolve into phyllo after the tenth century when the Turks traveled to the Near East and encountered the refined cooking of the Muslim courts. Several centuries later, when the Turks conquered Constantinople and renamed it Istanbul, the sultan initiated an age of patronage of the arts—including cookery. It was in his vast Topkapi Palace that phyllo rose to its present level of perfection. Later, when the Turks invaded Hungary, phyllo found its way into European kitchens and was reborn as the puff pastry so acclaimed in Western culinary techniques.

Today, sheets of frozen phyllo dough can be found in many supermarkets. While it still retains its mystique, its newfound availability has made phyllo a more common ingredient in everyday cooking. The paper-thin pastry leaves are traditionally used in recipes for baklava and strudel, but they can also be an imaginative replacement for a variety of outer wrappings from other world cuisines, such as tortillas, wonton skins, and crepes.

dried apricot cheesecake

serves 6 to 8

This was the obvious dessert to make for the Flavors of America *show on cheese. Most people think making cheesecake is difficult or involved, but this recipe proves that it's not the case. I have used ricotta, which gives a lighter texture than the traditional cream cheese. Apricots and pine nuts are a natural pairing, but you can use other similar combinations to flavor this dessert, such as dried apples and walnuts, or dried figs and hazelnuts.*

for the crust

½ cup finely crushed graham cracker crumbs

2 tablespoons melted butter

½ teaspoon ground cinnamon

for the cheesecake filling

2 pounds ricotta cheese

⅓ cup heavy cream

⅓ cup sugar

5 egg yolks

⅓ cup finely sliced dried apricots

2 tablespoons pine nuts

1 tablespoon flour

2 teaspoons minced orange zest

Pinch of salt

Preheat the oven to 350°F. Line an 8-inch springform pie pan with foil and lightly butter the foil.

To prepare the crust, mix together the cracker crumbs, butter, and cinnamon in a mixing bowl and evenly press into the pie pan.

To prepare the filling, place the ricotta, cream, sugar, egg yolks, apricots, pine nuts, flour, orange zest, and salt in a mixing bowl and thoroughly combine. Pour over the crust in the pan and transfer to the oven. Bake for 40 to 45 minutes, or until a toothpick inserted in the center comes out clean. Let the cheesecake cool for 30 minutes before unmolding.

tip If your dried apricots are less than pliable, soak them in warm water for 15 minutes and drain.

desserts

231

chocolate waffle and strawberry sundaes

serves 4

Although it is the Belgian waffle that is renowned, waffles actually origi-nated in Holland. When they were brought to the United States, they were embraced enthusiastically. There's no doubt they are a special treat, especially topped with fruit and whipped cream or ice cream, but many people I know never seem to use their electric waffle makers or old-fashioned waffle irons. That's almost a crime—this recipe should give them every excuse to put the irons to good use. These waffles are almost like light brownies, and they are very easy to make. I topped them with strawberries because that was the subject of the show, but raspberries or any seasonal berries will work just as well.

for the waffles

¼ cup (½ stick) butter

2 ounces chocolate chips (about ⅓ cup)

½ cup flour

1 teaspoon baking powder

Pinch of freshly grated nutmeg

Pinch of salt

3 eggs

½ cup sugar

1 teaspoon vanilla extract

¼ cup milk

for the sundaes

4 large scoops of vanilla ice cream

4 large scoops of strawberry ice cream

2 cups fresh strawberries, hulled and sliced

Preheat the oven to 250° F.

To prepare the waffles, place the butter and chocolate chips in the top of a double boiler or in a dish in the microwave, and melt together. Let the mixture cool. In a small mixing bowl stir together the flour, baking powder, nutmeg, and salt and set aside. In a separate large mixing bowl, beat together the eggs, sugar, and vanilla. Stir in the chocolate mixture and fold in the flour mixture. Add the milk and mix together until the batter is smooth; do not overmix.

Heat the waffle maker to a medium setting and pour in ½ cup of batter. Cook until the waffle is done, about 5 minutes. Remove and keep warm in the oven. Repeat for the remaining waffles (the batter will make 4 waf-fles). Transfer the waffles to 4 serving plates and top each one with a scoop each of vanilla and strawberry ice cream and ½ cup of the strawberries.

roasted pears
with gorgonzola

serves 4

Any diet that allows you to use Gorgonzola cheese gets my vote, and one of the principles behind Dr. Chud's Gourmet Prescription (see page 46) is that most things are healthy in moderation. This is an enjoyably flavorful way of getting protein from dessert, and the recipe is both simple and sophisticated. Blue cheese and fruit are a time-honored combination, and the richness of the cheese is cut nicely by the sweet roasted pears. Splurge on the best Gorgonzola you can find—you don't need much.

2 ripe pears, such as Anjou or Bartlett, peeled, cut in half, and cored

1 ounce Gorgonzola cheese, crumbled (about 3 tablespoons)

2 tablespoons nonfat ricotta cheese

1 tablespoon Grand Marnier

Preheat the oven to 375°F. Spray a nonstick baking dish, large enough to hold the halved pears in a single layer, with nonstick spray and place the pears, cut-side down, in the dish. Roast in the oven for 20 minutes, or until tender.

Place the Gorgonzola, ricotta, and Grand Marnier in a mixing bowl and blend well. Place the pears, cut-side up, on serving plates and top with the cheese mixture. Let the mixture melt slightly and serve.

children's party special
cookies and berries with chocolate–peanut butter dip

serves 4

Most kids love to get involved with making their own food, and the more responsibility you give them, the more likely they are to eat and appreciate the end product. For older kids, you could present the dip and the strawberries with some skewers and make it into a fondue party. The combination of chocolate and peanut butter is always a winner with children, as Reese's could probably tell you.

3 ounces cream cheese, at room temperature

¾ cup creamy peanut butter

1 teaspoon ground cinnamon

¼ teaspoon freshly grated nutmeg

¼ cup chocolate syrup

2 tablespoons milk

12 assorted cookies

12 fresh strawberries

Place the cream cheese, peanut butter, cinnamon, and nutmeg in the bowl of an electric mixture fitted with a paddle attachment and beat until smooth. Gradually beat in the chocolate syrup and milk and mix until well blended. Dip the cookies and the berries into the chocolate–peanut butter mixture.

When the English and the Dutch arrived on American shores, they brought with them their craving for butter. Cattle had been transported to the continent years before by the Spanish, and cows in the colonies were prized commodities. The first American dairy herd was established in 1625, and rural dairies began supplying the growing urban areas with milk and butter. In the early years, city dwellers were often subject to dairy products hauled in open containers for miles before making their unappealing appearance at the market. The invention of railroads and refrigeration made fresh dairy products available to the masses, and milking machines and automatic churners developed in the 1830s enabled dairy farmers to meet a growing demand. By the end of the nineteenth century, visitors to America noted that its citizens ate practically everything dripping with butter.

American butter is always made from pasteurized cow's milk and is graded by the United States Department of Agriculture based on flavor, texture, color, and salt content. By law, butter in America must consist of at least 80 percent milk fat, and most commercial butters are produced with the minimum amount of milk fat required. Americans have grown accustomed to the industry standard in this country, but those who visit Europe notice a difference in the butter there. Europeans prefer butter with slightly more than 80 percent milk fat, making the product creamier and more versatile in the kitchen.

European-style butter produced in America, such as Keller's, is a boon for bakers aiming for flakier croissants and superior puff pastry. In other cooking uses, professional chefs find that European-style butter makes sauces smoother, silkier, and shinier. Also, because of the additional fat, the butter has a higher burning point than traditional American butter, which tends to smoke easily when used for frying or sautéing.

raspberry tart

Tarte aux framboises, *as this recipe is called in France, is a classic summer dessert in that country. While filming* Flavors of America, *I forced myself to try a rather large and inviting slice of raspberry tart at a pastry shop in Dijon. Its delicate texture, excellent flavor, and just-enough sweetness inspired me to include a version for the show. You can use a mixer for the dough recipe, but it's really best made in a food processor.*

for the pastry shell

- 2 cups pastry flour
- ¾ cup (1½ sticks) butter, softened
- 1½ tablespoons sugar
- 2 small egg yolks
- 1½ tablespoons cold water

To prepare the pastry shell, place the flour, butter, and sugar in a food processor and pulse for a few seconds just to combine. Add the egg yolks and pulse a couple more times. Remove from the processor and transfer the mixture to a mixing bowl. Work in the water with a wooden spoon until the dough is thoroughly combined and forms a ball. Wrap the dough in plastic wrap and refrigerate for 1 hour.

Preheat the oven to 425° F.

To prepare the pastry cream, place the milk in a medium saucepan and scald (bring almost to the boiling point). Place the egg yolks, flour, and cornstarch in the top of a double boiler over medium heat and whisk together until combined. Add a little of the hot milk to the egg mixture while stirring vigorously, and pour the mixture back into the pan, whisking until smooth. Remove from the heat and stir in the butter and liqueur. Set the pastry cream aside to cool.

for the pastry cream

4 cups milk

8 egg yolks

½ cup flour

2 tablespoons cornstarch

2 tablespoons diced chilled butter

1 cup raspberry liqueur, such as
   Chambord or Framboise

2 cups fresh raspberries

1 tablespoon confectioners' sugar

Unwrap the pastry dough and roll it out on a lightly floured work surface so that it will just cover the bottom and sides of a 9-inch tart ring or pie pan. Trim off any surplus pastry. Cover the dough with wax or parchment paper and fill with dried beans. Transfer to the oven and bake the shell for 4 to 5 minutes. Remove the beans and paper and continue baking for 10 minutes longer, or until the shell is golden brown. Let it cool.

Pour the cooled pastry cream into the pastry shell. Cover with the raspberries and sprinkle the sugar over the top. Serve at room temperature.

tip Don't let your pastry cream or custard overcook! Three signs will tell you it is time to take the pan off of the stove: If the foam moves in large bubbles toward the edge of the pan, the custard coats the back of a wooden spoon or spatula, or you can make a path through the sauce with the tip of your finger, it's ready!

desserts

georgia peach cobbler

serves 4

Georgia is famous for both its peaches and its tradition of cobbler, so it was no surprise to me that the best peach cobbler I have ever tasted was in Savannah. I enjoyed the cobbler in question at a restaurant called The Lady and Her Two Sons, while we were in town filming for Flavors of America. *I know my cobbler; my mother is from Georgia and I grew up with her superb peach and blueberry versions. This recipe is a little unusual in having a biscuit-type batter/topping that is layered with the fruit (it is important not to stir them together). Try this recipe with butter-pecan ice cream.*

2 cups peeled and sliced fresh ripe peaches (3 or 4 peaches)

2 cups sugar

¾ cup flour

2 teaspoons baking powder

Pinch of salt

½ cup milk

¾ cup (1½ sticks) butter

Preheat the oven to 350°F. Place the peach slices in a mixing bowl, sprinkle 1 cup of the sugar over, and set aside. In a separate mixing bowl, combine the flour with the remaining 1 cup of sugar, the baking powder, and salt. Add the milk and mix well to form a batter.

Melt the butter in an 8-inch square baking dish, pour in the batter, and arrange the peaches on top. Do not stir. Transfer to the oven and bake for 1 hour, until a toothpick inserted in the center comes out clean. The batter will puff up around the peaches. Remove the cobbler from the oven and spoon portions onto 4 warm serving plates.

tip When a recipe calls for peeled peaches, try this trick. Drop the peaches in boiling water for 20 to 30 seconds, then remove them with a slotted spoon and place in ice water. Use a paring knife to easily slip the skins off.

blueberry-merlot cobbler

serves 6

Two of the food products for which the Pacific Northwest is justly famous are blueberries and red wine grapes, especially Merlot and Pinot Noir (for more on blueberries, see page 60). The climate of the region suits both products perfectly, and they make a natural match. Using biscuit mix rather than flour for the topping makes it lighter and airier, and the mixture of wine and berries makes this recipe a little moister than other cobblers in this chapter. The alcohol in the wine will cook out, so don't be concerned about serving this dessert to kids.

½ cup Merlot wine

1 teaspoon cornstarch

2½ tablespoons butter

3 tablespoons (packed) light brown sugar

1 pound fresh blueberries, washed

½ cup plus 2 tablespoons granulated sugar

¼ teaspoon ground cinnamon

1½ cups biscuit mix, such as Bisquick

¾ cup milk

Preheat the oven to 375°F. In a small bowl, stir the Merlot and cornstarch together. Pour into a saucepan and set over medium high heat. Add the butter and brown sugar and stir until the butter melts and the sugar dissolves.

Butter six 1-cup ramekins and divide the blueberries among them. Pour the wine mixture over the berries evenly and sprinkle evenly with ½ cup of the granulated sugar and the cinnamon. (You can stir the cinnamon and sugar together before sprinkling, if you like.) In a mixing bowl, stir together the biscuit mix, the remaining 2 tablespoons of sugar, and the milk until thoroughly combined. Pour the batter evenly into the ramekins and place in a baking dish. Transfer to the oven and bake for 35 minutes, or until a toothpick inserted in the center comes out clean.

coffee and walnut cake

serves 8

When I began doing some research in my cookbook library for the Flavors of America *program on coffee, I was surprised by how many recipes, both historical and contemporary, include the noble bean. Coffee was first written about in fifteenth-century Constantinople (Istanbul), where it was used as a drug so imbibers could stay awake to pray. The active ingredient in coffee, caffeine, is a drug, of course, and until the 1800s, it could be purchased only in drugstores (the same was true of chocolate, for the same reason!). For more on the history of coffee, see page 52.*

½ cup freshly brewed coffee

1½ tablespoons cornstarch

¾ cup granulated sugar, divided

½ cup dark raisins

½ cup golden raisins

½ cup chopped walnuts

½ cup (1 stick) butter, at room temperature

½ cup (packed) light brown sugar

2 cups flour

¼ teaspoon salt

1½ teaspoons cream of tartar

1½ teaspoons baking soda

½ cup milk, at room temperature

1 teaspoon vanilla extract

3 eggs, beaten

Preheat the oven to 350°F. Stir together the coffee and cornstarch in a saucepan set over medium-low heat, and when smooth, add ½ cup of the granulated sugar. Cook for about 5 minutes, or until the mixture has thickened and the sugar has dissolved. Add the dark and golden raisins and the walnuts and set aside to cool.

In a mixing bowl, beat the butter with the brown sugar and the remaining ¼ cup of the granulated sugar until thick and light in color. Add the flour and salt and beat in. Add the cream of tartar and baking soda, and slowly beat in the milk. Add the vanilla and then slowly add the eggs, while beating. Mix until the batter is completely blended.

Pour half of the batter into a buttered 9-inch cake pan. Carefully pour in the coffee mixture (do not stir) and cover with the remaining batter. Transfer to the oven and bake for about 50 minutes, or until a sharp knife inserted in the center comes out clean.

mother's day pancake soufflés

serves 8

These pancakes masquerading as soufflés make Mother's Day just that little bit more special. As with regular pancakes, the topping determines the flavor of the dish, so feel free to use Mom's favorite. For children, I would recommend plain butter or chocolate syrup as alternative toppings. If you are serving these pancakes for brunch, omit the sugar; I have added it here for those who would like to make the soufflés as a dessert.

¼ cup (½ stick) melted butter

5 eggs

1 cup flour

1 cup milk

¼ cup sugar (optional)

¼ cup strawberry jam, apple butter, maple syrup, or honey

Preheat the oven to 425° F. Thoroughly coat eight 1-cup ramekins with the melted butter. In the bowl of an electric mixer, or by hand, beat the eggs for 1 minute, or until fluffy. In ¼-cup increments, add the flour and milk alternately, and stir in the sugar, if using. Place the ramekins on a cookie sheet and transfer to the oven to warm for 2 or 3 minutes. Remove and pour the batter into the ramekins, no more than three-quarters full. Transfer to the oven and bake for 20 minutes, or until a toothpick inserted in the center comes out clean. Take the soufflés out of the oven, split them open, and add the jam or topping of your choice.

desserts

241

cherries

For many Americans, spring officially begins when the cherry blossoms burst open in the nation's capital, but decorating our political arena with cherry trees was not a homegrown idea. Instead, they were a gift from the mayor of Tokyo in 1910, and making them part of Washington's landscape was merely a matter of good politics. Although we cherish the story of young George Washington owning up to chopping down a cherry tree, the truth is that a writer named Parson Weems invented the yarn to pad the future president's reputation. Since our only two historical references to cherries are either foreign or fabricated, how American can cherries be?

Actually, cherries were one of the handful of fruits already here for the picking when the first European explorers arrived. The bite-size treats had long been a favorite of Native Americans, who used dried cherries to perk up the flavor of pemmican, an otherwise bland mixture of dried meat and fat that sustained them on long journeys. Colonists brought European cherries to their new home, and the cross-pollination between the wild and domestic types of the fruit resulted in the many cherry varieties now growing in the United States.

Today, cherries are one of America's most impressive crops, ranking with better-publicized fruits such as Florida oranges and California strawberries. Traverse City, Michigan, is the cherry capital of the world, producing 70 percent of all sour cherries—up to eighty million pounds a year. (Sour cherries are often used in canning and baking, and in savory dishes.) Along the sandy shores of Lake Michigan the cherry orchards boast almost 23,000 trees per square mile. That area and the cherry orchards in the Pacific Northwest have allowed the United States to blossom into the world's leading cherry producer, and our exports satisfy the taste for cherries worldwide.

cabernet-cherry pudding

Many wines, and especially Cabernets, are described as containing fruit tones, including cherry, so the combination in this simple recipe is a natural. Licorice and tobacco are other common wine descriptors, but I draw the line there! Chocolate, cherries, and almonds are also successful partners in many desserts around the world. If fresh cherries are unavailable, use jarred cherries that have been drained.

6 ounces semisweet chocolate pieces or morsels

1 cup sugar, divided

¾ cup (1½ sticks) butter

9 eggs, separated

¼ cup Cabernet Sauvignon wine

1⅓ cups ground almonds (about 8 ounces)

⅓ cup plain dried bread crumbs

1 pound fresh cherries, pitted

1 cup whipped cream (optional)

4 to 6 sprigs of fresh mint (optional)

Preheat the oven to 350° F. Place the chocolate in the top of a double boiler or in a dish in the microwave and melt. Remove and let cool. In a mixing bowl, cream together ¾ cup of the sugar and the butter. Add the egg yolks to the mixing bowl one at a time. Beat in the melted chocolate and add the wine. Stir in the almonds and bread crumbs and add the cherries.

In a separate bowl, whisk the egg whites until medium peaks form. While whisking, slowly add the remaining ¼ cup of sugar. Fold the mixture into the chocolate batter and pour into a 2-quart baking dish that has been buttered and lightly floured. Transfer to the oven and bake for 1 hour, or until a sharp knife or toothpick inserted in the middle comes out clean. Scoop out the pudding with a serving spoon and serve with the whipped cream and mint sprigs, if desired.

tip Pitting cherries can be done either by smashing the fruit like garlic—using the flat blade of a knife—and then removing the stones, or by using a cherry or olive pitter.

apple strudel tart with brandy whipped cream

serves 4

This untraditional "open" strudel is a great example of how to use phyllo creatively (see page 230). Strudel is Austrian or German in origin (the word means "whirlpool"), and apple is the typical filling, but all kinds of fruit can be used. In some countries, for example, cherries are the favored filling. Purists will tell you that tart apples such as Gravensteins must be used, and they are a good choice if available, but Granny Smiths work well. However, only fresh apples will do.

for the strudel filling

1½ tablespoons butter

2 Granny Smith apples, peeled, cored, and finely sliced

¼ cup granulated sugar

3 tablespoons brandy

3 tablespoons golden raisins

3 tablespoons chopped walnuts

Pinch of ground cinnamon

Pinch of freshly grated nutmeg

for the phyllo cups

4 sheets of phyllo dough, thawed

2 tablespoons melted butter

⅓ cup plain cookie crumbs

Preheat the oven to 375° F.

To prepare the filling, melt the butter in a sauté pan set over medium-high heat. Add the apple slices and sprinkle with the sugar. Cook for about 35 minutes, or until caramelized. Place the brandy and raisins in a small saucepan set over medium-high heat and bring to a boil. Add to the sugar and apples while stirring, being very careful as the mixture could ignite. Let the mixture boil for 4 or 5 minutes, or until the brandy has evaporated. Stir in the walnuts, cinnamon, and nutmeg, and remove from the heat.

To prepare the phyllo cups, spray a muffin tin with nonstick spray. Place one phyllo sheet on a flat work surface, brush with butter, and cut into quarters. Carefully place a piece of phyllo in each of 4 muffin cups, pressing down lightly, so the points are sticking upward. Sprinkle with one quarter of the cookie crumbs. Place another piece of phyllo on a flat

for the brandy whipped cream

⅓ cup heavy cream

2 teaspoons confectioners' sugar

2 teaspoons brandy

work surface, brush with butter, cut into quarters, and place one piece on top of each in the muffin tin, arranging them with the points offset, or in the opposite direction as the first pieces of phyllo. Sprinkle with crumbs. Repeat until there are 4 pieces of phyllo dough forming a basket in each muffin cup. Spoon the apple mixture into the phyllo cups and transfer to the oven. Bake the strudels for 15 minutes, or until golden brown.

To prepare the brandy whipped cream, pour the cream into a mixing bowl and whisk until stiff peaks form. Stir in the confectioners' sugar and brandy. Place the strudels on serving plates and spoon the cream over the top.

tip For a quick and simple homemade dessert, bake empty phyllo cups using the same method as in this recipe in a 375°F. oven for 8 to 10 minutes, or until golden brown. Then fill with whatever fruit, mousse, or ice cream tickles your fancy.

cranberry-walnut cake
with caramel sauce

Fresh cranberries are such a treat, and when they come into season, I look for as many ways to use them as I can (for more on cranberries, see page 139). Their extreme tartness demands a balancing sweetness, and that's especially true for a dessert. That is where the rich, gooey caramel sauce comes in, and you can also use it with other cakes or drizzle it over ice cream. The cake makes delicious breakfast bread if baked in a loaf pan.

for the cake

2½ cups flour, divided

2 teaspoons baking powder

Pinch of ground cinnamon

Pinch of ground allspice

Pinch of salt

3 tablespoons butter, at room temperature

1 cup sugar

2 eggs

1 cup milk

2 cups fresh cranberries

½ cup walnut pieces

for the sauce

½ cup granulated sugar

½ cup (packed) light brown sugar

½ cup (1 stick) butter

1 cup heavy cream

Preheat the oven to 350° F.

To prepare the cake, place 2 cups of the flour, the baking powder, cinnamon, allspice, and salt in a mixing bowl. In the bowl of an electric mixer, or by hand, cream together the butter and sugar. Add the eggs one at a time and beat in. Alternately add the milk and the flour mixture in increments. Place the cranberries and walnuts in a bowl, toss with the remaining ½ cup of flour, and fold into the batter (do not add any of the excess flour). Butter a 9-inch cake pan or baking dish and pour the batter in. Bake for 25 to 30 minutes, or until a toothpick inserted in the middle comes out clean.

To prepare the sauce, place the granulated and brown sugars, butter, and cream in a large saucepan and bring to a boil. Stir well.

Place slices of the warm cake on serving plates and pour the sauce over. Any extra sauce can be stored in the refrigerator and warmed in the microwave oven.

butterscotch cookie ice cream sandwiches

serves 4

Inspiration can strike unexpectedly. Having some time to spare in Ocean City, Maryland, during a filming assignment on striped bass for the television show, I paid a trip to an ice cream parlor on the boardwalk. It's tough sometimes, doing research. But someone had to try their butterscotch ice cream sandwich, and it was so good that I was determined to try to replicate the flavor combination. No one really knows how butterscotch—a toffee-type mixture made from brown sugar and butter—got its name, and it does not seem to have any connection to Scotland.

½ cup (1 stick) butter, at room temperature

1 cup (packed) light brown sugar

1 egg

½ cup bran cereal (any kind)

1½ cups flour

1½ teaspoons baking powder

4 scoops ice cream (preferably butter pecan)

¼ cup chocolate syrup

tip You will have up to a dozen cookies left over, but I figure they won't last long! Keep them in an airtight container.

In the bowl of an electric mixer, or by hand, cream together the butter and sugar, gradually mixing until well blended. Add the egg and bran cereal and mix thoroughly. Scrape down the sides of the bowl with a spatula. Mix the flour and baking powder in a small bowl and blend into the batter. Remove the dough, transfer to a lightly floured work surface, and shape into a roll about 4 inches in diameter. Wrap it in waxed paper and refrigerate it until firm, 30 to 45 minutes.

Preheat the oven to 425°F. Cut the dough into ½-inch-thick slices and place on a nonstick cookie sheet. Transfer to the oven and bake for 10 minutes, or until the cookies are golden brown.

Place 1 cookie on each of 4 serving plates and top with a scoop of ice cream. Gently press another cookie on top of the ice cream and drizzle with chocolate syrup.

desserts

247

cuban diplomat bread pudding

serves 4

In preparation for our Flavors of America *show about Miami's Little Havana, I was browsing through some pre-revolution Cuban cookbooks. I have adapted this recipe from one prepared by a Havana hotel and casino that was favored by the diplomatic community. It would have been even more fun to visit the same hotel to demonstrate for TV how it was made. There is no mistaking the tropical touch in this bread pudding: Raisins and coconut are popular in Cuban desserts, and rum is another tradition. The papaya is a touch that I added both for flavor and color.*

2 tablespoons rum

3 cups cubed French bread

1 cup milk

2 eggs, beaten

¼ cup sugar

½ teaspoon vanilla extract

2 tablespoons unsweetened coconut flakes

1 tablespoon diced orange

2 tablespoons diced papaya

1 tablespoon golden raisins

Pinch of ground cinnamon

Papaya slices, for garnish

Preheat the oven to 350°F. In a large mixing bowl, sprinkle the rum over the bread cubes and toss to blend. In a separate bowl, whisk together the milk, eggs, and sugar and add the vanilla, coconut, orange, papaya, raisins, and cinnamon. Pour the milk mixture into the bread cubes and stir to combine. Butter four 1½-cup ramekins and spoon in the bread pudding mixture. Place on a cookie sheet and bake for 25 to 35 minutes, or until golden brown on top. Serve the pudding with the papaya slices.

boston brown betty

serves 6 to 8

This is a dessert I prepared for our Historic Boston television show, and it dates back to Yankee Colonial days. It still appears on menus in Boston, but I have never seen it anywhere else except as a novelty item. A betty is a baked dessert dish with layers of fruit (usually apples), brown sugar, and buttered bread crumbs, and it's simply delicious served with whipped cream or ice cream.

3 tablespoons melted butter

2 cups plain dried bread crumbs

Grated zest of 1 orange

¾ cup freshly squeezed orange juice

½ cup (packed) brown sugar

½ teaspoon ground cinnamon

½ teaspoon freshly grated nutmeg

4 Granny Smith apples, peeled, cored, and thinly sliced

Preheat the oven to 375° F. In a mixing bowl, mix together the butter and bread crumbs. In another bowl, combine the orange zest and juice, sugar, cinnamon, and nutmeg. Butter a 7- or 8-inch baking dish and make 3 alternating layers of the apples and the bread-crumb mixture, starting with the first layer of apples on the bottom and finishing with the third layer of bread crumbs on top. Sprinkle each layer of the apples with the orange juice mixture. Cover the dish with foil and bake for 30 minutes; uncover and bake for 30 minutes more, or until golden brown.

pineapples

When Columbus landed in the West Indies, the story goes, he and his crew were invited into native huts decorated with pineapples. The explorers learned that this exotic fruit was not only delicious, but also served as a local sign of welcome. This tradition found its way back to Europe, where the pineapple became very popular with the upper classes. Nobles took great pains to grow the fruit in hothouses long before refrigerated ships made pineapples available to the general public.

Pineapples came to symbolize not only hospitality, but also wealth and quality of life. Images of the fruit were carved and molded onto castles and manors across Europe and even found their way onto coats of arms. When the first Colonists braved their way across the Atlantic to North America, the symbol of the pineapple came with them, even though it would be centuries before the fruit became part of the diet here.

Today the golden fruit is available year round. Pineapples are loaded with vitamin C and dietary fiber, and the fact that they contain an enzyme that breaks down protein makes them a good choice for dessert after a meat-rich meal. Beyond bringing home a healthy snack, shoppers might be surprised to learn they have just picked up a European status symbol and the emblem of American hospitality. No wonder those bags are so heavy!

miami frozen fantasy

serves 8 *When I think of Miami, I think of tropical color and brightness, and I devised this dish to match. Limes, mangos, and papayas were all part of my Miami experience, and those were some of the luscious flavors I chose for this light dessert. It's wonderfully refreshing, and no matter where you are located, the combination of a graham-cracker crust with sorbet and fresh fruit will transport you to the land of swaying palm trees and sun-kissed beaches.*

3 cups graham cracker crumbs

¾ cup (1½ sticks) butter, melted

¼ cup (packed) light brown sugar

¾ quart lime sorbet, slightly softened

½ pineapple, peeled, cored, and diced

1 ripe papaya, peeled, seeded, and diced

1 ripe mango, peeled, pitted, and diced

2 pints fresh strawberries, stemmed and hulled, or raspberries

¼ cup toasted coconut flakes (see page 269)

In a mixing bowl, thoroughly combine the crumbs, butter, and brown sugar. Press the mixture over the bottom and sides of a 9-inch springform pan and transfer to the freezer for 15 minutes. Remove the pan and spread the sorbet evenly over the crust. Refreeze for about 45 minutes, or until firm.

Place the pineapple, papaya, mango, and berries in a mixing bowl and toss well to combine. Remove the pan from the freezer and release the sides of the pan. Cut into 8 slices, transfer to serving plates, and spoon the fruit mixture over each serving. Garnish with the toasted coconut flakes.

orange flan

serves 6 to 8

This dessert makes a terrific item for the holiday season. It contains no oranges; instead, the taste of oranges is provided by the Triple Sec liqueur, most commonly found in margaritas, and the orange color comes mainly from the sweet potato. Substitute Grand Marnier or Cointreau for the Triple Sec, if you wish. This dessert is the creation of Laurent Manrique, executive chef at the Campton Place Hotel (see page 22).

for the caramel

1¼ cups sugar

for the custard

Sweet potato (8 ounces), peeled and diced

3 cups milk (whole)

3 eggs plus 6 egg yolks

1 teaspoon vanilla extract

2 tablespoons Triple Sec

To prepare the caramel, place the sugar in a heavy-bottomed saucepan and set over medium-high heat. Cook the sugar, stirring constantly with a wooden spoon or heatproof plastic spatula, for about 20 minutes, or until the mixture turns a light amber color. Pour the caramel into an ungreased 1½- or 2-quart baking dish, tilting it to quickly cover the bottom and partway up the sides with caramel before it begins to cool and harden.

Preheat the oven to 325° F.

To prepare the custard, place the sweet potato in a saucepan of boiling water and cook for about 20 minutes, or until soft. Drain, transfer the potato to a food processor or blender, and purée. Transfer the potato to a mixing bowl. Scald the milk in a saucepan (bring almost to a boil) and add to the potato, while whisking. In a separate mixing bowl, whisk together the eggs and yolks until thick and lemon-yellow in color and add to the sweet potato mixture. Stir in the vanilla and Triple Sec. Pour the mixture into the baking dish and place in a large roasting pan. Add enough water to the roasting pan to come halfway up the sides of the baking dish and transfer to the center rack of the oven. Bake for 45 to 50 minutes, or until the flan is set but the middle is a little shaky; a sharp knife inserted in the center should come out clean. Remove the baking dish from the roasting pan and let the flan cool.

Run a sharp paring knife around the inside of the baking dish and dip the dish in hot water for 1 minute. Place a large serving platter over the baking dish and invert to unmold the flan. Let the caramel drip onto the flan. Spoon the flan and caramel onto serving plates.

tip A great way to store extra egg whites for use in another recipe is to place one in each section of an ice cube tray. When frozen, pop the cubes out into a resealable freezer bag. Thaw each egg white as needed by placing it in a dish overnight in the refrigerator.

blueberry and chocolate black-bottom pie

I associate chocolate-covered pastry crusts with Southern desserts, but it's a great flavoring technique for any fruit pie. The first time I tasted this combination, I was in the middle of a ten-day, 385-mile river float and fishing trip in Alaska. The guides on this adventure who prepared the pie at camp in the middle of nowhere were careful not to harvest the blueberries too far off the beaten path, as Alaskan grizzlies love the fruit, too. For more on blueberries, see page 60.

2 tablespoons milk

2 tablespoons heavy cream

1½ cups milk chocolate chips

2 teaspoons vanilla extract, divided

1 store-bought cookie-crumb pie crust

12 ounces cream cheese, at room temperature

½ cup confectioners' sugar

⅓ cup toasted slivered almonds (see page 269)

4½ cups fresh blueberries, washed

⅓ cup blueberry preserves

1 cup whipped cream, for garnish

4 sprigs of fresh mint, for garnish

Place the milk, cream, and chocolate chips in the top of a double boiler set over medium heat. Stir until the chocolate is melted and the mixture is smooth. Remove from the heat and mix in 1 teaspoon of the vanilla. Pour the mixture over the cookie-crumb crust and let it cool until the chocolate is firm.

In a mixing bowl, combine the cream cheese, the remaining 1 teaspoon of vanilla, and the sugar. Spread this mixture over the layer of chocolate in the crust and sprinkle the almonds on top. Evenly spread the blueberries over the almonds.

In a saucepan, melt the blueberry preserves over low heat and stir until smooth. Pour the preserves over the top of the pie and cover with plastic wrap. Transfer the pie to the refrigerator and chill for at least 2 hours, or until firm. Slice the pie and serve with the whipped cream and mint sprigs.

old-fashioned new england indian pudding

Native Americans of the region probably shared a rudimentary version of this traditional pudding with the early settlers in New England. It was most likely sweetened with maple syrup, and the spices and flavorings would have been different, but I am sure it was more than welcome. It makes a hearty, filling dish that seems best suited to fall, and especially to the Thanksgiving season.

⅓ cup yellow cornmeal (preferably stone-ground)

3 tablespoons skim milk powder

4 cups boiling water

1 cup dark molasses

2 tablespoons vegetable oil

½ teaspoon ground cinnamon

½ teaspoon ground ginger

½ cup raisins

2 eggs, well beaten

1 cup milk

Ice cream or heavy cream, for serving (optional)

Preheat the oven to 325°F. Combine the cornmeal, skim milk powder, and boiling water in the top of a double boiler. Cook for 15 to 20 minutes, stirring constantly. Stir in the molasses, oil, cinnamon, ginger, and raisins. Stir in the eggs and pour the mixture into a buttered baking dish. Pour the milk over the mixture; do not stir.

Transfer the pudding to the oven and bake for 1 hour, or until firm. Serve warm with ice cream or heavy cream, if desired.

desserts

bittersweet chocolate cupcakes

I had just read an article in a food magazine about how cupcakes were making a comeback on fashionable menus when, a few days later, Carole Peck (see page 58) created this dessert for the show. Talk about serendipity. Sure enough, since then, I've seen cupcakes featured in stores as well as on restaurant dessert menus. These flourless cupcakes are notable for their simplicity—just six ingredients in all—yet the results are impressive. If you wish, you can make the recipe as a single larger cake and serve with a fruit coulis and/or fresh berries.

for the cupcakes

- 1 pound good-quality bittersweet chocolate
- 5 eggs plus 3 egg yolks
- 1 cup sugar

Preheat the oven to 375° F.

To prepare the cupcakes, melt the chocolate in the top of a double boiler over barely simmering water. While the chocolate is melting, combine the eggs, yolks, and sugar in the bowl of an electric mixer fitted with a balloon whisk attachment. Beat on high speed until the eggs are pale yellow in color and tripled in volume. With the machine running, add the melted chocolate and mix quickly. Turn off the machine and use a rubber spatula to scrape down the sides of the bowl; fold in until the chocolate is evenly distributed.

Spray a mini-muffin tin with nonstick cooking spray, or lightly grease with oil. Spoon the batter into the cups so the tins are three-quarters full. Transfer to the oven and bake for about 12 minutes, or until the cupcakes have risen and the tops are cooked and cracking. Remove and let the muffin tin cool to room temperature.

for the chocolate glaze

½ cup heavy cream

8 ounces semisweet chocolate chips

¼ cup (½ stick) butter, diced

Remove the cupcakes carefully, tapping the tin on a counter to loosen them. Most of the cupcakes should lift out; use a paring knife or small metal spatula to nudge out any reluctant ones.

To prepare the chocolate glaze, pour the cream in a small saucepan and scald it by bringing it almost to a boil. Place the chocolate chips in a food processor, and with the motor running, pour the hot cream through the feed tube and mix until smooth. Gradually add the butter and blend in. Transfer the glaze to a small bowl and let it cool. Hold each cupcake by its base and dip it into the glaze to coat the top

tip This recipe makes approximately 24 mini-cupcakes or 12 regular-size ones. Serve up to 4 mini-cupcakes per person, or 2 regular ones.

carolina rice pudding with benne wafers

serves 4

Having already created a savory rice to commemorate the history linking Charleston, South Carolina, with the grain (see page 196), here I offer a sweet dish. Rice pudding is another old-fashioned dessert that has recently become a popular menu item, in common with other comfort foods. Benne wafers are sesame-seed cookies that are recognized as a specialty of the Charleston area. Benne was the African name for sesame seeds used by the slaves who brought the ingredient with them to the plantations of the Carolinas and Georgia. These wafers have been made there for centuries.

for the rice pudding

- 2 eggs, beaten
- ¾ cup milk
- 2 teaspoons melted butter
- ¾ cup granulated sugar
- ¼ teaspoon vanilla extract
- ¼ cup raisins
- 1 cup cooked Carolina rice
- ½ teaspoon ground cinnamon

Preheat the oven to 350° F.

To prepare the rice pudding, thoroughly combine the eggs, milk, butter, sugar, and vanilla in a mixing bowl. Fold in the raisins, rice, and cinnamon, and pour the mixture into a small buttered baking dish. Place the dish in a roasting pan and fill with enough hot water to come halfway up the sides of the dish. Transfer to the oven and bake for 1¼ hours, or until the custard is set. Remove the pudding and let it cool.

While the rice pudding is baking, prepare the wafers. Sift the flour, baking powder, and salt into a mixing bowl. In a separate mixing bowl, cream together the butter and brown sugar, and whisk in the egg and vanilla. Stir in the flour mixture and sesame seeds. Using a teaspoon, drop the mixture onto a nonstick cookie sheet, allowing room between each wafer for the dough to spread. Transfer to the

for the benne wafers

¼ cup flour

⅛ teaspoon baking powder

Pinch of salt

¼ cup (½ stick) butter

½ cup (packed) light brown sugar

1 small egg

½ teaspoon vanilla extract

½ cup toasted sesame seeds
(see page 269)

Coarse salt, for sprinkling

oven and bake for 8 to 10 minutes, or until the wafers are set. Let them cool for 3 or 4 minutes, sprinkle with coarse salt, and carefully remove the wafers to a cooling rack. Let the wafers cool completely.

Spoon the rice pudding into dessert bowls and garnish with 1 or 2 of the wafers per serving.

tip The wafers can be made ahead and stored for 3 to 4 days in an airtight plastic container. This recipe makes more than you will need for the pudding, so store the extras the same way.

almond cake with honey-orange glaze

serves 4 to 6

Almond cake is a tradition during Passover, at least on the East Coast, and Stanley Keenan, our outstanding pastry chef at the Rittenhouse Hotel, makes the best. This is a slightly adapted version of his recipe. Almonds (see sidebar) and honey (see page 131) are natural flavor partners and two of the oldest foods; both are mentioned several times in the Bible. The glaze is what really sets this dessert apart: The cake absorbs the syrup, leaving it moist and delicious.

for the cake

- 2 cups slivered almonds
- 2 cups granulated sugar
- 2 cups flour
- 1½ teaspoons ground cinnamon
- ½ teaspoon ground allspice
- 7 eggs
- ½ cup melted butter
- 1 tablespoon minced orange zest

for syrup

- ⅔ cup freshly squeezed orange juice
- 1 cup honey
- ⅓ cup confectioners' sugar

Preheat the oven to 350° F. To prepare the cake, place the almonds and ½ cup of the granulated sugar in a food processor and grind together. Transfer to a large mixing bowl and mix in the flour, cinnamon, and allspice. In a separate mixing bowl, whisk the eggs with the remaining 1½ cups of granulated sugar for about 10 minutes, or until very thick. Whisk in the melted butter and the zest, and then fold in the almond mixture.

Spray a 2-quart baking dish with nonstick spray. Pour the batter into the pan and bake for about 1 hour, or until a toothpick or sharp knife inserted in the center comes out clean.

Meanwhile, to prepare the syrup, place the orange juice, honey, confectioners' sugar, and ¼ cup water in a saucepan set over medium-low heat. Warm through, stirring to dissolve the sugar. Remove the cake from the oven and drizzle the warm syrup over the cake. Let the cake sit for 30 minutes to absorb the syrup. Cut the cake into squares and transfer to serving plates.

Almonds, the world's most popular nut, are actually drupes and belong to the same family as cherries and peaches. In the case of the almond, we eat the inside and throw away the rest. Almond trees are thought to have first taken root in Asia Minor, and are one of only two nuts mentioned in the Bible. Their popularity spread throughout the Middle East and they became very important in Islamic cooking, where they replaced meat on holy fasting days. The Romans discovered almonds through the Greeks and helped to popularize them throughout Europe. Almonds became a key ingredient in medieval cuisines and were prominent in the first known French cookbook, written in 1300.

European settlers brought almonds with them to America, and it was not long before the United States went nuts over almonds, becoming the world's largest producer. California is home to more than 400,000 acres of almond groves, a crop second only to grapes in that state, and the huge Blue Diamond Cooperative in Sacramento processes more than two million pounds of almonds every day. In addition to their flavorful contribution to a wide range of recipes, almonds boast a sizable dose of vitamin E, fiber, and calcium. Like other nuts, they are high in calories but low in cholesterol, and legend has it they have the added benefit of reducing the risk of a hangover if consumed with alcohol.

coeur à la crème
with berry sauce

This classic French dessert (translated as "heart with cream") is tradi-tionally made in a heart-shaped wicker basket or mold, making it the perfect choice for Valentine's Day. I have used individual heart-shaped molds that can be found at most kitchenware stores. I have also made the recipe with a mixture of soft mascarpone cheese (see page 224) and cream, rather than the standard cream cheese and sour cream. It's still rich and decadent, but a little lighter on the palate and waistline.

for the coeur à la crème

- 1 cup mascarpone cheese, at room temperature
- 1¼ cups heavy cream
- 1 teaspoon vanilla extract
- 1 tablespoon freshly squeezed lemon juice
- 1 teaspoon raspberry liqueur, such as Chambord
- 1 teaspoon Triple Sec
- 1 teaspoon orange extract
- ½ cup sifted confectioners' sugar

Cut a piece of cheesecloth into four 6-inch squares. Dampen it and wring it out lightly. Press a cheesecloth square into each of four 3- or 4-inch heart-shaped molds or cookie cutters and set aside.

To prepare the coeur à la crème, in the bowl of an electric mixer fitted with a paddle attachment, whisk together the mascarpone, ¼ cup of the cream, the vanilla, lemon juice, raspberry liqueur, Triple Sec, and orange extract until thoroughly blended. Transfer the bowl to the refrigerator and chill. In a small mixing bowl, whisk together the remaining 1 cup of cream and the confectioners' sugar until stiff peaks form. With a rubber spatula, fold the whipped cream into the chilled cheese mixture in three increments, incorporating each one thoroughly. Spoon the mixture into the prepared molds and fold the edges of the cheesecloth over the tops. Lightly tap the bottom of the molds on the counter to remove any air pockets between the mixture and the molds.

for the raspberry sauce

½ pint fresh raspberries

1 tablespoon sugar

1 teaspoon freshly squeezed lemon juice

½ pint fresh blackberries or blueberries

¼ cup fresh raspberries, for garnish

4 sprigs of fresh mint, for garnish

Refrigerate on a cookie sheet for at least 2 to 3 hours.

To prepare the sauce, place the raspberries, ½ tablespoon of the sugar, and ½ teaspoon of the lemon juice in a blender or food processor and purée until smooth. Taste the sauce for sweetness and adjust the sugar and lemon juice as necessary. Strain into a bowl, cover, and refrigerate. Repeat for the blackberries and the remaining sugar and lemon juice, and strain into a separate bowl.

Unfold the cheesecloth covering the molds and drape it over the sides. Invert each mold onto a serving plate. While pressing down on the corners of the cheesecloth, carefully lift off the molds. Remove the cheesecloth slowly and smooth the top of the heart with the back of a spoon. Spoon both berry sauces onto the plates around the heart and garnish with the fresh berries and mint leaves.

tip

While pouring liquids from a measuring cup, did you ever feel like someone had played a trick on you and put a dribble cup in your cupboard? Prevent those drips by rubbing a little butter or oil on the pouring lip. This is an oldie, but goodie.

desserts

263

basic recipes & tech

niques

chicken stock

yields 5 to 6 cups

This is a low-sodium recipe, with only about 8 milligrams of sodium per cup, compared to as much as 1,500 milligrams in some commercial canned stocks. You can substitute dried herbs for the bouquet garni, if you wish. If you find that the finished stock is not as flavorful as you would like, bring it to a boil and reduce it, uncovered, until the flavor intensifies.

for the stock

3 quarts cold water

3 pounds chicken bones

2 large onions, chopped

1 carrot, sliced

2 stalks celery, sliced

for the bouquet garni

1 stalk celery, with leaves

1 sprig of fresh flat-leaf parsley

1 sprig of fresh thyme

1 sprig of fresh basil

1 sprig of fresh marjoram

1 sprig of fresh tarragon

1 bay leaf

2 cloves garlic, sliced

To prepare the stock, place the water, chicken bones, onions, carrot, and celery in a stockpot or large saucepan and bring to a boil.

To prepare the bouquet garni, cut a piece of cheesecloth large enough to hold the celery. Place the herb sprigs, bay leaf, and garlic on the cheesecloth on top of the celery and tie the cheesecloth securely with kitchen twine. Add it to the stockpot. Reduce the heat to low, cover partially, and simmer the stock for about 5 hours, occasionally skimming off any fat or impurities. Add more water as needed to keep the ingredients just covered.

Strain the stock into a large bowl and let it stand for 15 minutes. Carefully skim the fat and then strain the stock through cheesecloth into another bowl. Refrigerate until the fat congeals on the surface, and then skim off the fat. Cover the stock and store it in the refrigerator for up to 1 week, or freeze it for up to 3 months.

beef stock

Like the previous recipe, this is a low-sodium stock. Many people think that making stock at home is hard, but it really isn't. I recommend that you make more than you need for a recipe and freeze the extra.

4 pounds beef bones, washed

3 quarts cold water, divided

1 onion, chopped

2 carrots, sliced

3 stalks celery, sliced

2 cloves garlic, crushed

1 bay leaf

1 sprig of fresh thyme, or ¼ teaspoon dried thyme

5 black peppercorns, crushed

2 tomatoes, chopped

½ cup white wine

Preheat the oven to 350°F. Place the beef bones in a single layer in a shallow roasting pan. Roast for 30 to 40 minutes, stirring occasionally. Transfer the bones to a stockpot, draining off the fat. Pour 2 or 3 cups of the cold water into the roasting pan and deglaze it over medium heat. Add this liquid to the stockpot with the bones. Add the remaining water to the stockpot and bring to a simmer.

Spray a nonstick sauté pan with a light coating of nonstick cooking spray and sauté the onion, carrots, celery, and garlic over medium heat for 6 to 8 minutes, or until evenly browned. Drain the vegetables well and add to the stockpot with the bay leaf, thyme, peppercorns, tomatoes, and wine. Return the stock to a simmer and cook, uncovered, for 6 to 8 hours, occasionally skimming any fat or impurities that rise to the surface. Add more water as needed to keep the ingredients just covered.

Strain the stock into a large bowl and let it stand for 15 minutes. Carefully skim the fat and then strain the stock through cheesecloth into another bowl. Refrigerate until the fat congeals on the surface, and then skim off the fat. Cover the stock and store it in the refrigerator for up to 1 week, or freeze it for up to 3 months.

roasting bell peppers
and chiles

This technique gives bell peppers and fresh chiles a roasted flavor and brings out their full sweetness. It also makes them much easier to peel.

Preheat the broiler or prepare the grill. Spray or brush each pepper or chile lightly with olive oil. Place under the broiler or on the grill and turn frequently with tongs until the skin is blackened on all sides. Take care not to burn the flesh. When the peppers are charred, transfer to a bowl, cover the bowl with plastic wrap, and let the peppers cool for 10 minutes or longer. Remove the plastic wrap and peel the blackened skin with the tip of a sharp knife. Remove the stems, cut the peppers or chiles open lengthwise, and remove the seeds, core, and pale internal ribs. Chop, dice, slice, or julienne the peppers and set aside until ready to use.

toasting nuts, seeds, and coconut flakes

Toasting nuts and seeds intensifies their aromatic qualities and flavors.

Preheat the oven to 375°F. Place the nuts, seeds, or coconut flakes in a roasting pan or on a cookie sheet and transfer to the oven. Slivered almonds will take 8 to 10 minutes, pine nuts 10 to 12 minutes, fennel seeds 6 to 8 minutes, and coconut flakes 4 to 6 minutes; they should be lightly browned. Watch closely and take care not to burn them.

clarifying butter

Clarified, or "drawn," butter lacks the milk solids and water content of regular butter, giving it a higher smoking point for cooking foods.

To prepare clarified butter, melt whole unsalted butter in a saucepan over low heat. The milky looking fat and residue will sink to the bottom of the pan. Skim off the surface foam, pour off the clear golden liquid—the clarified butter—and discard the solids.

For fruits and vegetables
Frieda's Inc.
1 (800) 241-1771
www.friedas.com

For foie gras, caviar, canned goods,
and all other ingredients
Caviar Assouline
1 (800) 521-4491
www.caviarassouline.com

index

index

equivalent imperial and metric measurements

American cooks use standard containers, the 8-ounce cup and a tablespoon that takes exactly 16 level fillings to fill that cup level. Measuring by cup makes it very difficult to give weight equivalents, as a cup of densely packed butter will weigh considerably more than a cup of flour. The easiest way therefore to deal with cup measurements in recipes is to take the amount by volume rather than by weight. Thus the equation reads:

1 cup = 240 ml = 8 fl. oz.   ½ cup = 120 ml = 4 fl. oz.

It is possible to buy a set of American cup measures in major stores around the world.

In the States, butter is often measured in sticks. One stick is the equivalent of 8 tablespoons. One tablespoon of butter is therefore the equivalent to ½ ounce/15 grams.

liquid measures

Fluid Ounces	U.S.	Imperial	Milliliters
	1 teaspoon	1 teaspoon	5
¼	2 teaspoons	1 dessertspoon	10
½	1 tablespoon	1 tablespoon	14
1	2 tablespoons	2 tablespoons	28
2	¼ cup	4 tablespoons	56
4	½ cup		120
5		¼ pint or 1 gill	140
6	¾ cup		170
8	1 cup		240
9			250, ¼ liter
10	1¼ cups	½ pint	280
12	1½ cups		340
15		¾ pint	420
16	2 cups		450
18	2¼ cups		500, ½ liter
20	2½ cups	1 pint	560
24	3 cups		675
25		1¼ pints	700
27	3½ cups		750
30	3¾ cups	1½ pints	840
32	4 cups or 1 quart		900
35		1¾ pints	980
36	4½ cups		1000, 1 liter
40	5 cups	2 pints or 1 quart	1120

solid measures

U.S. and Imperial Measures		Metric Measures	
Ounces	Pounds	Grams	Kilos
1		28	
2		56	
3½		100	
4	¼	112	
5		140	
6		168	
8	½	225	
9		250	¼
12	¾	340	
16	1	450	
18		500	½
20	1¼	560	
24	1½	675	
27		750	¾
28	1¾	780	
32	2	900	
36	2¼	1000	1
40	2½	1100	
48	3	1350	
54		1500	1½

oven temperature equivalents

Fahrenheit	Celsius	Gas Mark	Description
225	110	¼	Cool
250	130	½	
275	140	1	Very Slow
300	150	2	
325	170	3	Slow
350	180	4	Moderate
375	190	5	
400	200	6	Moderately Hot
425	220	7	Fairly Hot
450	230	8	Hot
475	240	9	Very Hot
500	250	10	Extremely Hot

Any broiling recipes can be used with the grill of the oven, but beware of high-temperature grills.

equivalents for ingredients

all-purpose flour—plain flour
baking sheet—oven tray
buttermilk—ordinary milk
cheesecloth—muslin
coarse salt—kitchen salt
cornstarch—cornflour
eggplant—aubergine

granulated sugar—caster sugar
half and half—12% fat milk
heavy cream—double cream
light cream—single cream
lima beans—broad beans
parchment paper—greaseproof paper
plastic wrap—cling film

scallion—spring onion
shortening—white fat
unbleached flour—strong, white flour
vanilla bean—vanilla pod
zest—rind
zucchini—courgettes or marrow